Treating Children with Sexually Abusive Behavior Problems
Guidelines for Child and Parent Intervention

Pre-publication
REVIEW

"We may not want to believe it, but it happens. Children twelve years and younger are sexually abusing other children. In *Treating Children with Sexually Abusive Behavior Problems*, Burton and Rasmussen show how their clinical work using the 'Trauma Outcome Process,' a cognitive-behavioral model, can extend and complement the work of others. This is accomplished in two parts. The first section of the book identifies the multiple factors (individual and socio-cultural) that contribute to the onset of children's sexually abusive behavior and the variety of treatments (individual, group, parallel) that are appropriate as children, parents, and families work toward healthy relationships. The second section of the book provides detailed exercises that address issues of accountability, empathy, sexuality, coping with trauma, developing and respecting boundaries, and learning relationship skills. The section concludes with a short chapter on 'The Power of the Treatment Team.'

Burton and Rasmussen's book is an extremely readable book that is well documented and a mine of valuable 'hands-on' information. Using a systems approach and focusing on both victim and perpetrator issues, this is a book that all those who work with sexually abusive children or want to work with them must read. Even those who have a variety of books on this topic will want to add this one to their collection."

Sharon K. Araji, PhD
Professor of Sociology,
University of Alaska,
Anchorage

Treating Children with Sexually Abusive Behavior Problems

Guidelines for Child and Parent Intervention

THE HAWORTH MALTREATMENT AND TRAUMA PRESS
Robert A. Geffner, PhD
Editor

New, Recent, and Forthcoming Titles:

Sexual, Physical, and Emotional Abuse in Out-of-Home Care: Prevention Skills for At-Risk Children by Toni Cavanagh Johnson and Associates

Cedar House: A Model Child Abuse Treatment Program by Bobbi Kendig with Clara Lowry

Bridging Worlds: Understanding and Facilitating Adolescent Recovery from the Trauma of Abuse by Joycee Kennedy and Carol McCarthy

The Learning About Myself (LAMS) Program for At-Risk Parents: Learning from the Past—Changing the Future by Verna Rickard

The Learning About Myself (LAMS) Program for At-Risk Parents: Handbook for Group Participants by Verna Rickard

Treating Children with Sexually Abusive Behavior Problems: Guidelines for Child and Parent Intervention by Jan Ellen Burton, Lucinda A. Rasmussen, with Julie Bradshaw, Barbara J. Christopherson, and Steven C. Huke

Bearing Witness: Violence and Collective Responsibility by Sandra L. Bloom and Michael Reichert

Sibling Abuse Trauma: Assessment and Intervention Strategies for Children, Families, and Adults by John V. Caffaro and Allison Conn-Caffaro

From Surviving to Thriving: A Therapist's Guide to Stage II Recovery for Survivors of Childhood Abuse by Mary Bratton

"I Never Told Anyone This Before": Managing the Initial Disclosure of Abuse Re-Collections by Janice A. Gasker

Breaking the Silence: Group Therapy for Childhood Sexual Abuse, A Practitioner's Manual by Judith A. Margolin

Treating Children with Sexually Abusive Behavior Problems
Guidelines for Child and Parent Intervention

Jan Ellen Burton, PhD
Lucinda A. Rasmussen, PhD

with
Julie Bradshaw, LCSW
Barbara J. Christopherson, LCSW
Steven C. Huke, MS

David H. Justice, MS
Contributor

HMTP

The Haworth Maltreatment and Trauma Press
An Imprint of The Haworth Press, Inc.
New York • London

Published by

The Haworth Maltreatment and Trauma Press, an imprint of the The Haworth Press, Inc., 10 Alice Street, Binghamton, NY 13904-1580

Cover design by Monica L. Seifert.

Library of Congress Cataloging-in-Publication Data

Treating children with sexually abusive behavior problems : guidelines for child and parent intervention / Jan Ellen Burton . . . [et al.] ; David H. Justice, contributor.
     p.   cm.
Includes bibliographical references (p.) and index.
ISBN 0-7890-0473-9 (alk. paper).
    1. Sexual disorders in children—Treatment. 2. Behavior disorders in children—Treatment. 3. Children—Sexual behavior. 4. Child psychotherapy—Parent participation. 5. Parent–child interaction therapy. I. Burton, Jan Ellen.
RJ505.P37T74 1998
618.92′858306—dc21   98-6095
                                                             CIP

CONTENTS

ABOUT THE AUTHORS

Jan Ellen Burton, PhD, is a psychologist at Valley Mental Health and in private practice in Salt Lake City, Utah. She currently coordinates the sexual abuse program for children and adolescents at Valley Mental Health. This program includes both victims and perpetrators. Dr. Burton previously worked with adult sex offenders at the Center for Family Development. In recent years she has made a number of presentations in connection with her work with sexually abused and sexually abusive children.

Over the past twenty-two years, Dr. Burton has primarily worked with children, adolescents, and their families. She provides individual therapy in conjunction with family treatment. Dr. Burton believes it is critical to create an environment in which children are able to verbalize their opinions, thoughts, and feelings. If victim issues are not addressed, there is a risk that victimization will lead to perpetration.

Jan Ellen Burton graduated from Purdue University in 1975, and has had individual therapy and group treatment experience with adults as well as juveniles. She has worked in the substance abuse and outpatient units at Valley Mental Health and has had experience within the public school systems in Salt Lake City, Utah, and Milwaukee, Wisconsin. In addition, Dr. Burton worked with physically and emotionally handicapped children at the Curative Rehabilitation Center in Milwaukee. The 1992 article "Precursors to Offending and the Trauma Outcome Process in Sexually Reactive Children," published in the *Journal of Child Sexual Abuse,* was an initial attempt to conceptualize responses to victimization as they relate to perpetration. This book developed as a continuation of that early conceptualization.

Lucinda A. Rasmussen, PhD, is an assistant professor at the School of Social Work at San Diego State University. She received her doctorate in social work in 1995 and her MSW in 1983 from the University of Utah in Salt Lake City.

Dr. Rasmussen was a licensed clinical social worker in Utah for over ten years. She coordinated the group treatment program for children with sexually abusive behavior problems at Primary Children's Medical Center's multidisciplinary Child Protection Team in Salt Lake City. Her clinical experiences include treating child sexual abuse victims and their families as well as adolescent and adult sex offenders. Her interest in understanding how victimization can lead to the development of perpetrating behavior led to her work with sexually abusive children.

In Utah, and now in San Diego, Dr. Rasmussen has helped create and improve treatment resources for juvenile sexual offenders and children with sexually abusive behavior problems. She is currently a member of the San Diego County Network on Sexual Offending and the California Coalition on Sexual Offending. She was previously a founding member of the Utah Network on Juveniles Offending Sexually (NOJOS). She coordinated a nine-day training symposium for practitioners on the assessment and treatment of juvenile sexual offenders. She co-authored two Utah state reports about juvenile sexual offending and helped develop state protocols for the identification and assessment of juvenile sexual offenders for Utah's juvenile justice system.

Dr. Rasmussen has published two articles on child sexual abuse intervention in the *Journal of Child Sexual Abuse.* She also authored a manual for the Utah Division of Family Services to train foster parents on parenting strategies for managing children with sexual behavior problems.

Julie Bradshaw, LCSW, is a clinical social worker currently serving as the Director of the Child Protection Team at Primary Children's Medical Center in Salt Lake City, Utah, where she has worked for seven years. The Child Protection Team specializes in assessing and treating victims of abuse and their families.

Ms. Bradshaw received her BA in 1975 and MSW in 1981 from the University of Utah, where she graduated with honors. She majored in psychology as an undergraduate and specialized in the treatment of abused children while in graduate school.

Ms. Bradshaw's career, which began in 1974, has included broad experience in the field of social services. She has worked extensively with troubled and delinquent youth within the Youth Corrections and Mental Health systems. She has also worked with abused and neglected children. within the Utah Division of Family Services. Ms.

Bradshaw served as a troubleshooter for the Executive Director of the Utah Department of Human Services, investigating child fatalities, complaints, and consumer concerns.

Barbara J. Christopherson, LCSW, is a licensed clinical social worker who has specialized in developing intervention programs and providing treatment for victims of abuse and domestic violence. She received her MSW in 1979 from the University of Utah in Salt Lake City. She helped establish the multidisciplinary Child Protection Team at Primary Children's Medical Center in Salt Lake City and served as the team's director for four years. She also served as president of the Utah chapter of the American Professional Society on the Abuse of Children (APSAC). Ms. Christopherson has actively collaborated with other child abuse professionals in Utah and Oregon to improve treatment services for victims of abuse and their families. She has given presentations at numerous local, regional, and national conferences. She is currently in private practice and is a family therapist at the Morrison Center Counterpoint Program in Portland, Oregon.

Steven C. Huke, MS, received his bachelor's degree in psychology from Reed College and his master's degree in clinical psychology from the University of Utah. He was a member of the Child Protection Team at Primary Children's Medical Center in Salt Lake City. Mr. Huke has given presentations at regional and national conferences on the treatment of youth with sexually abusive behavior problems and sexually victimized children. He is currently a family therapist at the Morrison Center Counterpoint Program and has a private practice in Portland, Oregon.

David H. Justice, MS, is a research specialist at Salt Lake Valley Mental Health and an instructor in sociology at Salt Lake Community College in Salt Lake City, Utah. His research interests are in the areas of medical sociology, the sociology of mental health, and social problems. He has presented papers on the effects of psychosocial stress on chronic disease. His teaching interests include the areas of the sociology of mental health, social psychology, research methods, and the sociology of race and ethnicity, particularly Native American issues.

Preface

The evolution of sexual abuse treatment is such that it was not until the late 1980s when clinicians and researchers identified that sexual abuse is perpetrated by children. We have developed our program for sexually abusive children over the past eight years. This process has been challenging, but rewarding.

There have been several serendipitous outcomes from writing this book. The treatment program for abusive children has of course become better defined and more organized. We developed therapeutic materials for children, using adaptations from techniques used with adolescents and adults, and found parents are also better able to understand and discuss treatment concepts in this simplified language. Many of these techniques have been useful in victim treatment as well.

We are often asked if we developed our theories regarding sexually abusive behavior problems prior to beginning our treatment program. We would like to say we were that organized but cannot do so in honesty. We did have some initial hypotheses based on our clinical experiences with children and offenders. Some of these ideas were not accurate. In addition, the more we talked, the more we realized we did not all share the same perceptions regarding sexually abusive children. This book is a compilation of our individual perceptions and experiences in this area. At this time we believe our thinking is very similar, as is evidenced by our faith that a group of clinicians can write separate parts of a book and have it appear as a unified whole.

Acknowledgments

Many people have contributed directly and indirectly to the development of this program, as well as to the writing of this book. First, we wish to thank the children and their parents; they have made an impact on our lives. Although many of their experiences are illustrated in this book, we have changed names and altered case examples so that specific clients cannot be identified. If our examples resemble any actual persons, this similarity is coincidental.

We appreciate the support our own families and friends have provided; their encouragement and patience made completion of this project possible. We especially acknowledge our colleagues at both Primary Children's Medical Center and Valley Mental Health: Kenneth J. Hopps, PhD, had the initial idea to begin a group for younger children with sexually abusive behavior problems. Without Randy Linnell, LCSW, Randolph G. Sorenson, PhD, and Linda Firneno, RN, the young children's program would have floundered due to lack of personnel. We appreciate the work of the many therapists at both Valley Mental Health and Primary Children's Medical Center who offered their services to cofacilitate both children's and parents' groups.

The treatment of sexual abuse is costly, both in terms of time and personnel. Without the support of administrators at both facilities, our treatment program would not have been possible. In addition, Catherine Carter, PhD, Coordinator of Research, Evaluation, and Training at Valley Mental Health, has assisted us with program evaluation.

Our initial readers, Thomas A. Halversen, MD, Poonam Soni, MD, Betty Vos, PhD, and Mary Anne Greenwell-Plautz, MLS, demonstrated substantial courage by their willingness to critique this work before it was sent to the publisher. Finally, Robert A. Geffner, PhD, who edited our manuscript, gave us invaluable feedback.

PART I:
GUIDELINES FOR PRACTICE

Chapter 1

Sexually Abusive Behavior Problems: Definitions and Current Knowledge

ALL I REALLY NEED TO KNOW about how to live and what to do and how to be I learned in kindergarten. . . . These are the things I learned:

- Share everything.
- Play fair.
- Don't hit people.
- Put things back where you found them.
- Clean up your own mess.
- Don't take things that aren't yours.
- Say you're sorry when you hurt somebody.
- Wash your hands before you eat.
- Flush.
- Warm cookies and cold milk are good for you.
- Live a balanced life—learn some and think some and draw and paint and sing and dance and play and work every day some.
- Take a nap every afternoon.
- When you go out into the world, watch out for traffic, hold hands, and stick together.
- Be aware of wonder . . . .

—Robert Fulghum*

*Quoted from Robert Fulghum's (1986) *All I Really Need to Know I Learned in Kindergarten.*

Childhood: A picture emerges of a group of children in a kindergarten class behaving as Robert Fulghum describes. However, children often stand apart in classrooms, confused or rebelling against these simple kindergarten rules. Some children do not know how to "share everything" or "play fair." They have not known fairness. Many of these children have been victims of traumatic events, abused by those closest to them, unable to express their anger and pain. Without an acceptable way to express how they feel, they may hurt themselves or strike out and treat others abusively, as their abusers treated them. If they display harmful, sexually inappropriate behavior, they have "sexually abusive behavior problems."

It has taken a long time for society to admit these children exist. The societal myth that only "strangers" commit sexual abuse persists. In reality, the ever-increasing number of child sexual abuse referrals documents that most sexually abused children are victimized by someone they know—a parent, relative, friend, baby-sitter, or another child. The myth that children do not commit sex offenses is no longer tenable. When children experience sexual abuse, observe others' sexual activities, or discover explicit sexual material, they become more aware of their own sexual feelings. Unless abused and sexualized children can express their feelings, they remain vulnerable to developing maladaptive behavior patterns, including sexually abusive behaviors.

Research on adult sex offenders has indicated that approximately 50 percent began offending as juveniles (Abel, Mittelman, and Becker, 1985; Groth, Longo, and McFadin, 1982). Adolescent sex offenders in treatment programs have reported beginning offending patterns as early as age five (Stickrod and Ryan, 1987). Children who exhibit sexually abusive behavior problems are at risk to continue offending as adolescents or adults. Early assessment and treatment are therefore essential; it is important to intervene when these children's inappropriate sexual behaviors are first identified. Cunningham and MacFarlane (1996) stated:

All sex offenders come from somewhere . . . if we ignore them in their youth, they will likely revisit us in their adulthood when they will be harder to reach and when the results of their behavior will have left its painful mark on other young lives. (p. 262)

There is a growing body of literature that focuses specifically on children with sexually abusive behavior problems, including research on the characteristics of these children (Berliner et al., 1996; Cantwell, 1988; Friedrich and Luecke, 1988; Gil and Johnson, 1993; Glasgow et al., 1994; Gray et al., 1993; Gray et al., 1994; Gray and Friedrich, 1996; Johnson, 1988, 1989) as well as discussion of family dynamics, etiology, and treatment approaches (Araji, 1997, Cunningham and MacFarlane, 1991, 1996; Gil and Johnson, 1993; Gray and Pithers, 1993; Johnson, 1995a; Johnson and Berry, 1989; Lane 1991a, 1997a; MacFarlane and Cunningham, 1988; Ryan, 1991a, 1997a). In addition, a few resources have been developed to help parents (Gil, 1987; Johnson, 1995b; Pithers et al., 1993; Ryan and Blum, 1994). A recent survey conducted by the Safer Society Foundation identified 390 treatment programs that work with children with sexually abusive behavior problems (Knopp and Freeman-Longo, 1997). Unfortunately, the field of treatment for sexually abusive children is young, and research on individual characteristics, family dynamics, etiology, and treatment outcomes is still limited. Clinicians who treat these children must often rely on their own clinical experiences or make developmental adjustments to treatment approaches used with adult and adolescent sex offenders.

The purpose of this book is to help clinicians recognize and interrupt sexually abusive behavior in children. Clinicians need to simultaneously address children's sexually abusive behaviors as well as prior experiences that may have contributed to that behavior. It is important that interventions focus on the entire family system. Parent involvement is critical when teaching children to make responsible choices regarding their sexual thoughts and feelings. Many of these children can learn to express their feelings appropriately.

This book presents a multidimensional treatment program for children who have sexually abusive behavior problems. Although the primary practice model is cognitive-behavioral, there is a strong family systems component. Psychodynamic and play therapy approaches are also incorporated in the therapy process. Treatment strategies are derived from the authors' clinical observations and experience. This treatment program attempts to teach sexually abusive children healthy ways to manage their feelings and confront incorrect thinking. A parallel group treatment model is presented, as children and parents attend therapy groups at the same scheduled times.

DEFINING SEXUALLY ABUSIVE BEHAVIOR PROBLEMS

The literature lacks congruence regarding what to call sexualized behavior in children. Cunningham and MacFarlane (1991; 1996) have referred to children who act out sexually as abuse-reactive. Others have called them sexually aggressive or reactive (Friedrich and Luecke, 1988; Gray and Pithers, 1993), children with sexual behavior disturbances (or problems), (Berliner et al., 1996; Berliner and Rawlings, 1991; Gray et al., 1993; Gray and Friedrich, 1996; Lane 1997a), child perpetrators (Johnson, 1988; Lane 1991a), sexualized children (Gil and Johnson, 1993), and children who molest (Cunningham and MacFarlane, 1991; Johnson, 1995a). Friedrich (1995) has clearly objected to labeling children as sexual perpetrators. The National Task Force on Juvenile Sexual Offending (1993) has opposed describing sexually abusive behavior manifested by young children as reactive or acting out, as such terms deny or rationalize the abusive nature of the behavior. The National Task Force advocates, "when the behavior of children is potentially abusive, it is referred to as sexually abusive behavior" (p. 64).

We have chosen to use the terms *children with sexually abusive behavior problems* or *sexually abusive children* to refer to children who act out sexually toward others. These terms indicate the problematic nature of the sexual behavior without implying causation. Similarly, Araji (1997) advocates for the term "sexually aggressive." However, some young children appear less aggressive than sexualized, and it is our opinion that the word "abusive" connotes the effect of their behavior on their victims.

Age-Appropriate Sex Play

Not all forms of sexual behavior in children are problematic. For example, masturbation is common among infants, toddlers, and preschoolers (Martinson, 1991, 1997). Once they discover their genitals, toddlers may attempt to see or touch the genitals of others. It is not unusual for young children to take their clothes off, look at one another's bodies, and sometimes touch one another. This can be normative sexual behavior (Friedrich, 1990), age-appropriate sex play (Gil, 1993a), or expectable sexual development (Gil and Johnson, 1993) for children who do not have a history of sexual trauma or exposure to explicit sexual material. Curiosity may motivate this typically naive experimentation.

Activities such as "playing house" or "playing doctor" are common games among young children. However, the sexual content of their play is likely based on what they have observed or experienced (Gil, 1993a). Unless the children involved have been previously exposed to sexuality (through abuse, observation, or pornography), play activities are generally limited to undressing, looking, and touching. These activities are typically between same-age peers, without coercion, and the affect of the children involved is often spontaneous, playful, or embarrassed (Gil, 1993a; Johnson, 1988; Ryan, 1997a). When adults discover children engaged in age-appropriate sex play, they may "educate, redirect, or limit behavior, but the behavior itself is not deviant" (Ryan, 1997a, p. 439).

Some children engage in sexual behavior that is problematic for themselves but not necessarily abusive to others. Excessive masturbation and explicit sexual talk are examples of such behavior. These behaviors may interfere with a child's normal developmental progression, provoke rejection from others, increase risk for victimization, and/or cause distress for the child (National Task Force on Juvenile Sexual Offending, 1993). Individual therapy and psychoeducation can be sufficient interventions for these children. If placed in group therapy, it is usually best not to include them with others who act out more severely. The treatment program discussed in this book focuses specifically on children who act out sexually against others.

Sexually Abusive Behavior

It is important to differentiate developmentally appropriate sexual behaviors from behaviors that are sexually abusive. Research on sexual development in children (Gil, 1993a; Johnson, 1993a, 1993b; Martinson, 1991, 1997; Ryan, 1991a, 1997a; Sgroi, Bunk, and Wabrek, 1988) has provided guidelines for distinguishing age-appropriate from abusive behaviors. The type of sexual behavior exhibited helps discriminate abusive sexual interactions from age-appropriate sex play. Friedrich and colleagues (1991) studied normal sexual behavior in children. Of their sample of 880 children ages two to twelve, 45.8 percent were reported to have touched their own sexual parts, and 6.0 percent were reported to have touched others' sexual parts. Only .1 percent of this normative sample were reported to have put their mouth on another's sexual parts. Other sexual behaviors rarely noticed by the caretakers of these children (e.g., asks others to engage in sexual acts, inserts objects in vagina/anus, imitates intercourse) tended to be behaviors that were "more aggressive or more imitative of adult sexual behavior" (p. 462).

A sexually abusive child is one who initiates sexual behavior in a manipulative or coercive manner. The actual behaviors may encompass anything from fondling to sexual intercourse and include object insertion, oral-genital contact, frottage, and bestiality. Other less intrusive sexual behaviors can be abusive if they are repetitive and invasive. Examples of such behaviors include: exposing genitals, window peeping, grabbing others' breasts or buttocks, looking up skirts, etc. Ryan and colleagues (1988) described a "range of sexual behaviors in children." They defined the following behaviors as "no questions" as to their abusive nature: "oral, vaginal, or anal penetration of dolls, children, or animals; forced touching of genitals; simulating intercourse with peers with clothing off; and any genital injury or bleeding not explained by accidental cause" (cited in Ryan, 1997a, p. 440). Similarly, Johnson (1993b) described a "continuum of sexual behaviors." Typical behaviors of "children who molest" included "oral copulation, vaginal intercourse, anal intercourse, and/or forcibly penetrating the vagina or anus of another child with fingers, sticks, and/or other objects" (p. 48).

Abusive sexual behaviors are coercive and nonconsensual and exploit equality in relationships (National Task Force on Juvenile Sexual Offending, 1993). Ryan (1997a) stated, "It is the relationship and interaction that define sexual abuse rather than an isolated behavior that occurs out of context" (p. 439). Power differential, intimidation, manipulation, and coercion are abusive dynamics that help define sexually abusive interactions between children. The first abusive dynamic, power differential, refers to differences in age, size, intelligence, and physical ability. An offending child may be older, larger, more intelligent, or abuse a child who has a disability. Second, an abusive child may use status or authority to intimidate other children. Examples could include baby-sitting, being a class officer, being popular, etc. The third dynamic, manipulation, refers to deliberate actions used by sexually abusive children to secure their victims' cooperation and participation in sexual activity. Hamilton, Decker, and Rumbart (1986) define manipulation as "deliberately influencing or controlling the behavior of others to one's own advantage by using charm, persuasion, seduction, deceit, guilt induction, or coercion" (p. 191). Sexually abusive children manipulate their victims with verbal persuasion, games, tricks, and bribes or coerce other children into sexual activities by use of threats or force. The abusive dynamic of coercion is also apparent when children try to hide or cover up their sexually inappropriate behavior: they may carefully choose a hidden location for sexual contact, and they may either suggest or demand their victims keep silent, occasionally enforcing their silence with threats of bodily harm.

CURRENT KNOWLEDGE

A number of different theories have been proposed as explanations for the development of sexually offending behavior (Ryan, 1991b, 1997b). Araji (1997) and Gil (1993b) have reviewed various theories and practice models as they apply to the etiology of sexually abusive behavior problems in children. The following etiological theories and models are included in one or both of these reviews: psychodynamic trauma models (e.g., post-traumatic stress disorder model—Cunningham and MacFarlane, 1991, 1996); social learning trauma models (e.g., traumagenic dynamics model—Finkelhor and Browne, 1985, 1988); adaptation perspective and coping theory (Friedrich, 1990); four preconditions of abuse model (Araji and Finkelhor, 1986; Cunningham and MacFarlane, 1991, 1996; Rasmussen, Burton, and Christopherson, 1992); addiction model (Breer, 1987; Carnes, 1983; Cunningham and MacFarlane, 1991, 1996); and the Trauma Outcome Process (Brown and Rasmussen, 1994; Rasmussen, Burton, and Christopherson, 1992).

Our own perspective for the etiology of sexually abusive behavior problems in children is based on four major theoretical perspectives: psychodynamic, social learning, humanistic, and family system). We take a psychodynamic view in our belief that unresolved feelings related to prior trauma may be reenacted in abusive behavior. We also emphasize the role of developmental factors in modulating children's resilience to the effects of trauma and in shaping their social competence and capacity for empathy. We follow social learning theory when we acknowledge the importance of modeling and stress confrontation of maladaptive thinking processes. We highlight the importance of awareness (a humanistic concept) and believe that sexual awareness is an essential motivator of sexually abusive behavior problems in children. Our work is systemic because we believe that children develop sexually offending behavior as a result of the interaction of their individual characteristics and family dynamics.

Over time we have identified salient treatment factors common to children with sexually abusive behavior problems. These factors include: (1) effects of prior traumatization, (2) accountability, (3) social competence, (4) empathy, (5) establishment of boundaries, and (6) the sexual abuse cycle. These individual characteristics interact with other family dynamics and contribute to the development of sexually abusive behavior. Research pertaining to these factors is reviewed in the following material.

Prior Traumatization

Over the past ten years, much research has linked the experience of prior sexual abuse with increased sexualized behavior (Browne and Finkelhor, 1986; Cosentino et al., 1995; Cunningham and Mac-Farlane, 1991, 1996; Deblinger et al., 1989; Friedrich and Luecke, 1988; Gale et al., 1988; Goldston, Turnquist, and Knutson, 1989; Johnson, 1988, 1989; Johnson and Aoki, 1993; Kolko, Moser, and Weldy, 1988; Shapiro et al., 1992; Slusser, 1995; Wells et al., 1995; White et al., 1988; Young, Bergandi, and Titus, 1994). Gale and colleagues (1988) found that 41 percent of a sample of thirty-seven sexually abused children under age seven displayed sexually inappropriate behaviors, while sexually inappropriate behaviors were found in less than 5 percent of physically abused and nonabused control groups. In her sample of sixty sexually abusive children, ages four to thirteen, Johnson (1988, 1989) found that 49 percent of boys and 100 percent of the girls had histories of sexual abuse. Friedrich and Luecke (1988) reported similar findings. Of the sixteen sexually abusive children in their sample, 87.5 percent had histories of sexual abuse, as validated by the child's report, admission of an offender, medical/physical evidence, or an eyewitness report.

Little work has been done comparing the effect of sexual abuse on males and females. Young and colleagues (1994) did look at gender, and they found more similarities than differences between male and female latency-age victims of sexual abuse. The sexually abused children in their sample ($n = 20$ males and 20 females) expressed more feelings of isolation and depression and showed more problems relating to peers than the matched nonabused control group. Caretakers described them as more aggressive and socially withdrawn, as well as oversensitive to others' attitudes and rejections. They also reported a deficit in socially valued behavior, including more sexual problems. The only gender differences between the sexually abused children were that boys viewed themselves as more aggressive than did girls and that girls reported themselves to be more submissive and depressed. In comparing 237 male and thirty-four female adolescent perpetrators, Ray and English (1995) found males to often be more coercive and sophisticated in their sexual behaviors. Females displayed more empathy for their victims than did males.

Early research on sexually abusive children showed that many report a history of physical abuse. Johnson (1988, 1989) reported that 19 percent of boys and 31 percent of girls in her sample had histories of physical abuse. Friedrich and Luecke (1988) documented that fifteen of the sixteen sexually abusive children in their sample had problematic relationships with their parents, including physical abuse, emotional neglect, abandonment, and/or exposure to sexualized adult behavior. Johnson and Aoki (1993) compared 158 latency-age children between six to eleven years old in seven residential treatment centers. Children who were *both* sexually and physically abused ($n = 83$) exhibited significantly more sexualized behavior than children in the physically abused group ($n = 31$) or the nonabused control group (*n* = 29), and they approached significance as being distinct from the sexually abused-only group (*n* = 15) in the number of sexualized behaviors exhibited. Johnson and Aoki proposed that physical abuse may be a significant contributor to the development of sexual behavior problems in sexually abused children. Similarly, Araji (1997) discussed a link between prior physical abuse and sexually aggressive behavior by reviewing the work of Fatout (1990), Green (1985), and Fraser (1996) and observing a commonality between the development of aggressive behavior as described by these authors and Friedrich (1990). Friedrich proposed that children "model" or imitate aggressive behavior, and this aggression is reinforced when paired with a pleasurable (in this case, sexual) response.

Although many children with sexually abusive behavior problems are past victims of sexual or physical abuse, a known history of abuse is not always present. Our own clinical observations confirm that the specific factors motivating a child to act out sexually are often unclear. Some children who display sexually abusive behavior have no documented history of sexual or physical abuse. For these children, other emotional (e.g., neglect), behavioral (e.g., lack of accountability, social inadequacy, and lack of empathy), or family systems components (e.g., poor boundaries) may be salient.

Types of Abuse

Although sexual and physical abuse are more often studied, neglect, abandonment, and other losses adversely affect most children. Further study is needed to clarify the relationship between the type of abuse and the type of destructive behavior (self- and/or other-directed) that might result (Taussig and Litrownik, 1997). Often adverse effects persist past childhood (Neumann et al., 1996; Osofsky, 1995). Experiencing both physical and sexual abuse as a child can lead to less favorable outcomes as an adult (Wind and Silvern, 1992). However, a child does not necessarily need to be physically injured to experience trauma; witnessing the victimization of a parent or sibling can have both acute and long-term negative effects (Osofsky, 1995; Staub, 1996). Growing up in a family that experiences emotionally abusive communication (e.g., verbal put-downs or threats) can certainly impact a child (Garbarino, Gutt–

man, and Seeley, 1986; Patterson, 1976, 1982). Whether these adverse experiences result in trauma depends both on the severity of the stressor(s) and a child's unique capacity to respond to stress (Beitchman et al., 1992; McCann and Pearlman, 1990; Osofsky, 1995).

Kaufman, Hilliker, and Daleiden (1996) suggested that the methods used by a perpetrator to set up or cover up abuse also have an important impact on the victim. They posited that the extensive integration of prosocial behaviors (e.g., gifts, praise, positive attention, etc.) into the "grooming" process may complicate treatment. Victims may have difficulty identifying the manipulative motive of these positive, nonsexual acts and perceive themselves as "willing" participants in the abuse. This process may also reinforce an offender's denial and minimization of an offense.

Effects of Trauma

Trauma and/or exposure to sexual material can cause children to experience any of several victim outcomes (Ryan, 1989). Abusive experiences can alter a child's cognitive and emotional orientation to the world and result in the "traumagenic dynamics" of traumatic sexualization, betrayal, powerlessness, and stigmatization (Finkelhor and Browne, 1985, 1988). Other acute and chronic effects of sexual abuse can include the following: fear, anxiety, depression, anger, hostility, aggression, somatic complaints, self-blame, poor self-esteem, difficulty trusting others, feelings of isolation, vulnerability to repeated victimization, self-destructive behavior, dissociative states, attachment problems, and sexually inappropriate behavior (Briere, 1992; Browne and Finkelhor, 1986; Kendall-Tackett, Williams, and Finkelhor, 1993; James, 1989; Wyatt and Powell, 1988). Similar effects are found in children who are victims of physical abuse (Bonner et al., 1992; Briere, 1992).

Exposure to excessive sexual stimuli (perhaps through pornographic videos or magazines) may provoke some children to model what they observed. Some families manifest a sexualized climate, which Gil (1993c) referred to as covert abuse. In these families, "inappropriate attitudes (about sexuality) are communicated verbally or nonverbally" (p. 102). Both prior sexual abuse and indirect exposure to sexual activities can be sexualizing to young children.

When they witness the sexual abuse of other children, their trauma may be significant. Trauma incurred from watching sexual abuse may influence some children to act out sexually against others, just as exposure to repeated violence may lead to increased aggression (Osofsky, 1995; Staub, 1996). In some cases, exposure to sexual stimuli and prior abuse may interact to influence behavior. As previously noted, "Enhanced sexual awareness coupled with anger associated with physical and/or emotional abuse can lead to an [sexual] offense" (Rasmussen, Burton, and Christopherson, 1992, p. 36).

When traumatic events occur, symptoms of post-traumatic stress disorder (PTSD) often result (Courtois, 1988; Cunningham and Mac-Farlane, 1991, 1996; Donaldson and Gardner, 1985; Eth and Pynoos, 1985; Goodwin, 1985; Kendall-Tackett, Williams, and Finkelhor, 1993). This disorder results from experiencing or witnessing an event involving "actual or threatened death or serious injury, or a threat to the physical integrity of self or others" (American Psychiatric Association, 1994, p. 427). An adult's response to a traumatic event often involves "intense fear, helplessness, or horror," while children may respond with "disorganized or agitated behavior" (Ibid., p. 428). Primary symptoms of PTSD include intrusive recollections of traumatic memories (e.g., flashbacks, nightmares, physiological reactivity to cues symbolizing aspects of the traumatic event), avoidance of stimuli associated with the trauma (e.g., "numbing" of feelings, detachment, restricted range of affect), and increased arousal (e.g., sleeplessness, anger outbursts, loss of concentration, hypervigilance).

Increasing evidence clearly indicates that even in the earliest phases of infant and toddler development an association exists between exposure to violence and PTSD symptoms (Garbarino et al., 1992; Osofsky, 1995; Pynoos, 1993; Staub, 1996). In addition, it appears that PTSD symptoms may vary according to the type of abuse the child has experienced. Deblinger and colleagues (1989) found that twenty-nine sexually abused children had significantly more PTSD symptoms indicative of reexperiencing trauma than the physically abused ($n = 29$) or nonabused ($n = 20$) control groups. Nonetheless, many victims experience symptoms relating to trauma but do not necessarily exhibit primary PTSD symptoms. Finkelhor

(1988) stressed that abuse is often a relationship or situation that evolves over time, rather than a discrete traumatic event. Briere (1997) described a continuum of trauma consisting of a variety of symptoms as sequelae to abuse.

Some abused children reenact their trauma through symbolic play. This repetitive play then becomes a means to express and work through their trauma (Gil, 1991; Terr, 1983). Children who engage in sexualized play may be reenacting the same events they experienced in their own abuse. In their effort to master their trauma and regain a sense of personal control, some may victimize others as they themselves were victimized (Cunningham and MacFarlane, 1991, 1996; Gil and Johnson, 1993). Friedrich (1990) stated, "It's safe to say that children who are sexually abused who then become victimizers are making a powerful statement that their earlier victimization was not resolved" (p. 244).

Dealing with Trauma Effects

Abused children experience differing degrees of trauma, depending on the circumstances of their abuse and their own and others' reactions. For some children, abuse and loss may result in a sudden interruption of their usual experiences. For others, frequent, intermittent abuse and loss become chronic and expected aspects of living.

The authors have observed that, for the most part, the more frequent, violent, or intrusive the abuse, the more severe the trauma. This hypothesis has been substantiated by several studies (Beitchman et al., 1992; Briere, 1988; Elliott and Briere, 1992; Everstine and Everstine, 1989; Harter, Alexander, and Neimenyer, 1988; Herman, 1992; Hindman, 1989; Katz and Mazur, 1979; Peters, 1988; Roesler and McKenzie, 1994; Tsai, Feldman-Summers, and Edgar, 1979). Peters (1988) found frequency of childhood sexual abuse to be the strongest predictor of depression and substance abuse in adults who were molested as children. Tsai and colleagues (1979) indicated that abuse of longer duration aggravates long-term symptoms of abuse. Similarly, Elliott and Briere (1992) found adults molested as children had more severe symptoms if they had experienced greater duration of abuse, higher frequency of abuse, and most significantly, if they perceived their abuse to be especially traumatic. Other studies have not found a significant correlation

between outcome and the duration of abuse (Einbender and Friedrich, 1989; Mennen and Meadow, 1994). It may be that duration,
frequency, and the extent of abuse are interactive.

Use of force and the intrusiveness of the abuse appear to contribute to more severe outcomes. Roesler and McKenzie (1994) found
use of force to be the single most significant factor associated with
adult abuse survivors' depression, post-traumatic stress disorder,
and other symptoms. Other studies found more intrusive sexual acts
(i.e., offenses involving penetration) to be associated with more
severe long-term outcomes (Beitchman et al., 1992; Briere, 1988;
Harter, Alexander, and Neimenyer, 1988; Tsai, Feldman-Summers,
and Edgar, 1979). The relationship a child has with a perpetrator
also appears to affect the degree of trauma experienced. Abuse by a
known and trusted friend or relative, rather than a stranger, may
result in additional feelings of betrayal, loss, and ambivalence
(Beitchman et al., 1992; Conte and Schuerman, 1987; Everstine and
Everstine, 1989; Hindman, 1989; Katz and Mazur, 1979; Mennen
and Meadow, 1994). Abuse by multiple perpetrators, both in and
out of the home, can multiply the negative effects of trauma (Briere,
1988; Briere and Runtz, 1988).

Research on the impact of child sexual abuse effects has often
focused on retrospective studies of adults. In the last decade, more
research has focused specifically on sexually abused children. Kendall-Tackett and colleagues (1993) reviewed forty-five studies of
child victims in which all subjects were eighteen years old or younger. The findings of the various studies reviewed indicated that
child victims experienced more severe symptoms if they had been
abused by a perpetrator close to them, had had a high frequency and
long duration of sexual contact, and had experienced oral, anal, or
vaginal penetration.

The ability of children to cope with traumatic events depends
both on their intrapsychic resources and the support available in
their environment at the time of the trauma (Kendall-Tackett, Williams, and Finkelhor, 1993; McCann and Pearlman, 1990; Osofsky,
1995; Staub, 1996). Children are less able to cope with trauma
when previous deprivation or loss have damaged their internal and
external resources (Staub, 1996). In contrast, their own physical,
cognitive, and emotional strengths and a supportive family environ-

ment can help children be resilient to the effects of abuse (Bagley and Ramsey, 1986; Everson et al., 1989; Fromuth, 1986; Kendall-Tackett, Williams, and Finkelhor, 1993). A supportive response in the child's home environment can modulate the impact of trauma (Friedrich, 1990; Friedrich, Luecke, et al., 1992).

Children who receive emotional support at the time of disclosure typically experience less trauma than those who lack this support and are often able to reach a restored level of adaptive functioning more quickly (Everson et al., 1989; Kendall-Tackett, Williams, and Finkelhor, 1993). "A hostile or unprotective environment" can complicate a child's recovery from abuse (Herman, 1992, p. 165). Negative responses of parents, peers, teachers, or the legal system can be confusing and overwhelming to the abused child (Everstine and Everstine, 1989; Katz and Mazur, 1979). Hindman (1989) studied 282 adult survivors of childhood sexual abuse. Those subjects categorized as most severely traumatized had experienced a disastrous response from their environment when they revealed their abuse.

Accountability

Our clinical experience demonstrates that children with sexually abusive behavior problems often have difficulty accepting responsibility for their behavior. All children sometimes avoid responsibility for misbehavior when they perceive they will get in trouble. However, unless they have major behavior problems, most children will typically admit they caused a problem when significant adults help them talk about it. In contrast, children with behavior problems may continue to deny responsibility for their inappropriate behaviors, even when evidence clearly shows their culpability. Manifestations of lack of accountability include distorted thinking patterns, impulsiveness, and aggression.

Similar to children with other behavior problems, sexually abusive children often use "thinking errors" (Berenson, 1987; Salter, 1995; Stickrod and Mussack, 1986; Yochelson and Samenow, 1976) when confronted with the negative impact of their actions. Thinking errors are cognitive distortions used to justify hurtful behaviors. Offenders use these distortions to give themselves permission to hurt others, plan offenses, and justify their actions. Similar to adult and adolescent sex offenders, children with sexually abusive behavior problems may lie, deny, blame others, minimize the impact of their behavior, or rationalize their actions. They may assume they know how others think or feel and then act according to their assumptions. In their attempts to avoid responsibility, they often try to distract others from focusing on their behavior. When they talk about their actions, they may be vague or change the subject. They frequently take a "victim stance" and attempt to get others to feel sorry for them. These children may manipulate others either with angry outbursts or by pretending to be nice.

When people use thinking errors to justify their behavior, it is easier for them to commit actions that hurt or exploit others. Lane (1997a) noted that sexually abusive children often exhibit "a tendency to rely on a compensatory coping style that involves a misuse of power and control in many situations" (p. 330). She described examples of "power-based behaviors," including fights, disobeying rules, anger outbursts to get their own way, hitting, and provoking younger children and peers. Similarly, Johnson (1993b) described severely disordered children whose sexual behaviors had "an impulsive, compulsive, and aggressive quality" (p. 49).

Children with sexually abusive behavior problems are often impulsive and fail to consider the consequences of their behavior (Cunningham and MacFarlane, 1991, 1996; Gil and Johnson, 1993; Lane, 1991a; 1997a). They often have difficulty delaying gratification and place their wishes above those of others. A combination of harsh treatment and lack of structure and guidance can adversely affect a child's capacity to effectively self-guide (Staub, 1996). Staub further stated that self-control does not develop when there is chaos. Children need external structure to develop internal structure and the capacity for effective self-guidance. When external structure is lacking, aggression and lack of accountability often result. Similarly, Araji and Finkelhor (1986) indicated that internal and external barriers which inhibit sexual perpetration prior to the occurrence of an offense.

Early intervention is important to decrease the adverse effects of impulsiveness. Eyberg (cited in Burnette, and Murray, 1996) developed a program for children ages two to six years who meet DSM-IV criteria for the diagnosis of oppositional defiant disorder in an effort to stop the development of conduct disorders. Much of the focus of this program was to teach parents to manage their children's behaviors. Children learn to make more responsible choices when adults hold them accountable. Children who take responsibility for their behavior are more likely to consider others' feelings and are therefore less likely to engage in sexual offenses or other victimizing behaviors.

Social Competence

A deficit in social skills is a common behavioral characteristic of sexually abusive children (Beichtman et al., 1992; Cunningham and MacFarlane, 1991, 1996; Friedrich and Luecke, 1988; Gil and Johnson, 1993; Johnson, 1988, 1989; Johnson and Berry, 1989; Lane, 1991a, 1997a; Ray and English, 1995; Shapiro et al., 1992; Trickett and Putnam, 1993; Young, Bergandi, and Titus, 1994). These studies found that such children frequently have difficulty relating to peers. They may be self-centered, controlling, aggressive, or hostile; others are socially withdrawn and are uncomfortable relating to other children. Tong, Oates, and McDowell (1987) found relatively long-term (two and one-half years after abuse) effects of abuse on social interactions of a sample of forty-nine children and adolescents, specifically related to self-confidence, number of friends, and aggression, as reported by parents.

The sexually abusive children in the authors' treatment program have shown social skill deficits in problem solving, anger management, assertiveness, and communication. We learned from our clinical experiences that sexually abusive children have a variety of problems associated with their social skill deficits. Their difficulty relating to peers can make them targets of other children's put-downs or verbal abuse. When they are rejected by their peers, they may experience feelings of worthlessness and self-depreciation and show signs of depression (Cunningham and MacFarlane, 1991, 1996; Lane, 1991a, 1997a). Feelings of inadequacy and inferiority become problematic when sexually abusive children attempt to compensate through control-seeking behaviors. They may seek out, manipulate, and intimidate younger children in an attempt to meet their own needs. Some may use sexualized behaviors to interact socially with others.

Sexually abusive children often engage in inappropriate attention-seeking behaviors rather than openly acknowledge their need for help. They may manipulate others through sulking, passive-aggressive behavior, or temper outbursts (Lane, 1991a, 1997a). For some children, feelings of inadequacy, impulsiveness, and oppositional behavior may relate to biological conditions such as a learning disability or attention deficit hyperactivity disorder (ADHD). In fact, Lane (1997a) noted that the most prevalent psychiatric diagnosis of the sexually abusive children treated in her program was ADHD. The negative reactions children with these conditions receive from their environment contributes to their sense of personal inadequacy and diminished self-esteem. Therefore, it is important to consider both biological and environmental factors when assessing and providing treatment to sexually abusive children.

Empathy

Empathy is "the capacity to read the cues of others and thus imagine the experience of the other" (Ryan, 1997c, p. 127). Children with sexually abusive behavior problems frequently display lack of empathy (Cunningham and MacFarlane, 1991, 1996; Johnson, 1993b, 1995b; Lane, 1997a). They often have difficulty noticing the cues of others and may harm other children without recognizing that they are causing others pain. Their lack of empathy separates them from other children who display caring behavior. Feeling resentful, sexually abusive children may become opportunistic, aggressive, and show predatory behavior.

Parental practices and "the totality of the child's experiences in the home and the outside world form the child and shape aggressiveness in general, and forms of aggressiveness in particular" (Staub, 1996, p. 122). An empathic, caring environment helps children to develop caring behavior. "Empathy occurs throughout numerous and frequent interactions with an attuned and responsive caregiver" (Friedrich, 1995, p. 72). Landry and Peters (1992) noted that infants who experience empathic care begin to demonstrate empathic reactions to the cues of others as early as eighteen months.

Several studies have provided information about young children's capacities to empathize with others. Aggressive preschoolers were found to have delays in interpersonal awareness and perspective taking, relative to their peers (Minde, 1992). Similarly, empathy (operationalized as perspective taking) was strongly related to prosocial behavior in ten- to eleven-year-old children (Bengtsson and Johnson, 1992). There is some evidence that early intervention programs such as Head Start can reduce aggression (Ziegler, Taussig, and Black, 1992). However, conflict mediation and social skills training can probably do most to facilitate the development of social competence and empathy and reduce aggression in children, if conducted within a community of caring that includes adults and peers in the children's lives (Staub, 1996). In fact, Zahn-Waxler, Radke-Yarrow, and King (1979) found empathic caregiving by mothers was related to caring behavior displayed by children as young as one and one-half to two and one-half years old.

Other studies have examined the association between lack of empathy and aggressive or antisocial behavior. This research has generally found antisocial behavior in children to be associated with deficits in empathy (Damon, 1988; Feshbach and Feshbach, 1969; Feshbach et al., 1983; Miller and Eisenberg, 1988; Selman, 1980; Zahn-Waxler et al., 1995). There is indication that abuse interferes with the development of empathy and prosocial behavior very early in life. Main and George (1985) and Klimes-Dougan and Kistner (1990) studied preschoolers' responses to peers' distress. Both studies indicated that children who were physically abused exhibited a greater number of inappropriate responses (aggression and withdrawal) toward peers than nonabused children. The nonabused children in these studies tended to respond with interest, concern, empathy, or sadness. Howes and Eldredge (1985) even noted that maltreated preschool children resisted friendly overtures from others.

Interference with the process of learning emotional regulation may lead to disruptions in the development of empathy and other prosocial behaviors (Osofsky, 1995). Zahn-Waxler and colleagues (1995) focused on empathic and prosocial orientations in preschool children who were considered to be at low, medium, and high risk for developing disruptive behavior disorders, based on their current behavior problems. When these children first witnessed someone in distress, they all initially reacted with similar levels of empathic concern and prosocial behavior. However, moderate- and high-risk children were less likely to remain positively engaged with distressed victims.

Many sexually abusive children do not live in an environment that is conducive to developing empathy; they tend to live in troubled homes. Strayer (1980) noted that sadness is less related to empathy than are happy emotions. Therefore, it is perhaps unreasonable to expect children living in abusive or neglectful circumstances to develop empathy. Nonetheless, there are numerous case examples of individuals surmounting the effects of environmental degradation to engage in prosocial activities. Since the precise circumstances of a child's early social development are most often unknown or only partially understood, it may be these individuals were able to form a close attachment with someone at a young age. Cunningham and MacFarlane (1996) noted that securely attached children "have developed self-empathy and empathy towards others, and will be able to form intimate, positive relationships with others" (p. 24). Conversely, children who lack a secure attachment with a caregiver are more likely to lack empathy for others. Cunningham and MacFarlane pointed out that children with sexually abusive behavior problems often have "disruptions in their attachment to a significant caregiver" (p. 24) and "have not developed self and other-directed empathy" (p. 25). Certainly, "In the interest of preventing further victimization . . . it is important to have some focus [in treatment] on understanding the perspectives of others" (Friedrich, 1995, p. 72).

Establishment of Boundaries

Boundaries are limits that define the separateness of individuals within systems (Katherine, 1991). They are "invisible and symbolic 'fences' that serve three purposes: (a) to keep people from coming into our space and abusing us; (b) to keep us from going into the space of others and abusing them, and (c) to give each of us a way to embody our sense of 'who we are'" (Mellody, 1989, p. 11). In a family system, boundaries define limits between a family and the outside world as well as divisions between the spousal, parental, and sibling subsystems (Minuchin, 1974). Families in which sexual abuse takes place typically have dysfunctional boundary patterns (Burkett, 1991; Larson and Maddock, 1986; Maddock and Larson,

1995; Madonna, Van Scoyk, and Jones, 1991; Regina and LeBoy, 1991; Sgroi, 1982; Will, 1983). Boundary disturbances are frequently evident in four areas: (1) external (between the family and its social environment); (2) generational (between adult and child generations); (3) interpersonal (between family members); and (4) intrapsychic (within individuals) (Larson and Maddock, 1986; Maddock and Larson, 1995).

Disturbance in external boundaries is exhibited in the families of sexually abused and sexually abusive children in several ways. First, the family may isolate itself by establishing rigid rules that limit interaction with nonfamily members. These rules may protect the secret of sexual abuse by insulating family members and forcing them to depend solely upon each other for emotional support (Larson and Maddock, 1986). Lack of environmental feedback reinforces the closed nature of the external boundaries and makes change less likely. Systems theorists contend that "the extent to which a family allows new information and experiences to enter the system, determines in part its potential for growth and change" (Hartman and Laird, 1983, p. 64). While open systems have permeable boundaries and are receptive to environmental input, closed systems move toward "entropy, randomness, or lack of organization and differentiation" (Ibid.).

The difficulties sexually abusive children have establishing social competency may be related to disturbances in the boundary between the family and its outside environment. Families of sexually abusive children often lack a supportive network of extended family and friends, which, if present, would help them build social competency. Following disclosure regarding sexual abuse, a family comes into contact with social and/or legal systems. Boundaries may "rigidify even more as they [family members] attempt to maintain homeostasis and keep the family intact" (Larson and Maddock, 1986, p. 29). Treatment professionals must be aware of these rigid boundaries and focus first on family members' fears and defensiveness as they establish a relationship.

Disturbance in generational boundaries results in confused role distinctions (Burkett, 1991). Parents may involve their children in conflicts in their marriage, creating triangles in which children are pressured to side with one parent against the other (Bowen, 1978).

They may also abdicate important responsibilities while children take on household tasks and care for younger siblings. Parents may either fail to set appropriate expectations for their children's behaviors or set limits so inconsistently that parental authority is unclear or ignored (Sgroi, 1982). In the chaotic environment of conflictual relationships, blurred roles, and unclear parental authority, children are at risk to develop parentified behavior and "a false self" (Winnicott, 1965) focused on meeting the needs of others. They may then be more likely to misuse the authority given them by their parents by becoming abusive.

Sexually abusive children and their family members sometimes have enmeshed interpersonal boundaries that inhibit individuals from developing separate identities (Bowen, 1978; Minuchin, 1974). Family members must yield their autonomy in order to belong; in fact, "differentness is experienced as distance and individuality is viewed as alienation and disloyalty" (Larson and Maddock, 1986, p. 30). Families in which attachment has not occurred contrast with enmeshed families. In these disorganized families, the parents may function as independent entities while siblings provide little support or socialization for each other. Affectional relationships remain superficial, parental supervision is poor, and family organization is chaotic (Ryan, 1991c, 1997d).

In families with sexually abusive children, disturbance in interpersonal boundaries most commonly involves lack of respect for family members and violations of privacy and personal space. Disrespectful communication may include name-calling, blaming, and other forms of verbal or emotional abuse. This type of communication may create an environment of power and control, and "when power dominates, the stage is set for competition and conflict" (Maddock and Larson, 1995, p. 56). Power domination includes the abusive dynamics of power differential, intimidation, manipulation, and coercion and may lead to sexually abusive behavior. Violations of privacy (e.g., involving bathroom use, dressing, or undressing) may also create an unsafe environment in which sexual contact between family members may occur (Gil, 1993c; Johnson, 1995a, 1995b; McNamera, 1990).

The thinking errors described earlier in this chapter are a way in which disturbance in intrapsychic boundaries is manifested in families of sexually abusive children. Psychopathology, or disturbance in intrapsychic boundaries, involves a lack of fit between an individual's internal personality structure and the environment, "resulting in distortions of meaning and behavior" (Maddock and Larson, 1995, p. 81). Defense mechanisms such as denial are used "to help minimize the cognitive dissonance and emotional pain created by the familial abuse while maintaining . . . emotional dependency and interpersonal enmeshment" (Ibid.).

The Sexual Abuse Cycle

Clinicians who treat sexually abusive children often apply intervention models that were originally developed for adult and adolescent sex offenders. One such model, the sexual abuse cycle (assault cycle, offense cycle) is a construct that describes the "process" of sexually offending behavior. It was initially created to describe the offending process of violent adolescent sex offenders (Lane and Zamora, 1984) but is now widely used with all types of adolescent sex offenders. Although research has begun to confirm elements of the sexual abuse cycle concept, it has not been empirically validated (Lane, 1991b, 1997b). There are several versions of the sexual abuse cycle (Kahn, 1990; Lane, 1991b, 1997b; Ryan et al., 1987; Ryan, 1989; Stickrod Gray and Mussack, 1988), to including one version adapted for use with sexually abusive children (Isaac and Lane, 1990; Lane 1991a, 1997a). A version presented by Stickrod Gray and Mussack (1988) is shown in Figure 1.1.

Ryan (1989) defines the sexual abuse cycle as "a predictable pattern of negative feelings, cognitive distortions, and control seeking behaviors, leading to a sexual offense" (p. 328). Some view the sexual abuse cycle as having three phases: precipitating, compensatory response, and integration (Lane, 1991b, 1997b). The precipitating phase involves being exposed to a stressful event, negatively misinterpreting the event, and coping through avoidance. The compensatory phase involves increasing self-esteem and reducing anxiety through power-based or compensatory behavior. In the integration phase, the individual rationalizes the offending behavior in order to avoid self-depreciating feelings.

Clinicians who use the sexual abuse cycle as a conceptual framework tend to focus on helping young offenders to (1) identify trig-

FIGURE 1.1. The Assault Cycle

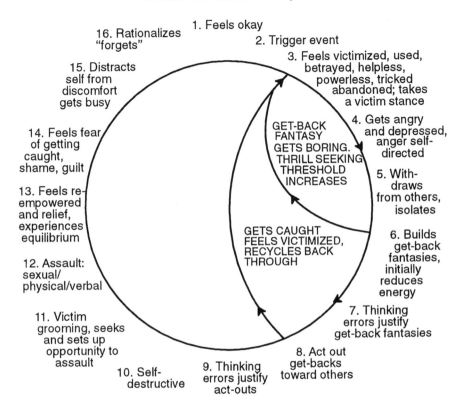

Source: *Teaching the Juvenile Sex Offender to Clarify the Assault Cycle* by A. Stickrod Gray and S. Mussack (1988). Reprinted by permission.

ger events and negative feelings about those events, (2) recognize and correct cognitive distortions, (3) interrupt power-based or compensatory thoughts and behaviors, and (4) acknowledge responsibility for offending behaviors. Sexually abusive children can learn to identify the steps in the sexual abuse cycle and use these steps to avoid sexually inappropriate behaviors. For children, these steps include identifying triggers, recognizing and correcting thinking errors, and setting up a plan to prevent a reoffense.

SUMMARY

Children who commit harmful sexual acts against other children are known as sexually abusive children or children with sexually abusive behavior problems. It is critical to differentiate sexually abusive behaviors from age-appropriate sex play. Children with sexually abusive behavior problems often use power differences, intimidation, manipulation, and coercion to initiate inappropriate sexual behaviors with other children.

We have reviewed the literature describing factors that appear salient for children with sexually abusive behavior problems—prior traumatization, accountability, social competence, empathy, establishment of boundaries, and the sexual abuse cycle. A number of factors may contribute to the etiology of sexually offending behaviors. Any model intended to predict sexually abusive behavior must consider a combination of factors and account for the interaction of developmental issues. Whether they are additive or interactive or whether any one factor in isolation can be a necessary precursor to sexually abusive behavior has yet to be empirically explored.

The remaining chapters in Part I present our treatment approach for intervention with sexually abusive children. Chapter 2 presents the Trauma Outcome Process, a practice model that addresses both victim and offender issues. Chapter 3 presents guidelines for assessment and describes our integrated treatment program. Finally, Chapter 4 describes the structure of the parallel group treatment program for sexually abusive children and their parents.

Chapter 2

A Treatment Approach

Parallel child and parent treatment addresses individual and family dynamics concurrently throughout the therapy process. Although therapy is initiated to address the child's inappropriate sexual behavior, parental involvement is critical to successful treatment. Family dynamics often contribute to and help maintain a child's sexually offending behavior. In most cases, a child cannot make the changes needed to overcome sexual behavior problems without changes taking place in the family environment as well. If further abusive behavior is to be prevented, the principles learned in therapy need to be generalized to home, neighborhood, and community. Whether a family situation is permanent or temporary (e.g., foster care), this generalization cannot take place without an established partnership between therapists and parents. Parents are an integral part of the treatment process and a child's relapse prevention plan (i.e., a plan to interrupt further abusive patterns of behavior to prevent reoffenses).

Children, their parents, and other family members are frequently in a state of crisis when therapy begins. Children are often embarrassed, defensive, and anxious about their parents' reactions to their offenses. Often parents are still in shock after finding out that their child has committed a sexual offense. Parents may blame themselves for their child's problems and ask themselves what they did wrong. Some worry about the future implications of their child's behavior and fear that he/she may one day end up in prison as a child molester. Others may be so angry about the offense that they find it difficult to talk to their child or to offer support. In a few cases, parents may deny that their child has a sexual problem and instead claim that the victim and his/her family were overreacting or not telling the truth about what happened.

A therapist must first assess parents' reactions to the disclosure of sexually abusive behavior and evaluate their abilities to cope with the situation and provide their child adequate support and supervision. The stress of coping with sexually abusive behavior may place sexually abusive children at risk for abuse. This is especially true if parents are extremely stressed and lack impulse control. If the situation in the home seems volatile, it may be advisable to recommend that the sexually abusive child be temporarily placed in the home of extended family members or friends, until the parent has had time to contain and learn to manage the anger provoked by the discovery of the child's offense(s). Pianta, Egeland, and Erickson (1989) found:

> a child may become the victim of maltreatment, not because of his own behavior, but because the child places added burdens upon an already stressed or incapable family system, resulting in a breakdown in the processes of good parenting. For example, parents who have yet to resolve their feelings about their own upbringing, who are involved in dysfunctional interpersonal relationships, or who are experiencing environmental stress such as unemployment may also find it difficult to meet the needs of any child, especially one who presents challenges for caretakers. It is also possible that children with substantially deviant behavioral or temperamental characteristics might place extreme stress on otherwise competent caretakers who may engage in maltreating behavior. (pp. 209-210)

It is important to begin treatment with a clear explanation of what is expected in therapy. Children and parents may be told that during the course of treatment children will be expected to tell what they did (accountability), describe what has (perhaps) happened to them (prior traumatization), learn how their victim(s) might feel (empathy), and learn to respect others by treating them appropriately and giving them space (social competence and boundaries). Parents sometimes avoid talking to their children about their offenses because they feel embarrassed and uncomfortable when they approach the topic of sexual behavior. Children are often painfully aware that their parents are having difficulty coping with their offenses. Therapists may help by calmly presenting to both children and their parents that children who have "learned to touch others' privates" can usually "learn to stop." They can emphasize to the child that other children do not like being touched on their private parts or may feel confused or scared. It is usually reassuring when therapists send a clear message to both children and parents that therapy can help them.

TRAUMA OUTCOME PROCESS

The Trauma Outcome Process (Brown and Rasmussen, 1994; Rasmussen, Burton, and Christopherson, 1992) (see Figure 2.1) is an adaptation of the sexual abuse cycle that delineates recovery, self-victimization, and abuse as three potential responses to trauma. It is both an explanation of the etiology of sexually abusive behavior problems and a treatment approach. This framework, based on psychodynamic, social learning, and humanistic theories, views the abusive process of the sexual abuse cycle as only *one* possible response to traumatic experience(s). The recovery response represents healthy coping, while the self-victimization and abuse responses represent maladaptive coping styles. Similar to other psychodynamic trauma models (e.g., the PTSD model), the Trauma Outcome Process views internal conflicts and unresolved feelings related to traumatic events as important motivators of behavior. However, similar to the sexual abuse cycle and social learning models (e.g., traumagenic dynamics of abuse model [Finkehor and Browne, 1985, 1988], four conditions of abuse model [Araji and Finkelhor, 1986]), the Trauma Outcome Process highlights the role of adaptive and maladaptive thinking processes. In addition, this framework is humanistic because it stresses awareness and choice as factors that determine an individual's response to traumatic events.

The Trauma Outcome Process is useful as a practice model for treating victims and offenders. Clinicians use this conceptual framework to help sexually abusive children identify their individual responses to traumatic events, determine if their responses are healthy or dysfunctional, and replace dysfunctional responses with adaptive responses. In similar fashion, parents are encouraged to confront any prior traumas of their own, identify their individual reactions to stress, and strengthen their positive coping styles.

FIGURE 2.1. Trauma Outcome Process

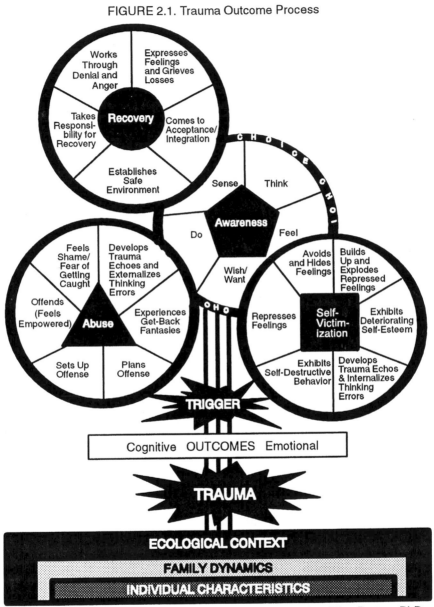

©1997 Revised, ©1995, Lucinda A. Rasmussen, PhD, Jan Ellen Burton, PhD, Barbara J. Christopherson, LCSW, Julie Bradshaw, LCSW, Arthur H. Brown III, PhD.

In the Trauma Outcome Process, individual and family characteristics interact to influence a child's responses to traumatic events (Brown and Rasmussen, 1994; Rasmussen, Burton, and Christopherson, 1992). Each child has unique individual and family characteristics and dynamics. Resilience or vulnerability to the effects of trauma depends on the interaction of the child's cognitive and personality strengths and weaknesses. Family dynamics and ecological factors influence this interaction. For example, if a child's family provides adequate emotional support at the time of a trauma, negative impacts may be lessened. Similarly, a child's response to trauma may be influenced by cultural, societal, and other ecological factors. Support provided within a child's environment (e.g., by extended family members, teachers and other school personnel, neighbors, church members) may help the child and his/her family to cope with the effects of trauma. Child protection and mental health resources in the community may provide additional environmental support.

Individual Characteristics

Specific characteristics often present when children develop sexually abusive behavior problems have been addressed in the previous chapter (i.e., effects of prior traumatization, accountability, social competence, and empathy). The following presentation is intended to illustrate those factors and clarify how they interact to influence the development of sexually abusive behavior in children. "Most sexually abused children who exhibit sexual behavior are not thinking about their next action nor are they linking it to the abuse they experienced" (Friedrich, 1995, p. 111). However, most can later identify steps they took as they planned, initiated, and covered up their offenses. Treatment is a process of helping children to become aware of their feelings and vulnerabilities prior to offending. Some appear to act out sexually in response to current feelings. Others may have particular difficulty inhibiting their sexual impulses when they are aroused by external circumstances or situations reminiscent of prior victimization (Friedrich, 1995).

We initially anticipated that work with young children would be short-term because they would not be as highly motivated to offend as older perpetrators. Clinical experiences soon indicated that initial impression was false. Unfortunately, many children engage in repeated sex offenses because they are highly sexualized. Some of these children may later become conduct-disordered offending adolescents. Others may continue to be vulnerable to sexual overtures from peers or adults. They may exhibit behaviors that illustrate both the assault and self-victimizing cycles of the Trauma Outcome Process. For example, Georgia, age nine, was a victim of repeated sexual abuse by her father and uncle. She was placed in foster care and then molested her three foster siblings and a neighbor boy. She told her foster mother that she wanted to have her own apartment when she grew up so she could have men stay over. She consistently emulated teenage hairstyles and pulled out the braids and ponytails her foster mother tried to convince her to wear. Georgia's excessive interest in physical attractiveness and sexuality, acquired through the modeling of adults in her traumatic past, was self-destructive in preventing her from enjoying the age-appropriate activities of a latency-age child. Furthermore, her fixation on sexual themes led to further abusive actions. It is the premise of this book that the interaction of prior traumatic and socialization experiences as well as accountability and empathy impacts an individual's choice of behavior.

Friedrich (1995) describes common themes that become the focus in treating sexual abuse: these are decreased power and control, a sense of differentness, guilt and shame, and impaired self-integrity. Abused children often carry scars from past trauma that alter their perceptions of the world and affect the way they interact with others (Finkelhor, 1988). Unless they have an opportunity to express their feelings and correct their misperceptions, they remain at risk to act out their ambivalent feelings in inappropriate or abusive behavior. For example, when he was five years old, Nathan witnessed an adolescent boy performing anal sex on his ten-year-old brother. He tried unsuccessfully to get the older boy to stop. Although Nathan was not molested himself, he became fearful, angry, and later sexually abused his younger sister. Nathan's feelings of powerlessness contributed to his entering the abuse cycle.

Darren, a nine-year-old sexually abusive child, at first tried to deny he had molested several younger boys in his neighborhood. When his therapist confronted him with statements by the boys,

Darren finally admitted his sexual involvement. However, he justified his actions by saying, "They wanted to do it. I had to do it because they made me." Not only did Darren blame the other children for the behavior he initiated, he showed both "assuming" and "taking a victim stance" thinking errors when he claimed the other children wanted to do it and made him participate. When children are not accountable, it is often because their daily environment does not support self-disclosure. Therapists can sometimes help by providing a choice of whether to discuss problems now or later. It is preferable for children to say, "I don't want to talk about it," rather than to engage in repeated denial. Discussion of problems leads sexually abusive children in the direction of recovery and away from the destructive responses of self-victimization and abuse.

A sense of differentness, guilt and shame, and impaired self-integrity can inhibit the development of social competence, although positive social experiences can ameliorate these effects and promote recovery from past traumatic events. Impaired self-integrity refers to the concept of the "false self" (Winnicott, 1965), in which a child may "become precociously mature superficially, almost always in the service of an adults' needs, but . . . feel empty internally," (Friedrich, 1995, p. 164). Abused children who have impaired self-integrity may relate precociously with adults. They may attempt to please adults by engaging in sexualized behavior. For example, Laura was molested when she was a young child by several adult perpetrators. At age eleven, she related seductively with adult men, often sitting on their laps or initiating hugs and kisses. When asked about this behavior, she became tearful and said she merely wanted someone to love her. Laura's behavior reflected both her desire to please adults and her own internal emptiness.

Sexually abusive children may also display evidence of impaired self-integrity by showing awkwardness in social settings. They sometimes have difficulties initiating conversations or asking friends to play games. As abused children move toward achieving developmental goals of self-integrity and competence (Erikson, 1963; Winnicott, 1965), they may attempt to gain control or seek affection from peers in inappropriate ways. Sexually abusive behavior may be one result. For example, Ray, a ten-year-old sexually abusive boy, was usually the last child chosen for teams at school. Other children frequently reacted negatively to his bossy and controlling behavior. His typical response when denied what he wanted was to shut down and refuse to talk for hours at a time. His inability to relate to his peers and his poor coping skills were evidence of his failure to achieve a sense of self-integrity and competence.

Some children act out sexually in an attempt to meet needs for affection and nurturing. Alan came from a family in which all siblings were acting out sexually with one another following molestations by various persons. He appeared shy and awkward in social situations. He fondled other children in school regularly, with incidents occurring each week over a period of months. As he became more accountable for his sexual behavior, Alan began to identify this behavior as an attempt to relate to others. He later learned to find more appropriate ways to interact socially.

When children complete therapy, they usually have some experience in making responsible choices directed toward recovery from trauma. It is much easier to redirect them to prosocial patterns of behavior once they have new social skills and have developed increased social competency. Mary acted out sexually with a same-age peer just after her discharge from treatment. She did so at the instigation of the other child. Although she had stopped initiating sexual activity herself, she did not pause to think before acting when approached by another. She later admitted to her therapist that she had felt sexually aroused and reacted impulsively rather than using techniques she had learned in therapy.

Empathy, or concern for others, "provides the highest level of deterrence for abusive behavior" (Ryan, 1997c, p. 127). Children with sexually abusive behavior problems lack the ability to understand how their manipulative and coercive behaviors harm others as well as themselves. Unless they learn empathy skills, they remain at risk to continue to act in self-destructive or abusive ways. Developing empathy can help them stop their behaviors before they hurt someone and help them cope more effectively with stressful situations. For example, Zack, age ten, did not understand how he had hurt the two boys he molested until his therapist asked him to mimic the cries they made during the offense. When Zack attempted to imitate the boys' cries, he became tearful and said, "I guess I really hurt them." Once Zack realized his behavior was hurtful, he was able to progress in treatment. He became more aware of others' feelings and started noticing their behavioral cues. He incorporated what he had learned in his relapse prevention plan when he wrote, "I will listen to others and notice how they feel."

Controversy exists among professionals as to whether young children can experience empathy. The disagreement seems to be related to the criterion that empathy involves putting oneself in another's place. This cognition is not typically observed in children by researchers until the age of seven or eight. Nonetheless, as described in Chapter 1, there is evidence that the concept of prosocial behavior and concern for others exhibits itself much earlier, perhaps at a preverbal level (Landry and Peters, 1992; Zahn-Waxler, Radke-Yarrow, and King, 1979). One of the authors recently observed Sara, age three years, one month, slowing down during a race so her four-year-old brother would win. She then proudly exclaimed, "Yeah, Ryan!"

Family Dynamics

Family dynamics are affected by individual child characteristics as well as by environmental and cultural factors. This discussion cannot be all-inclusive, as each person is affected differently by similar experiences in seemingly comparable family environments. However, it is possible to describe common topics or themes that frequently arise in treating sexually abusive children. Examples of potentially relevant family dynamics include the appropriateness of family boundaries, parents' levels of accountability, relationships between family members, prior trauma experienced by parents, and parenting skills.

Family Boundaries

It is important to question how family members define and respect privacy. In families of sexually abusive children, personal space and privacy are often ignored. Individuals may intrude upon one another's privacy without seeming to be aware of this intrusion. In some cases, appropriate rules for using the toilet, bathing, changing clothes, and/or sleeping arrangements have not been established. For example, a parent might allow a sexually abusive child to be unsupervised with another sibling while using the bathroom. Other children may sleep in various rooms throughout the night. Family members may bathe or shower together or walk through the house unclothed.

Cultural and socioeconomic factors sometimes affect the type of privacy practiced in families. What may appear to be a boundary violation in one culture may be acceptable in another. Most cultures still have adequate restraints in place to deter abusive behavior. In addition, socioeconomic conditions may influence how privacy is implemented. Many families live in small apartments with few bedrooms. Parents may need to be creative in their efforts to protect privacy. Even in small apartments, privacy may be respected by taking such steps as hanging curtains to section off rooms or establishing clear rules regarding bathroom use.

Emotionally intrusive behavior is also present in families of sexually abusive children. Some parents of sexually abusive children turn to their children rather than toward each other or peers to meet their emotional needs. This creates a blurring of boundaries between generations. The resulting enmeshment of family members inhibits their individual strengths and discourages attempts to develop relationships outside the family. Social isolation from neighbors and the community often results. For example, members of one family felt rejected whenever they dealt with the outside world. They began to consciously choose associations within the family rather than risk more rejection from neighbors and peers. This pattern of coping protected them from negative experiences but exacerbated their social isolation.

Another family, on first glance, appeared well connected to church, neighborhood, and community. When sibling incest was disclosed, an examination of the family system revealed that the parents discouraged outside friendships; family relationships were valued to the exclusion of others. Both parents justified enmeshment by espousing family closeness as a virtue. They had difficulty identifying problematic patterns governing personal space and interactions within their home. Unless specific questions were asked, problems such as missing bathroom doors and holes in walls were not disclosed.

Beverly, a young mother, felt helpless to confront continued intrusions and unrealistic expectations from her own parents and siblings. She lacked the assertiveness necessary to confront their invasiveness effectively. In an attempt to overcorrect for the enmeshed boundaries she had experienced as a child, she later chose to sever her relationships with her parents and siblings. She was then left without a support system, which led to social isolation.

Two sexually abusive brothers competed with and detracted from each other's progress in treatment. They set each other up for explosive episodes and belittled and demeaned each other in front of family and peers. In group therapy, this dynamic was illustrated when the brothers reported each other's problem behaviors. They did not support each other's efforts to do well. Their competitiveness at home created family discord and often ended in violence. Parental inconsistency in providing discipline and structure contributed to the chaos.

As emotionally immature parents try to meet their needs through one of their children, they sometimes emotionally isolate the other parent. Alignments can shift, with any of the three family members alternately playing victim, rescuer, and persecutor roles (Karpman, 1968). It becomes difficult in these families to clearly distinguish individual identities. As interpersonal boundaries become blurred, intimacy becomes difficult to achieve. One mother, Harriet, admitted using her adolescent son, Phillip, as an adviser and confidant, particularly when her husband, Don, removed himself from parental responsibilities. Don then began to feel left out and alternately took part in and avoided family issues. Phillip responded to his father's ambivalence with anger and defiance, thereby perpetuating negative interactions within the family.

Accountability

It is difficult to discuss what children must do to make progress without addressing parents' views regarding the seriousness of their children's offenses. Many parents do not initially know exactly what their child has done. Once they learn the details, they often express disbelief that their child has participated in such intrusive sexual behavior. Some parents initially tend to blame the victim for perpetrating the abuse. Others perceive "the system" as overreacting to the offense(s). Further discussions often show parents do not understand how the abuse affected their child's victims. One mother commented that she could accept her son's responsibility for the first time the abuse occurred, but she felt the victim was to blame when that child returned to her home and a second incident occurred. Another mother became enraged when her son's victim told other children at school about the molestation. Parents who blame others for their child's misbehavior, or who show a lack of understanding of the effects of their children's abusive actions, may later blame the therapist for failing to solve their child's problems. These responses are understandable since it is painful for parents to acknowledge the seriousness of their child's sexually abusive behavior problems.

Parents often have thinking errors (Berenson, 1987; Salter, 1995; Stickrod and Mussack, 1986; Yochelson and Samenow, 1976) of their own that affect how they view their children's behavior. Sexually abusive children have committed acts that involve a breach of trust. Taking responsibility involves an examination of both the abusive behavior and the thinking processes leading to that behavior. When children provide full descriptions of their offenses to their parents, the impact of such disclosures often enables parents to break through their own minimization or denial of the seriousness of the offenses. Once parents recognize how they avoid accountability, they can begin to see how their own thinking patterns are consistent with those used by their children. They can better understand how their children avoid being accountable for their behavior. Accepting responsibility for their own cognitive distortions can thereby help parents facilitate the same process in their children.

In addition to minimizing their child's offense and blaming others, parents frequently make faulty assumptions. These inaccurate assumptions can result in inappropriate responses. One common assumption is that a child's misbehavior is a direct attack against the parents' authority. If parents react punitively or engage in a power struggle with their child, they may further erode the child's sense of control. When parents learn to avoid making out an assumptions, they usually find misbehavior to have a completely different motivation. As parents acknowledge and correct inaccurate assumptions and other thinking errors, they are better able to help their children make progress in treatment.

Prior Traumatization

Many parents of sexually abusive children are victims of physical, emotional, and/or sexual abuse. Even though parents are often asked about prior trauma during an initial assessment, some do not recall abuse until they begin dealing with the dynamics of their child's sexual offense(s). Their child's perpetrating behavior may trigger memories of their abuse, which may rekindle past feelings of anger and helplessness. They may feel torn between their desire to support their children and anger toward their child, who has victimized another as they themselves were victimized. Parents who have a history of abuse may be reluctant to accept their child's sexual behavior as a sexual offense. It may be necessary for them to face their own victim issues before they can acknowledge their child's behavior as abusive.

Upon hearing their children's disclosures, parents sometimes make decisions relating to their own abuse history. One mother subsequently confronted her own father about their past incestuous relationship; another actually wrote a "divorce decree" stating she would have no contact with her incestuous father or her mother, as her efforts to communicate with them about her past abuse had been unsuccessful. It is important for parents to understand their own abuse issues so they can be active participants in their children's relapse prevention team (i.e., concerned adults who assist a sexually abusive child to avoid a reoffense [Gray and Pithers, 1993]).

Interpersonal Relationships

Relationships include interactions with family members, friends, and neighbors, and different types of relationships meet different needs. Although needs for love and affection may primarily be met through intimate relationships, casual relationships also meet needs for socialization and acceptance. An ideal intimate relationship is characterized as one in which both parties are allowed a sense of self, without the erosion of the other's identity. The enmeshed or disengaged boundaries frequently seen in families of sexually abusive children interfere in relationships and may preclude the development of true intimacy. It is difficult to achieve a sense of self when the family environment includes such characteristics as role confusion, disrespect, and violation of privacy. Family members may lack the sense of safety, predictability, and consistency that engender the development of secure and intimate attachments.

Parents of sexually abusive children often have problems in both their intimate and casual relationships. They may be socially isolated and lack close connections with family members (including extended family members living outside the home), friends, and neighbors. They may have particular difficulty forming and maintaining intimate relationships. Some parents struggle with unresolved conflict with their former spouses, including disputes over child custody and visitation. Parenting a sexually abusive child can be especially difficult for a single parent who lacks external support and who is unable to provide the vigilant supervision sexually abusive children often require. In two-parent households, marital discord may prevent parents from working together to nurture and discipline their children effectively. Parents may not support each other in their efforts to supervise. It is not unusual for the demands of therapy schedules, supervision of the sexually abusive child, court appearances, and doctor appointments to fall mainly on one spouse. These demands can add stress to an already troubled marriage.

Sexually abusive children often exhibit conflictual interactions with adults and peers. Parents may feel helpless when their child attempts to control and manipulate them with anger and defiance. Many parents tend to avoid their child's anger by giving in or diverting their attention elsewhere. Parents who have been victimized themselves may be especially prone to this pattern. Although they may have participated in prior treatment to address their victim issues, these parents may fall back into the victim role and feel vulnerable and out of control. This pattern of behavior interferes with effective discipline and may place children at risk both to be abused and to abuse others.

When parents are unable to effectively meet their own emotional needs, they can have difficulty nurturing their children. The children may then experience emotional deprivation and seek attention, nurturing, and affection from alternative sources. Siblings may turn to one another for comfort. This can be problematic when children have been traumatized through a prior molestation or other sexual exposure, especially in families that have unclear boundaries about personal space and privacy. Sexually abusive behavior may result.

While living with a neglectful and alcoholic mother, Charlie was molested by his baby-sitter's son. Since Charlie's mother was not physically and emotionally available to him and his brother, Larry, the brothers turned to each other as a consistent source of support. They became enmeshed and Larry developed little independent identity. He always turned to Charlie for approval before responding to questions or acting on his own. Their enmeshment was exhibited by their sexually abusive behavior with each other as well.

Family members' early attempts at socialization may be frustrated by poor social skills. In his discussion on the generational pattern of abusive parents, Rutter (1989) notes, "Social support is not only a feature of what is available in the environment; it also reflects personality strengths and weaknesses in eliciting or attracting support" (p. 320). In an attempt to elicit support, one mother engaged in victim/rescuer relationships that actually "burned out" her support networks one by one. One father, Wayne, provided assistance to neighbors whenever they asked for help. When his own request for help was refused, he felt used, hurt, and angry and became reluctant to ask again. It did not occur to Wayne that there may have been a legitimate reason his neighbors could not help him that day.

Sexually abusive behavior presents additional social problems. Parents may fear others will find out about their child's offense(s) and reject both their child and themselves. These fears become reality when children act out sexually with neighbors. The parents of neighborhood children may prohibit contact with an abusive child and his/her family. It is appropriate for parents of sexually abusive children to discourage sleepovers and baby-sitting, for fear of enabling the occurrence of another abusive incident. However, prohibiting children from social contacts with peers, which do not involve risks (e.g., supervised play), may complicate problems. The children then may be inhibited from developing socially appropriate relationships.

Parenting Skills

Parents must often learn new skills to help their children be accountable for their actions and stop their inappropriate sexual behaviors. Children need caretakers who are consistent, nurturing, and able to confront inappropriate behaviors. Their parents need to provide clear direction so their children can develop responsible and empathic values and behaviors. Parents are not always cognizant of how they teach their children coping responses. They can easily miss opportunities to help their children recognize available choices and solve problems by themselves.

When involved in power struggles, parents are unable to collaborate with their children to develop their children's sense of independence. When parents are harsh and punitive, their children may become hurt and angry. The children may then attempt to cope with their feelings of powerlessness, humiliation, and resentment by victimizing others they can control. To implement effective relapse prevention plans for sexually abusive children, parents need to (1) have adequate knowledge and awareness of age-appropriate sexual behaviors, (2) be empathic listeners, and (3) implement non-abusive discipline procedures.

When parents learn to communicate feelings, they appear more "authentic" or "spontaneously open, genuine and congruent with feelings, thoughts, verbalizations and behavior" (Hammond, Hepworth, and Smith, 1977, p. 344). When parents show an understanding of their child's feelings, thoughts, and actions, they are usually better able to help their child interrupt his/her abuse cycle. Empathic listening can help avoid negative interactions and power struggles. Parents with this ability can help a child achieve mastery. When adults validate a child's feelings, the child usually feels nurtured.

Parents sometimes benefit from education about child development and human sexuality. Many resist talking openly about sexual information, and others have questions regarding what they should consider to be normal sexual behavior. Although most parents are initially uncomfortable discussing sexuality, they generally believe more knowledge is essential to discriminate age-appropriate from deviant sexual behavior. They want to create an open and sensitive environment that facilitates communication about sexual issues. To interrupt and redirect inappropriate sexual behavior, children must be able to talk about their sexual thoughts and feelings. Several resources are available to help parents address sexual topics with their children: Gil (1987), *A Guide for Parents of Young Sex Offenders;* Johnson (1995b), *Child Sexuality Curriculum for Abused Children and Their Parents;* Pithers et al., (1993) *From Trauma to Understanding: A Guide for Parents of Children with Sexual Behavior Problems;* and Ryan and Blum (1994), *Childhood Sexuality: A Guide for Parents.*

Triggers

When trauma occurs, outcomes can be both cognitive and emotional. Responses in the Trauma Outcome Process are activated by "triggers." A trigger is any event or stimulus that causes an individual distress and elicits negative feelings (e.g., feeling afraid, powerless, devalued, controlled, put down, or criticized [Ryan, 1989]). Sometimes triggers are closely associated with memories of prior abuse. These may include visual, auditory, and olfactory stimuli or situations that provoke feelings similar to the abuse.

Some children may respond to triggers with symptoms of PTSD (e.g., intrusive thoughts, flashbacks, nightmares, or physiological reactivity to cues reminiscent of their abuse). For example, Melissa, age nine, who was frequently molested by a drunken stepfather, became physically ill when she smelled alcohol on anyone's breath. In contrast, other children may externalize their distress through acting-out behavior. Rachel, age twelve, was molested by a teenage male neighbor. While entertaining a group of friends in her backyard, she noticed that her perpetrator (now a young adult) had sneaked into the yard to watch the activities. Rachel felt afraid, helpless, and violated. She repressed her feelings, but she later became enraged and physically abusive toward her younger sister. In therapy, Rachel identified her perpetrator's invasion of her party as the trigger for her rage.

Awareness and Choice

Choices individuals make as they deal with trauma vary as a function of individual and family characteristics. Each choice is a product of human awareness (i.e., body sensations, thoughts, feelings, intentions, and actions [Miller, Nunnally, and Wackman, 1975]). Personal experiences impact choice by altering awareness, and individuals vary in the degree to which they are consciously aware. For example, some people are more aware of their thoughts and are cut off from bodily sensations and feelings. Others may not know what they think. Few people, if any, are consistently aware of how their body sensations, thoughts, and feelings influence their intentions and actions.

When individuals experience trauma or triggers, a reawakening of previous awareness occurs, and they make choices about how to respond. Young children are not necessarily consciously aware of their choices, but they nevertheless select one of three possible responses: self-victimization, abuse, or recovery. In therapy, most children can learn to recognize when they are making a choice. When awareness is impaired, individuals are less likely to make responsible choices and are more likely to experience dysfunctional outcomes. For example, children cut off from their feelings and body sensations may dissociate or engage in posttraumatic play in response to triggers. These actions can interfere with responsible decision making and eventually lead to self-destructive or abusive actions.

Children who have been previously exposed to sexuality through abuse, observation, or pornography often have enhanced sexual awareness that can affect their responses to triggers. Intervention needs to focus on enhancing all aspects of awareness, particularly feelings and thought processes. Clinicians can help children recognize and acknowledge their feelings, including sexual feelings. Thinking errors can be confronted and replaced with adaptive thoughts. Individuals can then make responsible choices to control their sexual feelings and avoid self-destructive or abusive behavior.

Self-Victimization

Individuals who repress, avoid, and hide their feelings often end up harming themselves. This behavior becomes self-defeating, and it is as if they are their own victims. Children often have difficulty sorting out who is responsible for a problem and who is the perpetrator or victim. They may develop "trauma echoes" (i.e., thinking errors expressed to them by their perpetrator(s) that contaminate their own thinking) (Gray, 1989). They may internalize these thinking errors and blame themselves for their own abuse. These thoughts lead to deteriorating self-esteem and increase the likelihood of self-victimizing or abusive responses to trauma. If these trauma echoes and thinking errors are not corrected, victims may engage in self-destructive behaviors (e.g., social isolation, suicidal gestures, eating disorders, chemical addiction, or codependent relationships).

Jesse, a nine-year-old sexually abusive boy, had low self-esteem and feared rejection by his peers. When playing with peers, Jesse was often bossy and controlling. When other children reacted to his bossiness by leaving and playing with others, he complained, "Nobody likes me! I'm stupid! I'll never have any friends." He would then withdraw and pout and make facial grimaces at the other children. By this socially inappropriate behavior, Jesse set himself up for further ridicule from his peers. His self-destructive thought processes led to depression and suicidal ideation when he thought, "I just wish I was dead. Nobody would miss me anyway."

Abuse

The abuse response in the Trauma Outcome Process is similar to other sexual abuse cycles (Lane, 1991b, 1997b; Lane and Zamora, 1984; Ryan et al., 1987; Ryan, 1989; Stickrod Gray and Mussack, 1988). While children who choose the self-victimization response hurt themselves, children who choose the abuse response hurt others. Similar to self-victimizing children, these children respond to their trauma or triggers by developing trauma echoes. However, they externalize their thinking errors by blaming others, rationalizing, and using anger to manipulate others.

Uncontrolled anger and externalized thinking errors often lead to the development of "get-back fantasies." These fantasies may provide a sense of control or empowerment. A child may justify physically aggressive behavior by thinking, "If I get in fights, the other kids will think I'm tough." Similarly, a child might engage in a sexual fantasy as part of a wish to gain compensatory control. When Scott decided to molest a younger boy in his neighborhood, he felt isolated from his peers and resentful that the boy was well liked by other neighborhood children. Other children seek empowerment and fantasize that sexual behavior will help them gain approval from their peers. These children may show off by bragging to others about their offenses. As Mike, age eleven, carefully planned the molestation of his six-year-old cousin, he thought to himself, "I'll tell my friends I had sex with a girl." He wanted his friends to think the girl was someone his own age.

Thinking errors can serve as a bridge for the process of the sexual abuse cycle to move from fantasy to reality (Kahn, 1990). Sexually abusive children set up offenses when they pursue a victim or develop a trusting relationship to create a situation in which an offense can occur. Specific examples of setups are rough housing and "accidentally" touching, purposely walking in on an unclothed peer, being nude in front of a younger child, and enticing an intended victim with gifts or games.

Children and adults who feel powerless in their lives often feel more powerful as they set up and commit an offense. Once the negative emotions present at the beginning of the abuse cycle diminish, a sexually abusive child may feel satisfied and reinforced for acting out. Often sexually abusive children continue to use thinking errors to rationalize feelings of guilt or the fear of being caught. When another trigger occurs, many return to the same response of abusive behavior.

Recovery

In contrast to the self-destructive and abuse responses, the recovery response in the Trauma Outcome Process represents healthy coping for victims of trauma. To enter the recovery response, individuals must regain a sense of personal safety in their environment, take responsibility for their recovery, get beyond denial and anger by expressing feelings associated with their trauma, grieve losses, and integrate the traumatic events as part of their life experiences.

Regaining personal safety is critical to a successful recovery (Herman, 1992). A safe environment includes protection from further abuse, freedom to express feelings related to the abuse, and validation of these feelings. When safety is not present, available choices are often limited to surviving the trauma and self-protection. For example, children who are ordered by the court to see a noncustodial parent who has previously been abusive tend to deal with these visitations much easier when that parent has acknowledged their past abusive behavior.

When a sense of safety is in place, victims can begin to clarify responsibility for their abuse. They can be accountable for their own choices and behavior, while refusing to take responsibility for the choices and behaviors of others. Recovery often involves correcting trauma echoes, confronting thinking errors, and replacing both types of cognitive distortions with accountable thinking. Individuals who accept responsibility for their own recovery can then express and manage feelings associated with their trauma.

USING THE TRAUMA OUTCOME PROCESS IN THERAPY

As an approach to treatment, the Trauma Outcome Process involves increasing awareness of body sensations, thoughts, feelings, intentions, and actions. It may be used with parents and children to help them identify their characteristic patterns of behavior and grasp the concept of recovery as an option for themselves. When shame and guilt are present, children who have been sexually abused are especially reluctant to discuss their own trauma and sexually abusive behavior(s). Shame erodes their self-esteem and makes them more vulnerable to enacting self-victimizing or abusive responses. Feelings of ambivalence toward their own perpetrations also may interfere with disclosure. Learning about the Trauma Outcome Process facilitates the understanding that others experience similar feelings in reaction to trauma and engenders greater acceptance of personal responsibility for one's behavior.

Jennifer was sexually abused over a period of three years by a teenage cousin. Her abuse began when she was eight and continued until she was eleven. By the time the abuse ended, Jennifer was experiencing pleasure during the sexual activities with her cousin, and at times, she initiated this contact. In individual therapy, Jennifer began to separate her helplessness as a child from her willing participation in more recent incidents. She also realized that she needed to make healthy choices regarding sexuality in her current relationships with boyfriends. As she shared her new awareness with others, Jennifer felt accepted and validated. Her improved self-esteem was evidenced by her choice of friends.

Robert, age ten, abused several younger boys over a few months. Discussion of the Trauma Outcome Process helped him acknowledge that he had initiated sexual activities because "it felt good" (body sensations), "it made me feel important" (feelings), and "I thought the other kids liked it too" (thinking error). As he confronted his thinking errors, he realized that the other boys did not share his enjoyment of sexual touch but were frightened and confused. He subsequently admitted his behavior was hurtful. Robert's recovery involved continuing to confront his thinking errors, implementing specific strategies to manage his sexual feelings, and finding positive and appropriate ways to feel important.

Adapting the Trauma Outcome Process to Children

Since the Trauma Outcome Process is a cognitive approach, it can be difficult for young children to understand. However, it is possible to make this concept more concrete. Because young children think in a linear fashion, their own abuse, reactions, and triggers may be presented as points on a line. Likewise, the three choices (self-victimization, abuse, or recovery) may be presented as three lines branching from a trigger point.

The Trauma Outcome Process can also be more easily understood when presented as a story or metaphor. One such example is the story, "The Fire," presented in Chapter 7. Through the use of this story, therapists can help children learn to choose to engage in more responsible behavior when they are triggered to think about their own abuse or trauma echoes. They can be taught that talking about their thoughts, feelings, and actions helps them to get better (i.e., reach recovery).

Most young children (and many older children as well) do not perceive themselves as making a choice to abuse. However, when asked why they offended in secret and not in front of an adult, they can readily explain they did not want to get in trouble and describe how they made some effort not to get caught. When confronted with the element of prior thought involved in this coverup, they usually acknowledge that there were other things they could have done besides offend sexually.

Sexually abused children and adults often minimize the impact of both their own trauma and the impact of their actions toward others. After children have acted out, it may be more difficult for them to deal with feelings associated with their own traumatization. To confront their own pain may entail more guilt, particularly if they identify with their victim. One eight-year-old boy, who had molested other children, denied he had been victimized. Only when he learned his sisters were in danger from his perpetrator did he overcome his shame and disclose his own trauma.

Although some children and adults have more difficulty discussing their own trauma than their abusive behaviors, others identify prior trauma as a trigger for their sexual offenses and thereby blame that past perpetrator for their own current actions. In one group of five- to eight-year-old children, everyone clearly stated that they had molested because the same thing had happened to them. The therapists acknowledged that the children had all learned to touch privates because they had been touched. However, the children looked confused when the therapists continued to explain that not all children who are molested go on to touch others' privates. The next several weeks in group were devoted to helping the children identify events and feelings that occurred just prior to their abusive actions and discussing how they could have made more appropriate choices.

Occasionally, extreme feelings of shame can trigger a new offense. After reviewing the Trauma Outcome Process in therapy, Randy, age eleven, burst into tears and disclosed he had been forced to fellate his father when he was about age four. This was the first time Randy had disclosed the nature of his own victimization. On the way home from group, Randy also told his mother he felt like remolesting his victim-sister Alicia. The reoffense was prevented by Randy and his mother working together toward recovery.

Lack of empathy is often connected to experiences of prior traumatization. To be empathic, individuals must understand feelings. Many children (and adults) who have been victimized avoid dealing with their feelings. They may lie to themselves and others in ways that create emotional voids rather than close relationships. This is particularly true in cases in which children are victimized by a much-loved and supportive person. Even when children have not actually been sexually or physically aggressive, they may feel afraid to deal with negative experiences. They may keep people distant by withdrawing or exploding with anger. These dysfunctional styles of relating to the world lead to lowered self-esteem and can result in self-destructive behaviors.

The primary goal of the Trauma Outcome Process is to help children talk about feelings related to their past trauma(s). Talking about these feelings usually relieves anxiety, anger, and hurt. The children often then begin to discuss strong feelings as they arise. For example, Kyle, age ten, sexually abused his younger brother and sister. His entire family was abusive, as the older children had molested their younger siblings. Kyle was sexually abused by both his father and oldest brother. It took a long time in therapy for Kyle to begin expressing his feelings about his own abuse. When he finally did, he expressed much sadness and loss. Ultimately, Kyle understood and accepted ambivalent feelings toward his father and older brother and took responsibility for abusing his younger siblings.

Using the Trauma Outcome Process with Parents

Parents sometimes have a more difficult time dealing with past abuse than their children. When parents do confront their own prior abuse, the impact can initially be debilitating. For example, one father, George, remembered two separate incidents of sexual abuse. As he began to understand the impact of this abuse on his life, he gained insight regarding his family dynamics. He recognized how his father had been excessively controlling, discouraging independence and individuation. He perceived his own pattern of avoiding conflict and giving in to demands of others as likely contributing to his ineffectiveness in dealing directly with the needs of his children. He became acutely aware of the problems he was generating within his immediate family. As a result, George felt overwhelmed and guilty and became depressed. Before he could fully participate in treatment related to his child's sexually abusive behavior problem, he had to deal with this depression. George's experience is consistent with that of other parents who are depressed and who have difficulty providing emotional support to their children (Belsky and Vondra, 1989).

When individuals understand they are using self-victimizing behavior, they are more amenable to discussing their feelings and choosing recovery. For example, Veronica admitted that she did not talk to anyone, even relatively close associates, about her home life. Her marriage was relatively successful, but her husband did not understand why she would not make any personal calls from work. Veronica shared an office, and she did not want anyone overhearing her conversations. When reviewing the Trauma Outcome Process, she uncovered that this fearfulness stemmed from hiding alcoholic and abusive parents from her friends in her childhood years. She was able to identify how she was unnecessarily inconveniencing herself in many current instances in which self-disclosure would only bring her closer to other people who were interested in her life. She began to question the effect of her fears on her children and was able to make steps toward more rational behavior.

Parents of sexually abusive children must learn to recognize their own abusive responses. Feelings of helplessness often trigger anger and lead to "striking out." Parents then enter their own abuse cycle. This reaction, in turn, may shape their children's behaviors, creating a vicious cycle of victimization and abuse between parents and children (see Figure 2.2). Feelings of inadequacy and powerlessness may result from this negative interaction. A parent may then try to avoid having to deal with his/her child. The child's response to this emotional unavailability may further trigger inappropriate responses from his/her parents. This coercive family process has been described by Patterson (1976, 1982).

One mother, Sandra, dragged her teenage daughter out of a room by the hair after her own mother, Edith, undermined Sandra's efforts at discipline. Edith's overt criticism triggered feelings of helplessness and anger in Sandra. Her daughter's condescending smirk of triumph when her grandmother took her side contributed to those feelings as well. Sandra's actions in turn triggered rage in her daughter, who engaged in get-back fantasies and later stole money from her mother.

In one family, the mother was overcontrolling and did most of the parenting. In parent group, the father, Bill, expressed feeling continually discounted and ignored by his children. This mirrored early feelings of inadequacy he had experienced as a child. When his son,

FIGURE 2.2. Dueling Cycles

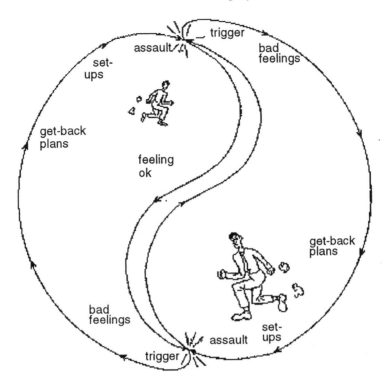

Chad, blatantly ignored his request to turn off the TV and complete homework, Bill impulsively cut the TV cord with his pocketknife. Chad stormed out of the room to enlist his mother's aid. She angrily confronted Bill, which further triggered his feelings of inadequacy. He then withdrew in frustration saying, "Nobody listens to me in this family!" Bill responded to this encounter with his usual pattern of isolating himself from his family and ignoring his children. Chad responded by ignoring his homework. Although he fantasized that he was getting back at his dad, he ultimately victimized himself, by barely passing in school.

Once children and their parents begin to use the Trauma Outcome Process to share information about themselves (e.g., how they enter the self-victimization and abuse cycles), they can work toward mutual understanding and support one another in reaching recovery. Siblings often are brought into family sessions to discuss ways in which they exacerbate problems and trigger abuse by other family members. After disclosures regarding abuse are made in family sessions, a discussion of how prior traumatization affects all family members usually takes place.

SUMMARY

Individual and family characteristics often interact to set the stage for sexual abuse to occur. A trigger event precipitates a response of recovery, self-victimization, or abuse in the Trauma Outcome Process. Treatment of children with sexual behavior problems focuses on developing individual and family resources, so that recovery is a clear option to both the child and family members.

Chapter 3

Integrated Treatment Planning

Assessment is the first step in developing an integrated treatment plan. The assessment process is ongoing throughout the course of treatment. Since children and their family members may experience considerable discomfort talking about sexual offenses, it is necessary to ask questions in an open, nonjudgmental manner, which sets the expectation that disclosures will be forthcoming. Initially, the child's disclosures may be guarded and incomplete. It is therefore important to obtain permission to contact adjunct professionals (e.g., caseworkers, juvenile court workers, former therapists) for corroborative information early in the evaluative process.

Parents are sometimes reluctant to report new incidents of abuse or behavior that they fear will be suspect. They may hide their own dysfunction for fear of additional outside sanctions or the potential breakup of the family. They may fear they will lose their children to foster care if further abuse continues. Some are afraid marital discord or discipline problems will make them appear to be unable to effectively manage their children. Sometimes parents hide information because they fear additional court action and extended treatment requirements. Nonetheless, it must be clear to both children and their family members that continuing victimizations of others will be reported to the appropriate authorities. Although clarification of reporting laws and procedures may initially be threatening to family members, the process of sharing this information up-front sets appropriate boundaries for therapy, establishes an atmosphere of directness and honesty, and assures the family that the therapist is skilled and comfortable working with the problem of sexual abuse.

ASSESSMENT FOR INTEGRATED
TREATMENT PLANNING

Since our treatment approach includes both children and their parents, our assessment includes questions pertaining to family functioning as well as individual characteristics. Specific questions are asked regarding the sexually abusive behavior, accountability (including thinking errors), empathy, family environment, and supervision issues, as well as sexual attitudes reflected in the family. If significant details emerge after treatment is initiated, treatment goals are updated to reflect the additional information.

General Information

A thorough intake assessment is conducted. Because treatment tends to be multidimensional (i.e., it is not possible to treat sexual abuse without dealing with family and social relationships), general information is gathered to get a full picture of the child's previous experiences, presenting problems, strengths, and weaknesses. Family background is carefully explored and includes the following information:

- Family composition
- Family history
- Family members' perceptions of their interactive behavior (including how discipline and conflict is handled)
- Significant disruption(s) to family life (including deaths or other losses and out-of-home placements)
- Substance abuse history of family members
- Physical, emotional, and/or sexual abuse history of family members
- Mental health history of family members
- Support system (e.g., extended family members, friends, and neighbors)

Information relating to the functioning of the child includes:

- Developmental data (e.g., prenatal and birth history, developmental milestones)

- Medical history and current health status (including medications)
- Mental health history (including psychiatric hospitalizations and former therapists)
- Details of physical, sexual, and/or emotional abuse that the child has experienced
- School functioning (e.g., academic performance, evidence of learning problems or attention deficit hyperactivity disorder [ADHD])
- Friendship patterns and peer relationships
- Prior delinquent offenses
- General level of cooperation and behavior at home, school, and in the neighborhood

A mental status examination of the child assesses the following:

- Sleep disturbances
- Nightmares
- Eating problems or weight change
- Symptoms of anxiety (e.g., shakiness, agitation, panic)
- Concentration problems
- Symptoms of depression (e.g., general loss of interest, suicidal ideation, suicidal plans, attempts, and risk)
- Psychosomatic complaints
- Mental capacities (e.g., orientation to time, place, and person; memory, judgment, insight)
- Thought processing (e.g., delusional thoughts, hallucinations, thought process and content)
- Dissociative symptoms
- Risk to others

After these data are gathered, a DSM-IV diagnosis (American Psychiatric Association, 1994) is formulated. Children who may benefit from medication are referred for psychiatric evaluations. Medication can have a necessary stabilizing effect. As children's moods stabilize, they can engage in treatment more effectively. Many children are depressed, and many have had periods of nightmares or other sleep disturbances associated with prior trauma. These problems usually diminish gradually as the children address their previous trauma and the guilt associated with their sexually abusive behavior. It is, of course, essential to monitor depressed children for signs of suicidal ideation and to intervene when a child becomes actively suicidal.

Children who have thought disorders can be successfully treated in outpatient treatment when their thought-processing problems are addressed. Occasionally children experiencing psychotic episodes fixate on sexual issues or self-blame. Parents may need guidance to limit their children's exposure to sexual content. Children with low impulse control can more readily act out their fantasies when they are not stable. Similarly, children with dissociative symptoms may present special challenges in treatment. They may focus too exclusively on traumatic issues or have upsetting flashbacks triggered by therapeutic discussions. Therapists need to assess these children's coping abilities and, when necessary, limit discussions pertaining to past trauma.

Assessment of Sexual Acting-Out Behavior

Once the sexually inappropriate behavior becomes the focus of discussion, it is important to determine the nature of the offense. Sometimes it is not clear whether a child has actually acted out in an abusive manner. As previously stated, occasionally peers engage in fondling behavior because they are sexually curious. At other times, children are wrongly accused of offenses. If a child denies engaging in sexual behavior and the reports implicating that child are vague (e.g., referrants cannot provide details of behaviors the child has been alleged to exhibit), we do not automatically include that child in a treatment program for sexually abusive behavior. When a child victimizes others, but not in a clearly sexual way, it is also important to avoid labeling that child as sexually abusive. For example, children are occasionally referred for treatment because they kicked or grabbed others in the privates.

When determining whether a sexual act committed by a young child constitutes an offense, clinical data are reviewed in relation to the definition of sexually abusive behavior presented in Chapter 1. Differences in power, use of authority, manipulation, method(s) of coercion, and use of coverups are assessed. The intrusiveness of the behavior is considered within the context of a child's developmental level. For example, five-year-old children do not normally know about oral sex. Although this behavior is highly intrusive, a five-year-old may be reenacting prior experiences rather than exhibiting sexualized aggression. However, he/she may also be highly sexualized. It is important not to minimize this behavior in treatment, but rather reassess the extent to which a child exhibits significant sexual aggression over time.

Similarly, the use of coercion is considered in conjunction with developmental factors. When same-age children act out sexually at one child's suggestion, they may be engaging in normal experimentation. It is often difficult to ascertain when behavior is motivated primarily by experimentation. However, if one child threatens another with a weapon and deliberately manipulates to cover up his/her actions, it is clear that sexual abuse has occurred.

It is important for information about specific sexual offenses to be detailed. We ask children to describe their actions and identify the thought processes they used to set up their offenses. It is usually easy to obtain some information about who was victimized and what occurred. Greater details about methods of coercion, thought processes, and the actual numbers of offenses are sometimes not disclosed until children and their families begin to trust the therapists involved in their treatment. Although a child may appear to immediately admit to the offense(s) for which he/she was caught, full accountability often does not occur until after months of treatment.

Table 3.1 is useful for recording details of a child's sexual offense(s) disclosed during treatment as well as in an initial assessment session. Since assessment and treatment are ongoing, it is advisable to periodically review all information regarding offenses. It is important children do not get the impression that they only need to deal with the offenses for which they were initially referred to treatment, when other offenses have also been committed.

Questions that are helpful in assessing sexually abusive behavior are presented in Table 3.2. It is important to ask questions in a calm, matter-of-fact manner to encourage children to fully disclose. It is important for them to identify the events that precipitated their sexual acting out behavior and be clear regarding the manner in

TABLE 3.1. Offenses Chart

A. Details of own offense(s) (including additional disclosure).

Victim Name	Age	Relationship to Child	Type(s) of Abuse	Number of Incidents	Types of Coercion
1.					
2.					
3.					
4.					

Types of Abuse—
"Hands-On" Offenses

1. Open mouth kissing
2. Fondling of breasts
3. Fondling of genitals
4. Forced victim to masturbate him/her
5. Masturbated victim
6. Digital penetration of vagina/anus
7. Oral sex (victim to perpetrator)
8. Oral sex (perpetrator to victim)
9. Dry intercourse (rubbing penis/vagina on legs, buttocks, or genitals of victim
10. Attempted anal/vaginal intercourse
11. Completed anal/vaginal intercourse
12. Object insertion in anus/vagina

"Hands-Off" Offenses

13. Sexual talk with victim
14. Showed victim pornography
15. Viewed victim nude
16. Voyeurism
17. Exposed genitals to victim
18. Exposed victim's genitals
19. Obscene telephone calls

Types of Coercion

1. Psychological manipulation/guilt
2. Superficial charm: "using charm to manipulate"
3. Games or tricks
4. Bribes
5. Requests or demands for secrecy
6. Threats
7. Use of weapons
8. Use of physical force
9. Unknown

B. Were others involved in the child's sexual offense(s) against other children? Yes _____ No _____
If yes, describe the role of others in the offenses (observed, participated, initiated, etc.)

TABLE 3.2. Assessing Sexually Abusive Behavior

I understand you touched someone's private parts.

Who did you touch?
How old were you when you did this?
How old was _____(victim)?
How did you touch _____(victim)?
Did you touch _____(victim) with your hand? mouth? privates (penis or vagina)?
Where were you? What room?
What did you think about before you did this? Did you think about doing this before?
How did you get _____(victim) to go along with this? Did you make threats? What did you say?
How did you feel?
How do you think _____(victim) felt?
Did anyone touch you in this way? How did you learn how to do this?
How did others find out you did this?
Have you ever done anything like this with an animal? Tell me about that.

Similar questions are asked regarding a child's own prior traumatization.

which they attempted to set up other children and cover up their actions.

Parents may also be asked to complete two measures developed to assess sexual acting out in children: the Child Sexual Behavior Inventory (CSBI [Friedrich et al., 1991]) and the Child Sexual Behavior Checklist (CSBCL [Johnson, 1993c]). Both measures involve asking the child's caretaker to estimate how many times the child was observed engaging in a variety of sexual behaviors. The CSBI is a thirty-six-item measure assessing a wide variety of sexual behaviors in children. It has been used to discriminate between the sexual behaviors of sexually abused children and children who have not been sexually abused (Friedrich, Grambsch, et al., 1992). The CSBCL contains "over 150 sexual behaviors in children ranging from natural and healthy childhood exploration to behaviors of children experiencing severe difficulties in the area of sexuality" (Johnson, 1993c, p. 142). Completing these questionnaires sometimes helps parents begin to think about sexual issues in regard to their child and to understand the need for supervision.

Accountability

An important measure of a child's accountability is often the degree to which parents are informed of the details of their child's offense. Parents sometimes complain their child is vague or responds, "I don't remember," when they ask about the offense. During treatment, it is expected that children will be able to talk to their parents about their sexually abusive behavior. As children become more accountable, they are usually able to disclose more details about their offenses to their parents. It is helpful to take the circumstances of disclosure into account. If the victim is a sibling and the parent is fully aware what occurred, a sexually abusive child may think he/she will get in trouble by failing to admit details of the offense. This admission under pressure may not indicate the abusive child will be fully accountable when such pressure is not present.

When parents are present during their children's disclosures, therapists must monitor their reactions. Children would not initially be referred for treatment without their parents' awareness that they have a sexual problem. However, parents are not always aware of the extent of the problem, and new disclosures are not uncommon. Due to their own discomfort, parents may inadvertently discourage their child from making full disclosures. Therapists may need to provide parents with considerable support to help them acknowledge and accept the full extent of their child's sexually abusive behavior. Parents can then more easily encourage their child to be fully accountable.

It may occasionally be necessary to ask a parent to leave when the child is having difficulty discussing his/her sexually aggressive behaviors. For example, Andrea, a young mother, began berating her son Timmy when he made a new disclosure. The therapist asked Timmy to play in the waiting room, while she talked to his mother about "figuring out what to do about this problem." Andrea then had an opportunity to express her feelings and plan how to handle the disclosure. When Timmy was brought back to the room, she conveyed her understanding that it is difficult but important to talk about sexual problems.

The Accountability Scale shown in Figure 3.1 is used to rate children's degree of acceptance of responsibility for the impact of

FIGURE 3.1. Accountability Scale

ACCOUNTABILITY SCALE
How Responsible I Am

0	1	2	3	4
UNTRUSTWORTHY	DISHONEST	EVASIVE	HONEST	TRUSTWORTHY
Admits no thinking errors and never corrects them.	*Admits very few thinking errors and hardly ever corrects them.*	*Admits some thinking errors and sometimes corrects them.*	*Admits most thinking errors and usually corrects them.*	*Admits all thinking errors and always corrects them.*
Denies abusive behavior occurred.	*Admits abusive behavior occurred but won't talk about it.*	*Discusses some details about abusive behavior.*	*Discusses most details about abusive behavior.*	*Discusses all details about abusive behavior.*

their behaviors on others. This is a subjective scale the authors developed to rate the children's behavior in group therapy sessions. It is usually possible to track a child's progress over time using this and other similar scales (Empathy, Participation, and Cooperation). The Accountability Scale may be used in group, individual, and family therapy. Children who consistently deny any misbehavior during group earn a 0 on accountability. On this scale 0 = untrustworthy, 1 = dishonest, 2 = evasive, 3 = honest, and 4 = trustworthy. Children are clearly informed that they may improve their scores by admitting to their problem behaviors.

Empathy

We regularly assess the extent to which both sexually abusive children and their parents have empathy for victims. This is initially done by asking children about the impact of their sexually abusive behavior on their victims and how they might feel if molested. Some parents and children come to therapy with genuine concern for the child's victim(s), while others exhibit ambivalent feelings. It is important to assess both the child's and parents' understanding of the impact of the sexually abusive behavior and their sensitivity to the feelings of the victim(s).

Parents are sometimes so worried about their own children that they appear unconcerned about the child who was victimized and his/her family. Children may be more worried that they have gotten "in trouble" than concerned about their victims. These children can experience empathy for their victims only when they feel safe. Some parents and children have difficulty experiencing empathy because they are cut off from their feelings. As they learn to identify their own feelings, they are better able to communicate empathy to others.

An empathy scale is presented in Figure 3.2. On this scale a score of 0 = abusiveness, 1 = rudeness, 2 = not noticing, 3 = sympathy, and 4 = empathy. This scale can be used to rate children's level of concern for others in group therapy. Victim empathy does not occur unless children generally exhibit more empathy for the people around them, including other group members. Children who tend to not help others, but avoid hurting others, would earn a score of 2 on

FIGURE 3.2. Empathy Scale

EMPATHY SCALE
How I Treat Other People

0	1	2	3	4
ABUSIVENESS	RUDENESS	NOT NOTICING	SYMPATHY	EMPATHY
Very little concern for others.	*Little concern for others.*	*Average concern for others.*	*Much concern for others.*	*Very much concern for others.*
Very hurtful action.	*Somewhat hurtful action.*	*Neutral or no action.*	*Somewhat helpful action.*	*Very helpful action.*
"Bullying."	*"Put downs."*	*"Don't hurt, don't help."*	*"Lend a hand."*	*"Goes the extra mile."*

the empathy scale. Empathy development is a slow process, and most children will not attain true empathy (a score of 4).

Sometimes children learn to label feelings and compliment others, but they do so to gain an advantage. This opportunistic behavior is usually obvious over time. It is important to note when children are feigning empathy because they hope to graduate from treatment soon or wish to be complimented by the group leaders or other children. The authors have found genuine concern for others is generally exhibited with quiet consistency, while attention-seeking behavior is more often dramatic and inconsistent.

If children (or parents) focus on how they have been maltreated by juvenile authorities, neighbors, or therapists, it becomes easy to avoid both personal accountability and victim empathy. Therapists may need to remind them of the harmful effects of abuse and help them be accountable without blaming. Empathy and accountability are critical elements in treatment which are assessed continually, even after all the details of the offense(s) have been obtained.

Family Environment and Supervision

Suggested questions to evaluate boundary and supervision issues are presented in Table 3.3. Additional information regarding boundaries and supervision is obtained over time. An initial assessment of family boundaries helps identify problem areas that need to be included in the treatment plan. As problems are identified, clinicians can help parents initiate changes in the structure of their home environment to reduce opportunities for their child to act out sexually, while respecting cultural differences and economic constraints.

A positive treatment outcome is more likely when parents provide both support and supervision. Supervision includes the establishment of a structured home environment with firm boundaries to protect the privacy of individual family members. The questions regarding supervision included in Table 3.3 can help assess risk to the community. It is often necessary to determine who must be informed regarding a child's sexually abusive behavior (e.g., baby-sitters, relatives, friends, other parents, school personnel, etc.). Parents may choose to withhold information about their child's sexually abusive behavior because they perceive their extended family members and/or friends to be judgmental. Therapists can help par-

TABLE 3.3. Assessment of Family Boundaries

I. **Personal Space**

    A. Identifying personal space issues (as observed in therapist's office)–Does the child:

        1. Move about your office without permission?
        2. Touch objects in your office without asking?
        3. Destroy objects in your office?
        4. Try to physically touch, kiss, or hug you?
        5. Hit, kick, bite, or shove?
        6. Touch his/her own genitals in front of you?
        7. Lift his/her clothing or begin to show underwear?

    B. Respecting personal space–
    What are family members' attitudes about personal space?

II. **Privacy: Assessment of the Home Environment**

    A. Structure of the house—
    Have family members draw a "floor plan" of their house:

        1. Note areas of multiple use (bathrooms, bedrooms, etc.).
        2. Note lack of structural boundaries (no doors, peek spaces and open doorknob holes, holes in walls, no draperies, no shower curtains). Note any locations in the house where sexually abusive behavior has taken place.
        3. Does each family member have a space for his/her individual belongings (e.g., closets, chest of drawers, dressers, toy boxes, etc.)?

    B. Bathroom use—
    What are existing rules regarding bathing? Who bathes with whom? Who can go in the bathroom with whom? What happens if someone needs to get into the bathroom quickly?

    C. Sleeping arrangements—
    What are house rules regarding sleeping? Who sleeps with whom? Do people change beds in the night? Do people change beds during a storm or after a nightmare? Are bedclothes worn?

    D. Dressing/Undressing—
    What are family members' attitudes about nudity? Do family members change clothes in front of one another?

III. **Generational Roles**

    A. Identifying each parent's issues—

        1. Is the parent comfortable in the parenting role?
        2. Does the parent use a child as a confidant?
        3. Does the parent show evidence of codependent relationships with the child or others?

TABLE 3.3 *(continued)*

4. Were there boundary disturbances in the parent's family of origin?
5. Does the parent make excessive demands of the therapist's time?
6. Does the parent show a lack of respect for his/her children's needs or privacy?

IV. **Family Interaction**

    A. Assessing interpersonal boundaries—

      1. How do family members communicate with one another? Are there any signs of physical or verbal abuse?
      2. Do family members treat one another with respect?
      3. Do family members respect one another's personal belongings?
      4. Do family members show trust in one another?
      5. Do family members keep harmful secrets from one another?

V. **Supervision of the Children**

    A. Assessing supervision—

      1. How are the children supervised when inside the house (especially when a parent is cooking, cleaning, on the telephone, showering, etc.)? How long are phone calls, and how distracted do parents get by calls? Is the phone cord long enough to allow for supervision?
      2. How well are children supervised when outside of the house? At neighbors' houses?
      3. When a parent is gone for a short time (to the store or neighbors'), who watches whom? For how long? What instructions are given to baby-sitters?
      4. What information is given to teachers and principals?
      5. Is the child allowed to go to or have sleepovers? Under what conditions?

Source: Adapted from Friedrich, W. N. (1990). *Psychotherapy of sexually abused children and their families.* New York: W. W. Norton.

ents decide what to say to whom, to ensure both community protection and maintenance of their child's confidentiality. It may be necessary to implement new rules to protect siblings, neighborhood children, and the sexually abusive child from additional incidents of abuse. Safety is a prerequisite for successful treatment. Suggested rules and guidelines for improving family boundaries are listed in Table 3.4. Included are suggestions for protecting personal space

TABLE 3.4. Boundary and Supervision Guidelines for Families of Sexually Abusive Children

Personal Space

1. No one should enter another family member's personal space without that family member's permission. ("Personal space" consists of the space around the person in all four directions when the person's arms are extended.)
2. There will be *no inappropriate touching* (i.e., touching another person on the private parts of the body, or the parts of the body that are covered by one's swimsuit). If someone tries to touch a family member in the private parts, that family member should immediately tell a parent. If the family member feels uncomfortable telling a parent, he/she should tell an adult who can help (e.g., caseworker, therapist, school teacher, police officer).
3. Appropriate touch is allowed if both family members feel comfortable with the touch (e.g., hugs, arm around the shoulder, pats on the back, kiss on the cheek, handshakes, holding hands). When a family member is not sure that the other person wants the touch, he or she should ask the other person for permission (e.g, "May I give you a hug?" "May I have a hug?" "May I hold your hand?"). Family members should remember, "When in doubt, ask."
4. A family member always has the right to say "no" to any kind of touch (e.g, "I'd rather not have a hug right now" or "Please don't kiss me on the cheek. I don't like that").
5. Wrestling and horseplay are not allowed. (This rule is necessary in homes with sexually abusive children. Some sexually abusive children use games such as wrestling to manipulate other children into participating in sexual touching.)
6. Family members should not touch their own private parts in front of others. If family members masturbate, they need to do it in private, avoid doing it excessively, avoid hurting themselves, and avoid infringing on the rights of others (e.g., avoid spending extended time in the bathroom).
7. Family members should not tell sexually explicit jokes or stories to each other. They should not use any inappropriate sexual talk or write inappropriate sexual notes (e.g., vulgar language, derogatory terms for private parts of the body).

Privacy

A. House Structure

1. All bedrooms and bathrooms should have doors that close or some other way to ensure privacy (e.g., curtains).
2. Repairing holes in walls or peek spaces helps protect privacy.
3. Family members' privacy is enhanced when they have their own places to store their belongings (e.g., a clothes closet and/or dresser for clothes, a box for toys and books, etc.).

TABLE 3.4 *(continued)*

B.   Bathroom Use

1.   One person at a time uses the bathroom (exception—parents helping preschool-age children).

2.   Family members will not bathe or shower together.

C.   Sleeping Arrangements

1.   It is best if each child has his/her own bedroom. However, if this is not possible due to the size of the house, it is important that each child has his/her own bed.

2.   Avoid having sexually abusive children share a bedroom with another child.

3.   It is important that family members sleep in their own beds and do not change beds during the night.

D.   Dressing/Undressing

1.   Family members should get dressed in private (exception—parents dressing preschool-age children).

2.   Prior to leaving their bedrooms or the bathroom, it is important for family members to be dressed.

3.   Family members should knock on closed doors and ask permission to enter.

Respect for Generational Roles

1.   Adult family members should avoid discussing adult concerns with children (e.g., marital conflict, finances, child support, employment difficulties) or having discussions with each other about these concerns when children are present. However, if the family is experiencing stress that affects the children, it is important for parents to explain the problems to the children in a way they can understand.

2.   Children are not confidants. Parents should not use children to meet their own emotional needs. When parents need to talk about personal problems, it is best that they talk to adult friends or adult family members.

3.   Children should be allowed adequate time to relax, have fun, and "be kids." Adults should encourage children to play and not overburden them with responsibilities that they are not developmentally ready to handle.

Family Interaction

1.   Family members should treat each other with caring and respect. This includes listening to each other and not interrupting.

2.   No physical aggression (e.g., hitting, kicking, spitting, or biting) is allowed.

3.   Family members will not swear at each other, call each other derogatory names, or use rude statements as put downs.

4. Family members need to respect one another's belongings. If they borrow an item, it is important that they take good care of it. They will not destroy another person's belongings.
5. Family members should keep each other's confidences. If a family member has disclosed personal information and requested it be kept private, other family members should not disclose the information to others. However, if the information is a harmful "secret" and involves illegal behavior such as abuse, it must *not* be kept private, but should be reported to parents or another responsible adult (e.g., teacher, principal, caseworker, therapist, doctor).

Supervision of the Children

1. After sexually abusive behavior has been discovered, children with sexual behavior problems must play in common areas (i.e., areas that are easily supervised by adults—no closed doors). As the children make progress in treatment and gain trust, parents may allow them to play with less intense supervision. Parents should consult with children's therapists before deciding to allow unsupervised play or sleepovers.
2. Sexually abusive children should not be involved in diapering or other caretaking activities for younger children.
3. Sexually abusive children should not be allowed to baby-sit.
4. When parents leave, they should make arrangements for adult supervision. They should inform the substitute caretaker (e.g., baby-sitter, friend, extended family member, parent of another child) of the need to provide adequate supervision of their sexually abusive child.
5. Parents may want to consult with their therapist about what information to disclose to other adult caretakers (e.g, baby-sitters, friends, extended family members, parents of other children, teachers, principals, etc.) about their sexually abusive child.

and privacy of family members, strengthening adult/child generational roles, and enhancing respectful interactions among family members. These guidelines can help parents establish a plan for supervision.

Sexual Information

When treating children with sexually abusive behavior problems, it is necessary for therapists to have an understanding of children's and parents' levels of sexual knowledge, as well as their comfort with sexuality. When adults (and children) are not comfortable, they often miss important information conveyed in a session. In contrast, some individuals are very open regarding sexual issues, even in an intake session. Suggested questions regarding sexual knowledge and fantasies are presented in Table 3.5. Additional questions regarding sexuality are presented in the exercise, "Communicating Sexual Values," in Chapter 9.

Children (as well as adults) often withhold specific information about their masturbation or sexual fantasies until treatment is well past the initial stages. Since trust and comfort in treatment are prerequisites for making these disclosures, it is inappropriate to insist that clients divulge this sensitive material during their first sessions. However, therapists need to be open to discussing this information if a child or parent brings it up on his/her own.

TABLE 3.5. Sexual Knowledge/Fantasies

A.   Sexual Knowledge

CHILD/PARENT

1. Appears to have limited knowledge regarding sexuality.
2. Appears to have distorted views regarding sexuality.
3. Appears to have accurate knowledge regarding sexuality.

B.   Masturbation/Sexual Fantasies

1. How often does the child masturbate?

2. Has the child ever been observed masturbating in front of others?

3. What type of fantasies accompany the child's masturbation?

    a. Noncoercive sexual contact with same-age peers
    b. Noncoercive sexual contact with younger children
    c. Coercive sexual contact with same-age peers
    d. Coercive sexual contact with younger children
    e. Sexual contact with adults
    f. Child reports he/she does not fantasize while masturbating

4. To what extent is masturbation involved in the child's sexual offense(s)?

    a. High degree of involvement (frequently masturbates prior to/during/following offending)
    b. Some degree of involvement (sometimes masturbates prior to/during/following offending)
    c. Minimal involvement (masturbation is rarely involved in the offense)

A parent's prior sexual abuse can impact the supervision he/she provides. Often mothers who have been abused are less able to set limits for their male children as their sons mature. Their early experiences have taught them to conform to males' wishes and fear reprisal for assertive behavior. Similarly, adult males who have been sexually abused may develop inaccurate assumptions about their own abuse, which potentially contaminate their relationships with their children. Dave was sexually abused at age thirteen by a thirty-year-old woman. He convinced himself that his experience was not abusive, but a "normal" experience for a teenage boy. When his ten-year-old son was abused by a male, he became convinced the experience would make his son gay and, in fact, communicated his feelings to his son.

TREATMENT MODALITIES

Complete assessments are necessary to plan treatment and select interventions to meet the needs of each individual child and family. Although sexually abusive children generally benefit from a combination of modalities (i.e., individual, family, and group treatment), the individual needs of a child or family may preclude the use of a particular treatment format. It is therefore important to be flexible and creative when planning and selecting treatment interventions. If family-of-origin members are unavailable, foster parents or other caretakers may be involved in family therapy. When treating children from cultures that emphasize extended family relationships, it may be useful to involve members of the extended family in the treatment.

Contracts for Treatment

The identification of common characteristics of sexually abusive children and their families is useful for planning interventions. Assessment of the child involves identification of specific treatment needs, formulation of treatment goals to address those needs, selection of treatment modalities, and the establishment of a treatment contract.

The establishment of a treatment contract requires the active involvement of the child, parents, and in some cases, siblings or extended family members. Clients are unlikely to work on problems they do not acknowledge or on goals they have not formulated. Clinicians must therefore ensure that the child and family are actively involved in identifying treatment needs, negotiating and formulating treatment goals, and selecting treatment interventions.

Individual Therapy with the Child

Individual therapy begins with the assessment process and usually continues throughout the course of treatment. Although we believe children with sexually abusive behavior problems do best when seen in a group that focuses on their specific treatment needs, we use individual therapy to reinforce themes introduced in group therapy and to explore problems in greater depth than is sometimes possible in the group setting. Individual therapists can help children develop specific goals to be achieved within the group and review their treatment progress. When a group is not available, individual therapy becomes the primary treatment modality.

The initial work in individual therapy usually focuses on increasing a child's accountability for offending behaviors and preparing children for group and family therapies. We usually expect the children to have disclosed at least some details of their offenses prior to beginning a group. They are told that they are expected to talk in group about "how they acted out sexually" and about "what happened to them," including prior abuse. Many children express reluctance to talk with others about their offenses. These disclosures can be practiced in individual therapy. We emphasize that all the children in the group have the same problem and need to learn how to stop their sexually abusive behavior. We also discuss the purpose of group therapy and carefully review the rules of confidentiality.

Children are more often able to talk first to their individual therapist specifically about how arousal contributed to their offenses. They may also be more likely to ask questions about sexual development and sexuality within the privacy of an individual session. These discussions may ultimately lead to the development of a relapse prevention plan. The children are characteristically encouraged to bring issues that arise in their individual sessions to the group and get feedback from their peers. In both individual and group therapy, children can develop specific strategies to improve peer relationships and prevent relapse. For example, a child may be asked to imagine a younger child asking to play house. A child can role play how to avoid such high-risk situations by suggesting alternative, "safe" play such as riding bikes, playing catch, or playing cards or board games.

Conjoint sessions with victims are usually planned and organized by a child's individual therapist. This most often occurs when a victim is a sibling or relative. As therapy focuses more on family issues, family therapy may replace individual sessions.

Individual Therapy with Parents

Parents of sexually abusive children need to know what treatment entails and what services are available. Therapy with children with sexually abusive behavior problems often takes one to three years. It is advisable for therapists to outline the nature and expected duration of the treatment process and to assist parents in accessing funding sources. Financing therapy is usually difficult, given the extensive level of treatment that is often necessary. Many parents are also initially concerned about how their child may be affected by the legal process. Therapists can provide support if there is a need to interact with caseworkers from child protective services or juvenile court.

Parents are involved in individual therapy sessions, based on need. Individual goals to be achieved within the parent group setting may be negotiated and monitored by the child's individual therapist. Collateral sessions with parents can provide an opportunity for the individual therapist to determine how much parents know about their child's offending behavior and to clarify any misunderstandings that might exist. As parents begin talking about their children's sexually abusive behaviors, they typically become more open to discussing their own feelings. They may then be referred to their own individual therapist.

To help prevent reoffenses, parents need to learn about their child's abuse cycle and attend to aspects of supervision not previously considered. Over time, it may be necessary to make modifications to the supervision plan. At first, parents must carefully monitor their child's interactions with other children, even with same-age peers. It is not always clear when to allow their child to visit other homes and whether to explain their child's problems to other parents. Supervision includes facilitating a child's social relationships while maintaining safety. As the child demonstrates increased responsibility, parents may modify the plan and allow increased social interactions, which eventually include parties and sleepovers. The individual therapist assists parents in deciding what information is shared with neighbors, friends, and extended family members. Potential implications of sharing this information must be cautiously considered.

As the events and behavioral patterns leading to abusive behavior are closely examined, parents begin to understand how the abuse cycle and thinking errors apply specifically to their children. They examine their own patterns of behavior that may lead to abusive parenting, such as slapping, spanking, and name-calling. In the later stages of treatment, parents learn to identify behaviors that their children exhibit which may trigger their own abuse cycle. They can learn how to disengage from their own cycles and to distinguish their cycles from their children's.

While learning about thinking errors, parents begin to identify how they avoid accountability. During a group session that focused on thinking errors, a parent looked up and stated, "This is not about them [the sexually abusive children], this is about *us*!" Once this realization occurs, parents are generally receptive to changing behaviors that contribute to maladaptive coping patterns within their families.

Family Therapy

The family therapist helps family members process and integrate newly learned behaviors. Family therapy is often the only therapeutic involvement for some family members. Safety concerns, supervision issues, family dynamics, and sibling rivalries are addressed in these sessions. Family members are taught the concept of thinking errors so they can confront these errors as they occur at home. They also learn to nurture and show respect for one another.

Family members must all be aware that a sexual offense has occurred. Some parents may wish to keep knowledge of the child's offense from other siblings. However, when some members of the family are not aware, these family secrets affect interactions, and communication is impaired. It is usually best for all family members to know about the offense so they can be part of the child's treatment and help to implement a relapse prevention plan. In family therapy, family members can express their feelings about the offense and ways in which it has disrupted their lives.

Siblings often resent the amount of time parents must spend with the sexually abusive child just to meet therapy schedules. They also complain about having to be involved in family therapy when they did not do anything wrong. Although individual family members may blame the sexually abusive child for a variety of problems, all family members need to commit to correcting interactional patterns that may have contributed to the abusive behavior. Siblings and the sexually abusive child often need to discuss differences in their privileges, such as sleepovers or sharing a room. Everyone must learn to adjust to the changes that take place to reduce high-risk situations.

Major goals of family therapy are to help individuals develop a safe openness with each other, discuss problems, and express feelings. The therapist can model empathy and encourage positive interactions in sessions. Everyone in the household can discuss boundary issues and make decisions that promote privacy and safety. Open discussion of these issues reinforces improved communication among family members. Use of "I messages" (e.g., I feel _____ when you _____ because _____) can curtail tendencies to blame others. Opportunities to solve problems in therapy sessions lead to the use of new strategies to resolve conflicts at home. Thinking errors can be corrected as they arise. As treatment progresses, parents and children report on how the relapse prevention plan has been activated at home and whether or not the plan has been successful.

Families members must deal with an additional set of problems when sexually abusive behavior occurs between siblings. If the sexually abusive child is not removed from the home, supervision requirements must be immediately addressed. Parents must somehow cope with both the grief they may feel because one child has been sexually abused and the anger they feel toward their perpetrating child. When a victim and perpetrator are both their own children, the combination of feelings can be debilitating. Unfortunately, these feelings occur just when parents need more energy to establish safety in their home.

When a child is removed from the home to protect siblings from further abuse, family members must adjust to this new arrangement. Parallel learning processes should begin immediately so that reintegration is a clear family goal. If a family has too much time to adjust to life without the problematic sexually abusive child in their home, reintegration is often more difficult. Reintegration requires special attention to the feelings of the victim and other family members regarding safety and supervision practices. The sexually abusive child must resolve anger over his/her removal from the home. All family members need to talk with one another until they feel confident they will be able to work together to prevent a new offense.

During a family session with the Green family, Aaron, a nine-year-old victim, described an incident that had disturbed him. While on a home visit, Steven, the twelve-year-old perpetrator, had held his six-year-old sister, Samantha, in his lap as they played on a swing. Aaron interpreted the swinging as breaking the family rules because Samantha's bottom was sitting on Steven's lap (genitals). In discussing the incident, it became clear that the siblings in this family would help to monitor high-risk behaviors, and the parents would listen to their concerns. Although Samantha had not interpreted Steven's behavior as threatening, she did admit to feeling more safe with her brother Aaron helping to protect her.

Therapeutic sessions between a sexually abusive child and the victimized sibling must occur if they are to live together. It is particularly helpful to have both children describe their prevention plans and identify high-risk behaviors and situations. Parents must be accessible so their children can talk with them. The sexually abusive child must identify someone he/she can talk to about sexual arousal. Once the child has returned home, family therapy sessions are a way to monitor progress and address problems as they occur.

Group Therapy for Children

Group therapy is an integral part of the treatment process. Sometimes children only begin to disclose detailed information about their sex offenses when they are included in group treatment. Group therapy helps address feelings of stigmatization associated with both prior abuse and sexually abusive behavior. For example, Tyson, a six-year-old, did not talk much about his offenses until another group member, Rhett, specifically approached him and told him he did not need to be so scared. Rhett commented that he and Tyson were a lot alike because they had done "the same thing." For a time, Tyson continued to avoid making disclosures unless his friend was present. Gradually he began to reach out to other group members.

Sexually abusive children can typically be treated in group; however, there are exceptions. For example, it may be necessary to work with some behaviorally disordered children individually and in family treatment to help them learn sufficient self-control to be integrated in group. When firm and consistent limits are set, many children with attention deficit or impulse control disorders respond quite well to the group process. Individual and family therapists can assess readiness for group treatment when individuals are too disruptive to be immediately included in a therapeutic environment with other children.

Brian, a seven-year-old child who began group therapy, was extremely oppositional. He distracted others and refused to sit apart from the group in time-out. He began kicking and screaming to the extent that it was impossible to continue the session with other children while he was in the room. On several occasions, he was removed to sit with his mother in the waiting area until he quieted down. When returned to the group, he immediately became disruptive again. Brian was removed from the group component of the treatment program until he was better able to respond to limits.

It is important to assess each child's level of cognitive ability to ensure he/she can understand the discussions. Young children ages four to eight tend to be concrete and will have difficulty grasping abstract concepts. To be effective with younger children, group therapists need to use concrete language and employ experiential interventions (e.g., play therapy, art therapy, role-plays with toys or puppets). Similarly, children with learning disabilities who have deficits in verbal skills may have some difficulty learning in group. To accommodate the needs of children with cognitive deficits, clinicians may decide to adjust the way they present treatment exercises. It is possible to treat a variety of children by selecting a variety of interventions.

Group therapy sessions are typically sixty to ninety minutes in length. Children need to be able to participate and attend to discussions for at least a thirty-minute period. All preschool children are not able to do this. Some preschool children who display severe ADHD or highly self-centered behaviors, which preclude group interactions, may need to be excluded from group. However, when clinicians finally establish the group structure, many preschool children can be successfully included in group therapy.

Children with thought-processing problems may occasionally be excluded from outpatient groups. For example, Nicole, a five-year-old diagnosed as having a pervasive developmental disorder, perseverated on issues related to sexuality. Weekly reminders of her sexual behavior problem became counterproductive for Nicole. She may, in fact, have acted out with siblings more often because of being in group treatment. However, it is not necessary to exclude all children who exhibit psychotic processes. Appropriateness for a particular group milieu can be assessed. The extent of disruption one child may create for other group members must be carefully weighed.

Group Therapy for Parents

Parents of sexually abusive children typically benefit from participation in educationally focused parent support groups. When forming parent groups, it is important to evaluate the homogeneity of the members and consider how parents relate to one another. Each parent in group needs an opportunity to talk about individual problems. Emotionally disturbed or personality disordered individuals who dominate much of the group discussion on an ongoing basis must be prevented from monopolizing group interactions. It may be necessary to exclude severely disordered individuals from group, particularly if their self-centeredness or emotional disturbance interferes significantly with the group process.

It also is important to evaluate parents' level of cognitive functioning when assessing them for participation in parent group. Similar to children with learning disabilities, parents who have cognitive deficits or who lack verbal skills may have difficulty following group discussion or grasping abstract concepts. As in groups with children with learning disabilities, therapists may employ experiential interventions to make information presented in parent groups more concrete and understandable. Parents who have cognitive deficits may then continue in group and experience the benefits of supportive interaction with other group members. One mother who exhibited signs of cognitive impairment spent considerable time in group discussing how to make arrangements for transportation to therapy. Group members helped empower her to solve this problem, and her child benefited from her more consistent group attendance.

Foster and adoptive parents need support and special training to deal with sexually abusive children. However, mixing foster and biological parents in the same group sometimes does present problems. Biological parents may believe that foster parents are critical of them, which limits their disclosures; they may subsequently avoid discussing family dynamics. Usually, when clinicians help biological and foster parents identify issues that they have in common, it is possible to form a cohesive group environment in which parents respect one another.

ASSESSING TREATMENT PROGRESS

As changes occur within a family, treatment must focus on the most relevant topic areas. Ongoing assessment ensures important issues are not missed as new problems surface and helps determine when treatment can be concluded or reduced in intensity. The Accountability and Empathy Scales presented earlier assist in making this determination, as does the group Progress Rating Form presented in Table 3.6. One of the authors (J. Burton) and two other raters obtained a reliability coefficient of .93 when using the Progress Rating Form.

It is generally expected that children will receive ratings of at least 3 on the Progress Rating Form prior to being discharged from group. Some allowances are made, given a child's developmental level and personality factors. For example, an exceptionally shy child who receives a rating of 2 in participation ("Talks in group") may be released from group if he/she has dealt with perpetration

TABLE 3.6. Progress Rating Form

Name_____   Date _____

Communication of personal responsibility to victim.

_____   Says he/she is sorry (in session or parent's report).
_____   Has written a letter of apology.
_____   Has admitted fault in a recontact session.

1. **Talks in group**   1   2   3   4   5   N/A*

Social Skills
    1.   Talks a little.
    3.   Talks when asked questions.
    5.   Talks on his/her own.

2. **Talks about problems**   1   2   3   4   5   N/A

Accountability
    1.   Does not talk about own problems.
    3.   Talks about own problems if asked questions.
    5.   Talks about own problems on his/her own.

3. **Sensitivity in group**   1   2   3   4   5   N/A

Empathy
    1.   Does not show awareness of others' feelings.
    3.   Sometimes shows awareness of others' feelings and needs.
    5.   Sensitive to other group members: pays attention to what they
       say.

4. **Cooperation with therapist**   1   2   3   4   5   N/A

Impulsiveness and Social Skills
    1.   Cooperates only after repeated direction.
    3.   Sometimes cooperates fully, but often needs repeated direction.
    5.   Usually cooperates without repeated direction.

5. **Discussion of touching**   1   2   3   4   5   N/A

Accountability
    1.   Denies touching (says he/she did not do it).
    3.   Admits to touching, but only if pushed to do so.
    5.   Talks about touching, and tells whole story.

6. **Talks about being a victim**   1   2   3   4   5   N/A

Prior Trauma
    1.   Does not talk about being a victim.
    3.   Talks about how he/she was a victim.
    5.   Expresses feelings/thoughts about being a victim.

_____

* If issue does not apply, rate as not applicable.

7. Ways of forcing victim   1   2   3   4   5   N/A

Accountability
1. Does not accept responsibility for touching
3. Talks about how he/she set up victim.
5. Talks in detail about how he/she took advantage of victim.

8. Talks about victim's feelings   1   2   3   4   5   N/A

Empathy
1. Does not talk about how his/her victim(s) felt.
3. States how victim(s) likely felt.
5. Talks about problems victim(s) may have experienced since being touched.

9. How touching happens   1   2   3   4   5   N/A

Accountability
1. Does not talk about how touching occurred.
3. Talks about situations in which touching can occur.
5. Talks about situations and feelings that lead to touching.

10. Thoughts about touching   1   2   3   4   5   N/A

Accountability
1. Denies thinking again about touching.
3. Admits to thoughts about touching.
5. Tells how he/she is changing thinking in order to stop touching.

The following ratings will be completed on individuals ages nine and older.

11. Gives feedback to other group members

            1   2   3   4   5   N/A

Social Skills
1. Does not give feedback to others.
3. Piggybacks on others' comments.
5. Gives helpful feedback to other group members.

12. Understanding how needs were met by the touching

            1   2   3   4   5   N/A

Empathy
1. Does not talk about how needs led to touching.
3. Talks about how some needs aremet by the touching.
5. Talks about how he/she used touching to meet needs.

TABLE 3.6 *(continued)*

13. Relationship with group members

1   2   3   4   5   N/A

Empathy
1. Does not act in a caring way with group members.
3. Sometimes acts in a caring way with group members.
5. Consistently acts in a caring way with group members.

14. Danger signs and safety   1   2   3   4   5   N/A

Accountability
1. Denies talking about further problems.
3. Talks about danger signs but has no plan in place to prevent further touching.
5. Talks about danger signs and has a good plan to prevent further touching.

_____

The following ratings will be completed on individuals ages 13 and older.

15. Relationship with family members

1   2   3   4   5   N/A

Accountability
1. Denies any family problems.
3. Talks about family problems without saying how he/she is a part of the problem.
5. Talks about own part in family problems.

16. Responsibility   1   2   3   4   5   N/A

Accountability
1. Superficially accepts responsibility for molestation but minimizes or rationalizes it.
3. Verbalizes personal responsibility without minimization or rationalization.
5. Demonstrates acceptance of full responsibility with appropriate affect.

17. Personality style/thinking errors   1   2   3   4   5   /N/A

Accountability
1. No understanding of thinking errors.
3. Able to recognize thinking errors in others.
5. Full understanding of thinking errors and how they related to molestation.

18. **Relationship with age-appropriate girlfriends/boyfriends**

1   2   3   4   5   N/A

Empathy
1. Interacts in a noncaring manner.
3. Sometimes interacts with girlfriend/boyfriend in an empathetic manner.
5. Evidence of consistent empathetic interaction with girlfriend/boyfriend.

Copyright © 1990 Barbara J. Christopherson, Jan Ellen Burton, Lucinda A. Rasmussen.

issues when questioned. Older children are usually expected to receive ratings of 4 or 5 prior to discharge from group, except those who have significant psychiatric problems.

In the event a child appears to deal fully with issues in group treatment (based on the rating form) but has molested in the past six months, group, individual, and family therapy are continued. In contrast, when one child stopped acting out sexually for a six-month period, staff remained wary and continued him in group therapy for an extended period. Since he was self-centered and lacked empathy, he had potential to harm other children without recognizing he was hurting them.

Treatment Planning for Severely Disordered Children

Some children cannot live at home due to the severity of their pathology. Some may have psychiatric problems such as severe depression with suicidal ideation or psychotic thought processes. Others may display severe behavior problems that make them a continued risk to hurt others, such as extreme physical aggression involving coercive threats or weapons. Greater supervision than can be provided in a home setting may be necessary. If a child is molesting other children in the neighborhood or school on a continuing basis or is engaging in extreme, intrusive offenses, it is necessary to stop this behavior immediately. To protect others, a child may need to be moved to a more restrictive environment (e.g., therapeutic foster care, group home, inpatient, or residential treatment facility).

Residential or inpatient treatment of sexually abusive children requires additional structure and interventions that are beyond the scope of our discussion. Outpatient treatment is most often tried prior to considering a referral to a more restrictive setting. Residential and inpatient modalities are generally reserved for those for whom outpatient therapy has been unsuccessful.

SUMMARY

This chapter illustrates the importance of integrating individual, family, and group treatment to address the problems presented by sexually abusive children. Prominent themes resurface throughout the children's and parents' therapies. Treatment goals must be coordinated between therapists using separate modalities.

Chapter 4

Parallel Group Treatment

Group treatment for sexually abusive children is intended to be an abuse-specific intervention. Perpetration issues are not adequately addressed when children are seen in less specific group settings, such as social skills groups. It appears that inclusion in a generic "victims" group is more often *not* helpful for dealing with perpetration issues; in fact, it can actually be *harmful*. If children (and adults) focus solely on their own victimization, they can successfully avoid dealing with how they victimize others.

We learned this lesson very early in our experience with sexually abusive children. When we began the very first session of the four- to eight-year-old group, we asked the children to describe how they had been molested. We assumed that it would be easier for them to begin this way, rather than to talk about their perpetrating behavior. During the second session of the group, the children were asked to tell whom they had sexually offended. Contrary to expectations, they all clearly stated that they had not touched anyone and to do such a thing would be "disgusting." The therapists had to do considerable work, reminding the children they had all been selected for the group because they *had* acted out sexually, before they would disclose their actions. As a result of this experience, we focus on perpetration and victim issues simultaneously.

Group treatment activities must be presented within the context of a therapeutic milieu. Group leaders should establish firm behavioral expectations and consistently model and reinforce a group process that is respectful. A milieu will be created whether or not the therapists direct the process. Given the maladaptive relationship patterns common to most children with sexually abusive behavior problems, one cannot expect a milieu established by them to be therapeutic. If therapists allow a countertherapeutic group milieu to develop before introducing appropriate behavioral expectations, the children will have to unlearn the milieu that has been established. Therefore, it is best to use a proactive, directive approach throughout the process of the group.

We conduct four different groups in our program for sexually abusive children. We hold separate groups for young and latency-aged children. Each of the children's groups includes eight to ten members. A parent group runs concurrently with each of the children's groups and is generally composed of eight to fifteen parents. About once per month or on alternate months, each of the children's groups and their parents meet in a parent/child combined group.

Similar behavioral management techniques are used in all of the children's groups. Group members must respect one another. This means that they wait their turn to speak, listen when others are talking, and treat others nicely. Most important, children are asked to not repeat to others what group members say in group. Respect and confidentiality create a trusting environment in which group members can talk about their most vulnerable feelings.

If a child is disrespectful, a short time-out is given. Time-outs are usually taken in the room, while seated in a chair facing a wall. When taking a time-out, a child is expected to sit quietly until a group leader indicates the time-out is over. On occasion, a seriously disruptive child will be asked to leave the room with one of the therapists to take a time-out. When further intervention is required, parents are asked to remain with their child until he/she calms down.

STRUCTURE OF GROUP TREATMENT PROGRAM

Young Children's Group

The young children's group meets once weekly for one hour. The session is divided into "talking time" and "playing time." During talking time, the children participate in an exercise developed to address one of the treatment goals. At the end of talking time, children are given cookies based on their level of participation and exhibited concern for others (i.e., one cookie for each of these two aspects of group performance). The group members themselves decide how many cookies each one has earned. Occasionally, additional treats or activities are provided, based on how well the group has worked together or the difficulty of the group session. During playing time, children either choose or make up games, with the requirement that they interact with one another. Sometimes a group leader will suggest a particular activity.

Latency-Age Children's Group

Older children meet in group once per week for ninety minutes. These sessions have a more complex structure than the group meetings with younger children. Sessions are divided into "check-in," "work time" and "social time." Check-in is the time to make announcements, introduce new members, and take care of other business. Check-in can also be used to talk about personal problems and successes. The children are encouraged to bring up personal issues and talk about their feelings.

During work time, which lasts about sixty minutes, the group engages in a therapeutic activity, which may be a game, an art project, or structured exercise. Children also can work on specific tasks needed to complete the group program. These include: "taking the hot seat" (see Chapter 5) to talk about their sexually abusive behaviors, sharing apology letters written to their victims, and describing their relapse prevention plans. At the end of work time, therapists give each group member structured feedback using the performance rating scales, as described next.

The last ten minutes of group are spent in social time. Social time is *not* a "free time" for group members to do whatever they want. As in the young children's group, the older group members are expected to spend social time interacting with one another. This time provides an opportunity for group members to improve and practice their social skills. Group therapists may deliberately suggest different interactive games and challenge group members to choose the activity through negotiation and compromise. If necessary, performance ratings are adjusted after social time.

The Accountability and Empathy Scales presented in Chapter 3 can be used to provide weekly feedback to each child regarding his/her progress. Although each child has individualized goals of treatment, most need considerable work in these two areas. The children are told they will be expected to explain how they set up and carried out their sexual offenses. In addition, they are expected to admit to other problems they create and demonstrate sensitivity to the other group members. Often, empathy is first clearly exhibited when the children talk about family members and close friends.

A Participation Scale is presented in Figure 4.1. On this scale a score of 0 = shut-down, 1 = minimal, 2 = involved, 3 = engaged, and 4 = self-disclosing. We use this scale to rate how well the children use group time to work on personal issues. For instance, children who initiate discussions about their own problems and make a genuine effort to find solutions would earn a 4 on participation. When children earn a 4 on participation, we compliment them on their decision to make good use of the group session.

The Cooperation Scale is presented in Figure 4.2. On this scale, a score of 0 = disruptive, 1 = distracting, 2 = compliant, 3 = responsible, and 4 = self-directed. We use this scale to rate children's compliance with group leaders, as well as their cooperation with one another. For example, children who make distracting jokes or comments would earn a score of 1. Children who follow directions when a group leader is present, but who stop working when they are not directly supervised, would earn a score of 2 on this scale.

When rating group members on these four scales, it is important to explain how individuals can improve their scores. The ratings are completed openly, as part of the group process. Although ratings are determined by therapist consensus, the children also give one another feedback. All of the group members then benefit from the feedback given to each individual. The ratings can be charted so the children can track their own progress. Figure 4.3 shows the group performance progress chart used to graph each child's performance ratings.

Individual and group rewards are contingent upon each child's performance ratings. Group members who earn two or more points on each of the rating scales are given a treat at the end of social time. If every member earns a treat, the group is awarded one "group point." Group points are used to obtain a special activity for the entire group (e.g., a pizza party or a softball game).

FIGURE 4.1. Participation Scale

PARTICIPATION SCALE
How I Use My Group Time

0	1	2	3	4
SHUT-DOWN	MINIMAL	INVOLVED	ENGAGED	SELF-DISCLOSING
Refuses to talk or answer questions. Does no work.	*Talks and answers questions only when asked. Work lacks effort.*	*Talks and answers questions freely. Work is thoughtful.*	*Discusses personal issues when asked. Work is very thoughtful.*	*Initiates discussion of personal issues. Work is self-disclosing.*

FIGURE 4.2. Cooperation Scale

COOPERATION SCALE
How I Follow Rules

0	1	2	3	4
DISRUPTIVE	DISTRACTING	COMPLIANT	RESPONSIBLE	SELF-DIRECTED
Much difficulty following directions.	*Some difficulty following directions.*	*Follows directions with reminders.*	*Follows directions without reminders.*	*Manages own behavior without reminders.*
Two or more time-outs.	*One or two time-outs.*	*One or two time-outs.*	*No time-outs.*	*No time-outs.*

Copyright © 1992 by Steven C. Huke, Lucinda A. Rasmussen, Barbara J. Christopherson, and Julie Bradshaw.

FIGURE 4.3. Group Performance Progress Chart

NAME: _____

GRAPH OF MY GROUP PROGRESS:

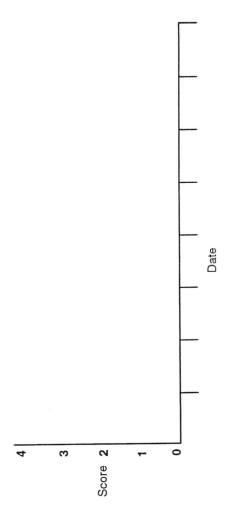

Weekly Scores for Accountability (A), Empathy (E), Participation (P), and Cooperation (C)

We show parents the children's rating scales and occasionally have them rate their own participation in parent group. The Accountability, Empathy, Participation, and Cooperation Scales may be adapted as a behavioral management tool for parents to use at home. The use of these scales at home can foster a sense of teamwork, with parents and therapists working toward the same objectives. It also provides therapists measurable feedback about a child's behaviors at home. Therapists may need to caution parents to use the scales only as a way to monitor and measure their child's behavior, not as a punitive disciplinary procedure.

TREATMENT TOPICS IN CHILDREN'S GROUP

Accountability

The children must accept accountability for their sexual acting-out behavior as well as any other activities that led to the victimization of others. Some have been involved in frequent fighting in school or in their neighborhoods. Others have tended to be quiet, but they engage in subtle ways of putting others down and/or attempting to control them. The need to feel powerful and in control is primary in both children and adults who have been sexually abused (Ryan, 1989). When children begin to exhibit sexually offending behaviors against others, they often show the same cognitive distortions or thinking errors that their own perpetrators used when abusing them. To interrupt sexually abusive behavior, clinicians need to directly confront these thinking errors, encourage accountability for perpetrating behavior, and redirect the children to examine their motivations for such inappropriate sexual behavior. We challenge group members to recognize their own thinking errors and confront the thinking errors of other group members whenever they occur.

Early group sessions focus primarily on accountability and building group cohesiveness. Whenever a new member joins the group, the purpose of the group is clearly stated. Children introduce themselves and state why they are in the group. The children who have been in group longest are asked to demonstrate accountability and be first to disclose information regarding their sexual acting-out behaviors. New group members then learn that they are not the only ones with sexual problems. They seem relieved to meet others who are struggling with the same issues; often they have not realized that others have problems similar to their own.

Disclosure of sexually abusive behaviors is sometimes difficult to facilitate. It is usually hard for children to begin talking about their sexually abusive behavior, and some are particularly resistant. Brad, a four-year-old, refused to talk about touching his cousin until his mother came into the group session and reported what another relative had witnessed. Although initially uncomfortable, Brad gradually began to self-disclose. The other children in the group were empathic and assured him they had all acted out in the same way.

The group process does facilitate open disclosure. At times we have begun sessions in which new group members have talked in some detail about their sexually abusive behaviors. In one early group session with young children, the therapists were surprised when the children gave full disclosures and freely talked about their offending behavior for the full hour, without asking for a break.

Sometimes problems with lack of accountability can be resolved by developing incentives for taking responsibility for any misbehavior. Jared, who initially refused to take responsibility for his perpetrating behavior, began being accountable by first reporting on his aggression. He was given stickers and other rewards for describing how he started problems with peers. It later became easier for him to accept responsibility for his sexual offenses. When children become accountable, they sometimes report additional offenses. As previously described, we help parents report these incidents to authorities.

Accountability continues to be addressed while group members work on understanding their motivation for offending (including arousal), developing empathy, and dealing with prior traumatization (if present). Children must understand how their own sexual offenses were a way to get their needs met. They must learn to cope with problems in more acceptable ways.

The final step in accepting accountability for inappropriate sexual behavior is to develop a plan to prevent reoffending. Before children can graduate from the group, they must have a plan detailing how they will interrupt their abuse cycle and avoid acting out sexually. Gray and Pithers (1993) have applied the relapse prevention model (Pithers, 1990; Pithers, Kashima, Cumming, and Beal, 1988; Pithers, Kashima, Cumming, Beal, and Buell, 1988; and Pithers et al., 1983) to sexually aggressive children. In this model, relapse prevention involves four critical aspects: self-management, trauma-induced reactions, compensatory responses, and external supervision.

Relapse prevention plans are developed to interrupt the abuse cycle and combine external and internal controls. The child must have a plan for managing sexual thoughts and arousal. For the very young child, the plan may be as simple as, "When I think about touching, I'm going to think about a great BIG stop sign, the biggest stop sign in the whole world. Then I'm going to find my Mom [or Dad] and tell her [or him or them] that I'm thinking about touching" (Thompson and Nelson, 1992). Latency-age children require more sophisticated plans, but the elements are the same—acknowledging feelings, stopping to think, and talking to a trustworthy person.

The children's relapse prevention plans include strategies for coping with their trauma-induced reactions rather than allowing these feelings to trigger a new abusive behavior. These plans identify to whom they can talk and specify coping techniques such as anger management and stress reduction. To interrupt compensatory responses that drive their abuse cycles, the children learn to confront their thinking errors and replace them with accountable thoughts.

Finally, external supervision of the child is crucial. Although we stress internal controls with the children, external controls must be in place to continually reinforce responsible behaviors. A child's prevention team consists of parents, therapists, caseworkers, and all other individuals who are concerned with the welfare of the child and are willing and able to be supportive (Gray, 1991). This prevention team must carefully outline a supervision plan. Parents must identify any reoccurrence of behaviors that may lead to reoffend and only high-risk situations such as baby-sitting or friendships with much younger children. An accountable child with supportive supervisors has a much greater chance of managing sexual thoughts and avoiding inappropriate sexual behaviors than a child lacking such support.

Empathy

Unless children begin to see how their behavior affects other people, they will not be motivated to change. If they do not care about others, they are at risk to continue to victimize and act out in sexual or aggressive ways. If they are able to imagine themselves in another person's place, they may be less likely to act out. Younger children may lack the capacity to view another person's situation and fully understand how they might feel in his/her place (Selman, 1980). However, they do show concern for one another, such as when they have hurt another in play or notice that someone has "hurt feelings."

As a first step in learning about empathic responses, the children are encouraged to try to identify what other group members are feeling during the group. In the beginning, these feelings may be confined to sad, mad, scared, or happy. Treatment exercises, such as "How Would You Feel If . . . ?" (see Chapter 6), are used to help children learn to identify a wider range of feelings. Even younger children can learn to identify more complex emotions such as embarrassed, shy, or jealous.

The focus of treatment shifts gradually from identification of feelings to victim empathy. Children are sometimes confused about why another child is a victim when they are the ones who got in trouble. It is necessary to educate them about the harmfulness of their offending behaviors. This is often done by encouraging them to express feelings about their own trauma or other problems and by helping them begin to understand the feelings of their victims. Rick, an eleven-year-old, disclosed his own victimization to the group while drawing the face of his victim. He was very upset by the parallel between his own feelings of traumatization and those of his victim. This session was a turning point, as his ability to show empathy was greatly enhanced.

The children are often able to experience empathy within the group because they are continually reinforced for showing respect to others. It is our belief that if the children learn to behave in an empathic fashion their aggression will diminish. Even if they do not acquire the quality of empathy, they can become more aware of their effect on others. Initially, the children are merely expected to avoid disrespectful behaviors. During the final stages of treatment, they are expected to show active concern for others. We encourage empathic responses to help others get through difficult experiences in group, such as a disclosure about their own victimization(s). The therapists help the children learn ways to demonstrate empathy both by modeling and by providing direct feedback.

Relationship Skills

When children begin to show concern for others, they are more likely to be accepted by peers. Then they are in a position to improve their relationship skills. When other children tend to avoid them, either because of their sexually abusive behavior and/or lack of empathy, sexually abusive children miss opportunities to develop their social skills. Often, sexually abusive children experience social rejection, become angry, act out in some fashion, and then experience more rejection. This pattern interferes with learning to relate on an intimate basis. Therapy stresses appropriate interactions with adults and peers. Throughout the group process, children receive immediate feedback regarding how their actions may have affected another group member.

Opportunities for social skills development also take place during the social time following group discussions. The children are asked to play with one another during this relatively unstructured time. Some try to avoid peer interaction by talking to the therapists and seeking their attention. These children appear to feel more comfortable with adults than peers. Other children are polite and appropriate during group discussions but attempt to control peers during unstructured times.

Positive reinforcement is given to those children who apply principles learned in group to the social setting. For example, in one group, a child was accidentally injured while playing a game. Tyler, the child who was responsible, obviously felt bad but did not talk about his feelings. He experienced more guilt than was necessary, given the situation. Other group members helped Tyler to understand that he had not intended any harm. This incident reinforced the importance of open expression of feelings.

Healthy Sexuality

Discussions about sexuality are encouraged in group to clarify values in sexual relationships and help the children understand the role of sexual arousal in their offenses. Most of the children need education regarding sexual development and acceptable sexual behavior. Many need to learn how to distinguish appropriate affectionate touching from sexual touching. It is also important for them to understand the concept of choice or consent in a sexual relationship. Specific goals regarding sexuality in the children's group include normalizing sexual feelings, differentiating appropriate sexual thoughts and behaviors from inappropriate ones, and recognizing how choice and self-control are involved in sexual thought and expression.

Therapists introduce the topic of sexuality when the children themselves do not. Young children tend to have less specific discussion about sexual feelings, but they usually acknowledge that they have acted out sexually in part because "it felt good." In groups of younger children, questions are answered as they arise. Specific lesson plans regarding sexuality are not presented.

To help older children become more comfortable discussing sexuality, colloquial sexual terminology is reviewed, and children are taught clinical terms to provide them with a common sexual vocabulary. Most children will prefer to use the colloquial terms, and this is permitted as long as the term is not offensive to anyone in the group. Younger children are usually allowed to use their own terms without sanctions. When children get silly during these sexually oriented discussions, therapists discuss the anxiety behind the laughter and allow the joking to continue as long as it is not offensive or disruptive.

Care is taken to respect parents' values and concerns about sexuality. Prior to discussions about sexuality, parents are informed of the purpose of such discussions with their children and asked for input. We ask parents questions about their beliefs and values regarding sexual relationships, masturbation, relationships outside of marriage, sexual orientation, etc. Many prefer to have the therapists help them talk with their children regarding the "facts of life" rather than face this task alone.

Individuals must learn to make choices regarding their sexual feelings and behavior. Ideally, when children mature, their sexual feelings can be expressed within the context of an intimate relationship. Unfortunately, many sexually abusive children have come to associate sexuality with "badness." Some may believe they have no control over their sexual behavior. They may view sexuality as something they must avoid in order to stay out of trouble. When assuming they have no control over what they do, children are likely to feel helpless, scared, and frustrated.

Children learn the concept of choice as they identify how they set up their victims. They begin to recognize how they took away the choices of their victims by the use of manipulation, bribery, or coercion. They begin to understand who is capable of consenting to sexual behaviors and who is not. We stress that children are not capable of legally consenting to sexual activity. When children begin to recognize that they can choose how to deal with their sexual feelings, they can become accountable for prior choices and discuss points at which they might have chosen differently. It is only after children acknowledge that they have choices that they can begin to exercise self-control.

Ted, a ten-year-old, reported feeling much better after disclosing an offense to the group. He was able to trace his offense through the abuse cycle and clarified for himself where he could have made better choices. Ted appeared to feel empowered and more hopeful by this experience, as he learned how to control a behavior that he felt had been out of control. His comment was, "I thought I was crazy and going to end up in prison or a hospital!"

The "basket of feelings" activity (James, 1989) can be adapted to discuss sexual arousal with older children. They first generate a list of feelings they associate with sexual excitement. These words, such as horny, weird, tingly, and guilty, are written on pieces of construction paper that are then spread out on the floor. The children then think of a time when they became aroused. They identify the way they felt at that time by placing markers on any of the feeling words that apply to their experience. The relative intensity of each feeling is reflected by the number of markers placed upon it.

Everyone can then talk about what thoughts were associated with each feeling. When group members begin to show signs of arousal, the discussion can shift naturally to exploring options for coping with sexual feelings. Arousal may be unavoidable, particularly in groups with highly sexualized members. In such cases, we recommend less specific exploration of this topic.

Sexual arousal may be reinforced through fantasies. Group members are encouraged to monitor their sexual thoughts to prevent the development of deviant fantasies. Inappropriate sexual thoughts and behaviors are those which contradict one's value system or are in any way disrespectful to the other person. Disrespectful thoughts and behaviors include objectification, force, coercion, or manipulation—in short, dismissal of consent. In contrast, appropriate sexual thoughts and behaviors are those which do not involve any of the previous factors, which would make them inappropriate. Following this discussion, the children are encouraged to review their fantasies and identify inappropriate elements. Finally, they work to replace the inappropriate elements of their fantasies with appropriate ones.

Sexually abusive children have the choice to act or not act upon their sexual thoughts and feelings. Acting upon these thoughts and feelings may be an appropriate choice, when it does not involve abusive actions; for example, masturbation may be an acceptable alternative. However, this option may need to be discussed in family therapy if parents' values prohibit masturbation. Certainly, masturbation would be considered abusive if used compulsively or in public. Masturbation must be done privately, and accompanying fantasies should be appropriate (i.e., nonabusive). Other options to cope with sexual thoughts and feelings include actively stopping thoughts, distraction, and problem solving. In group, children often share the strategies they use to interrupt sexual thoughts, such as talking with a parent, playing Nintendo, or forcing themselves to think about a nonsexual topic.

After children have learned to differentiate between appropriate and inappropriate sexual thoughts and behaviors and recognize how choice and self-control are involved in sexual thought and expression, they can apply this information in their lives. It is particularly important that older children understand how feelings of arousal were involved in their offenses. When they recognize their choices, they can develop individual strategies to exert self-control over their sexual expression and prevent relapse. Younger children must also understand how arousal led to their offenses and plan strategies to deal with sexual feelings. Talking with a parent about these feelings is usually the best relapse prevention plan for young children.

We recommend that groups be led by both a male and female therapist, although this is not always possible due to availability of staff. A male/female cotherapy team is useful to model male/female relationships that are not sexual. It also provides an opportunity for children to learn to talk with both male and female adults about sexuality. During one discussion regarding arousal, a group of older boys were surprised to learn that females not only think about sex, but enjoy it as well. The boys in another older group at first expressed discomfort due to the presence of a female therapist when they were asked to discuss their sexual feelings. After they agreed to discuss these feelings with respectful language rather than disrespectful slang terms, they became more comfortable with the idea of having a female present.

Discussions about sexuality and arousal need to be carefully monitored by group leaders. Some children may become sexually aroused when other group members describe their offenses or talk about trigger events. One twelve-year-old took great pleasure in describing his offenses in minute detail to the group. The therapists frequently interrupted his narration to keep him and the others focused on relevant issues, such as thinking errors and how he set up and covered up his offense. The stimulating aspects of these discussions can be inhibited by maintaining focus on treatment topics.

GROUP TREATMENT FOR PARENTS

Children and parents meet simultaneously in separate groups to learn and process related material. While the children are learning how to express feelings, their parents may be working on identifying feelings in others and giving empathic responses. The group is also used to communicate information presented in the children's groups to parents. In this way, the treatment process is integrated within the home environment.

Parents' groups provide parents with needed information and support. A parent may feel isolated from friends and families who "cannot understand what I'm going through." It is important for parents to learn how to establish functional boundaries between themselves and their children as well as between themselves and others in their environment. In group they learn they are not alone with their problems or their concerns.

Some parents are more likely to talk about child development and sexual issues with other group members than with their own therapist. One mother, Mary, was particularly offended when her ten-year-old son took pleasure in being "gross" (e.g., burping and passing gas in public). Typically she avoided taking him to social events. Although initially embarrassed discussing this problem, Mary was relieved when the other mothers assured her their sons showed the same type of behavior.

Early in the group process, parents generally focus on behavioral problems such as their children's angry outbursts. As they become more comfortable and trusting of group members, they tend to discuss more personal and private matters such as their own traumatization or problems in their marital relationship. Over time, sexual topics are also addressed more specifically. It is reassuring for parents to learn that others struggle with how to talk to children about sexual issues.

In some cases, a parental reluctance to discuss sexuality with a child goes beyond discomfort. Parents sometimes fear that talking to their children about sexuality will encourage future sexual behavior. They may therefore try to shelter their children from any discussion. However, sexually abusive children need to talk to the adults in their lives when they are tempted to reoffend. It is not likely they will do this, particularly as they grow older, unless a strong precedent for talking with parents about sexual thoughts and problem behaviors is set.

We work very hard with parents to prepare them to respond effectively to these disclosures. We teach that sexual feelings begin in infancy. In utero, fetuses are responsive to touch and may have erections (Johnson, 1993a; Martinson, 1991, 1997). From birth, infants may have occasional erections or vaginal secretions (Gil 1993a; Martinson, 1976). Even when parents have a difficult time accepting this information, they can accept that their children, who have acted out in a sexual way, have sexual feelings. Once parents acknowledge sexual feelings are present in children, they want to help guide their own children to handle these feelings.

COMBINED GROUPS

Parallel group treatment provides opportunities for parents and children to meet in a combined group. Then therapists in both groups can better understand how family members relate to one another. For example, one mother's eleven-year-old son lay almost prone against her on the couch. She seemed uncomfortable with this encroachment on her personal space. He did not respond to her subtle cues to move away from her until she became embarrassed and angry. During subsequent family sessions, the therapist used this observation from group to teach them about personal space, enmeshment, and appropriate discipline.

During combined sessions parents may watch therapists demonstrate how to use time-out and other types of discipline. They are also able to observe how other parents discipline their own children and make more informed decisions about which techniques are most helpful. Combined groups give parents the opportunity for feedback from other group members, as parents observe one another interacting with the children.

SUMMARY

The treatment process must focus on the specific needs of each child as well as address common characteristics of sexually abusive children. Common goals for treatment of sexually abusive children are to help them accept responsibility for inappropriate behaviors, develop empathy for the feelings of others, resolve feelings of prior traumatization and/or family dysfunction, increase competencies in both close and social relationships, and develop a healthy attitude toward sexuality.

As previously stated, all children with sexually abusive behavior problems are seen in individual and family treatment, and most are seen for group treatment. The parallel group experience facilitates similar learning experiences for children and parents. Both groups work toward making effective choices within a supportive environment. These parallel experiences allow children and parents to more easily begin to integrate new information and behaviors into everyday life.

Part II describes actual activities and techniques used to treat sexually abusive children and their families.

PART II:
TREATMENT EXERCISES

Introduction

Treatment of sexually abusive children and their parents entails the employment of a variety of activities and techniques. Interventions should enhance insight, stimulate affective responses, and facilitate behavioral change. Both children and their parents can benefit from treatment activities that combine cognitive and experiential interventions. By carefully balancing cognitive and affective techniques, therapists create a therapeutic environment to facilitate change.

Treatment techniques for sexually abusive children need to be more direct than traditional nondirective play therapy (Rasmussen and Cunningham, 1995). Sexually abusive children are unlikely to talk about their sexual problems on their own. Cognitive-behavioral techniques are used to confront the children's behavior and help them to become accountable, develop empathy for the feelings of others, express feelings related to prior trauma, and learn to appropriately manage their sexual impulses. In addition, experiential techniques, such as art therapy or role-plays with puppets or other props, help children express feelings related to prior trauma and develop empathy.

Part II presents activities and techniques we have found to be helpful in treating sexually abusive children and their parents. Periodic case examples are provided to illustrate the group process. Clinicians may find other useful activities in treatment workbooks such as the following: Cunningham and MacFarlane's (1996) *When Children Abuse: Group Treatment Strategies for Children with Impulse Control Problems*, Hindman's (1991) *The Mourning Breaks*, James's (1989) *Treating Traumatized Children: New Insights and Creative Interventions*, Johnson's (1995a) *Treatment Exercises for Child Abuse Victims and Children with Sexual Behavior Problems*, MacFarlane and Cunningham's (1988) *Steps to Healthy Touching*, Mandell and Damon's (1989) *Group Treatment for Sexually Abused Children*, and Steen's (1993) *The Relapse Prevention Workbook for Youth in Treatment*.

Chapter 5

Accountability

*ACTIVITY: DRAW THE OFFENSE**

Target Groups

Young and latency-age children.

Objective

To help children talk about their offense, including the setting and precipitating events.

Materials

Paper and pencils, crayons, or markers.

Description

The children are asked to draw a picture of their offense. ("Draw a picture of what you did when you touched another person's private parts.") After everyone has completed their pictures, they are asked to "tell" about what they drew.

Process

The children talk about the details of their offenses as they discuss their pictures. Therapists assist the children to disclose infor-

---

*Adapted from MacFarlane, K. and Cunningham, C. (1988). *Steps to healthy touching.* Mount Dora, FL: Kidsrights.

mation about how they set up the offenses. Questions regarding what occurred both before and after the circumstances depicted in the pictures are used to help the children understand what occurred. The children are asked questions such as, "When did you first think about touching?" and "How did you feel afterward?" To help them understand at what point they could have initiated a prevention plan, therapists emphasize the point in time when the idea to molest came to each child.

Precautions

Parents often express concern that their children will get new ideas as other children talk about their offenses. This matter does require some caution. During the discussion of the children's drawings, it is important for therapists to interrupt long, detailed accounts that appear arousing to any group members.

Young children do not always specifically understand the instructions to draw their offense. Some of them invariably draw themselves being molested. In some children, this is avoidance of accountability, but others have genuine difficulty sorting out their perpetrator's responsibility versus their own accountability. When children do draw their own molestation, it is important to discuss this work, as valuable information about prior traumatization may be obtained. Amy, a seven-year-old girl, drew everyone else in her family sleeping alone in their beds, but her father was drawn lying on top of her. Although she did not draw her offense as instructed, she did produce thoughtful and useful material regarding her prior trauma.

If a picture does not appear to represent a child's offense, it is important not to assume the child has ignored or misunderstood the directions. For example, Roland, age six, drew a single, vertical line that he later described was the wall against which he had pulled his brother when he molested him. It is important to ask each child to describe his/her drawing. Even when younger children take advantage of the time to draw a picture unrelated to their perpetration, it is usually possible to encourage them to talk about some details of their offense as they describe their picture. However, when older children clearly avoid accountability by drawing a picture of something other than their offense, it is important to redirect them to the task and, of course, make time later for them to tell about their offenses.

Adaptations

Latency-age children may be asked to draw pictures of how they set up and manipulated their victims. They may also draw what occurred before, during, and after their offenses. Young children have been able to complete these drawings over a couple of sessions. This exercise may be used in individual and/or family treatment as well as in group therapy.

ACTIVITY: TAKING RESPONSIBILITY
FOR YOUR PROBLEMS

Target Groups

Young and latency-age children.

Objective

To help children demonstrate accountability in their everyday lives.

Materials

None (although problems could be listed on poster paper or a chalkboard).

Description

A therapist explains to the children: "Everyone sometimes does things that hurt another person or make someone angry. When this happens, it is important to be able to admit you caused a problem." It is acknowledged that they all caused a problem when they molested, but during this exercise, the therapist asks them to talk about other times they caused problems. To facilitate this process, therapists model making such disclosures (e.g., overreacting to a co-worker's innocent comment) before eliciting examples from the children. Therapists then ask the children to take turns telling about a problem each one of them caused.

Process

The group discusses alternative ways of coping with feelings and handling situations. The children are asked to think about how other people might feel about the problems they caused. If an apology seems appropriate, individual children can role-play making an apology. However, it is important that the children themselves decide whether they wish to engage in such a role-play. When children do agree to role-playing or planning an apology, they are praised for being so "brave." Similarly, each time they make a disclosure during this exercise, the children are praised for being accountable.

Precautions

It is critical to maintain focus on problems the children actually have caused. Occasionally, a child will bring up "being bad" as a precipitant for a parent's problem, such as parental conflict, divorce, physical abuse, or drinking. At these times, the discussion shifts to whether a child can really be responsible for adult behavior. Numerous examples are elicited from the group to clarify what problems a child *can* cause versus those which are not within a child's control.

It usually takes continuing reassurance to convince young children that they will not get in trouble for their disclosures. This exercise is designed to encourage accountability, and it is important that the discussion *not* be judgmental or punishing. Parents are carefully prepared in parent group and family therapy to accept these disclosures at home.

Adaptations

This exercise generalizes to home more easily if addressed in a combined group or in family therapy. When taking responsibility for problems is modeled in group, parents better understand the importance of listening to their children without getting angry. They learn to praise their children for being honest and "telling" on themselves. Also, when children witness their parents being accountable, they learn it is acceptable to admit to problems themselves.

Young children who have difficulty with this exercise may be encouraged to use puppets to report a problem. For children who have particular difficulty admitting to problems, it is helpful to set up a positive reinforcement system. This can be easily monitored by the family therapist. A child and parent may be asked to spend five minutes at the end of the day to identify times when a child was responsible for a problem at home, school, or in the neighborhood. If a child spontaneously reports a problem he/she caused, the parent may reward the child with tokens, which can be cashed in for a trip to the ice cream store, playing a family game, etc. Rewards that encourage positive social interactions are better than money or toys.

ACTIVITY: STEPS AND SLIDES ABUSE CYCLE

Target Group

Latency-age children.

Objectives

To help abusive children:

1. understand how their abusive behavior problems are part of a sequence of feelings, thoughts, and actions;
2. understand how they use thinking errors to justify their progression through this sequence; and
3. develop a prevention plan that outlines specific behavioral alternatives they can use to interrupt their abuse cycle.

Materials

Steps and Slides Abuse Cycle (see Figure 5.1) as a handout or printed on large poster board; two worksheets based on Figure 5.1: Steps and Slides I: Sliding Down (see Figure 5.2), and Steps and Slides II: Climbing Up (see Figure 5.3).

Description

The Steps and Slides Abuse Cycle (see Figure 5.1) illustrates the sequence of feelings, thoughts, and actions that precede and follow abusive behavior. The sequence is presented on eight levels; on each level, the individual encounters a brick wall, a slide, and a staircase. The walls illustrate choice points at which an individual selects an action that will continue or interrupt the abusive sequence. Each slide represents a maladaptive choice that leads to increasingly hurtful behavior. Similarly, each staircase represents an adaptive choice that leads to increasingly responsible behavior.

The "Sliding Down" worksheet (see Figure 5.2) focuses on the slides, or maladaptive choices, and can help children understand their own abuse cycle. At each level of the sequence, children are

FIGURE 5.1. Steps and Slides Abuse Cycle

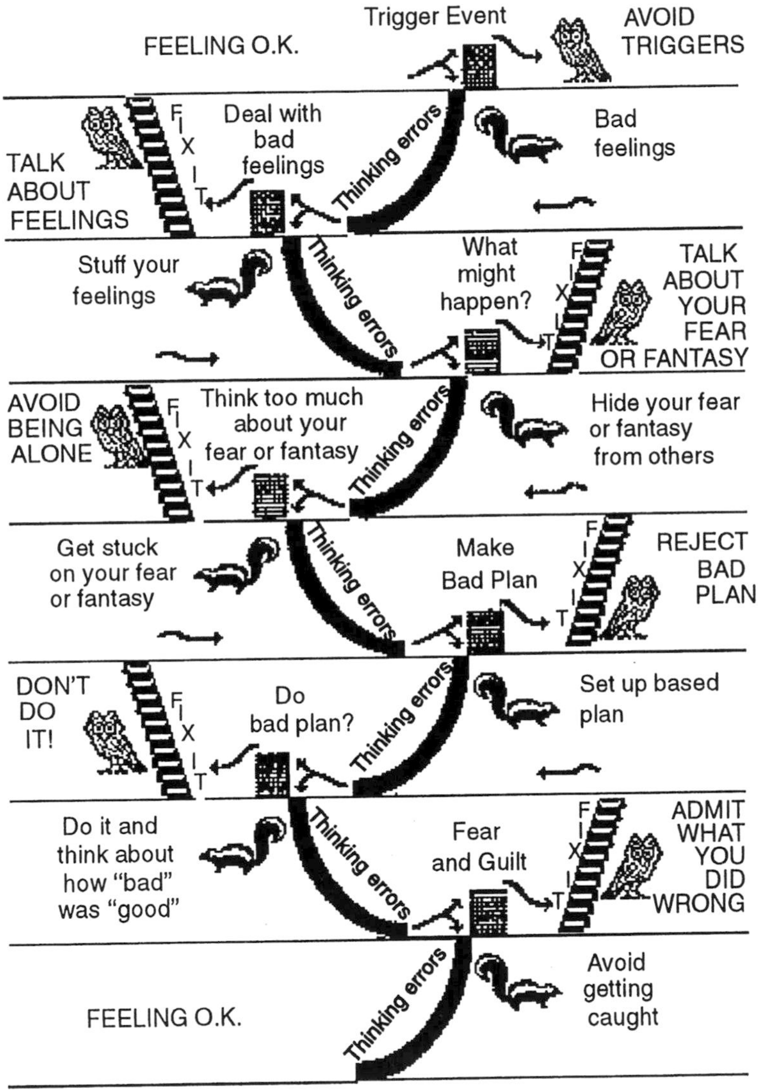

FIGURE 5.2. Steps and Slides I: Sliding Down
(Why Did I Do It?)

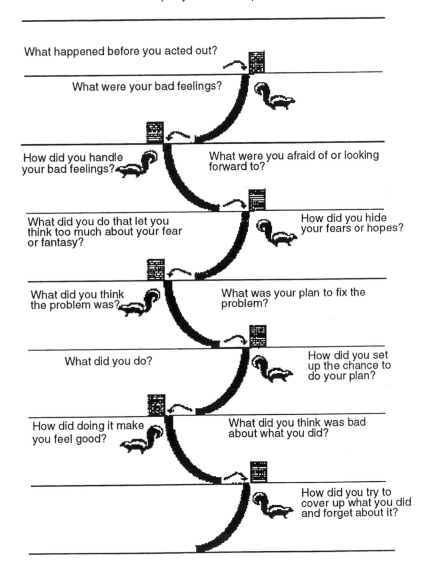

What happened before you acted out?

What were your bad feelings?

How did you handle
your bad feelings?

What were you afraid of or looking
forward to?

What did you do that let you
think too much about your fear
or fantasy?

How did you hide
your fears or hopes?

What did you think
the problem was?

What was your plan to fix the
problem?

What did you do?

How did you set
up the chance to
do your plan?

How did doing it make
you feel good?

What did you think was bad
about what you did?

How did you try to
cover up what you did
and forget about it?

FIGURE 5.3. Steps and Slides II: Climbing Up
(My Prevention Plan)

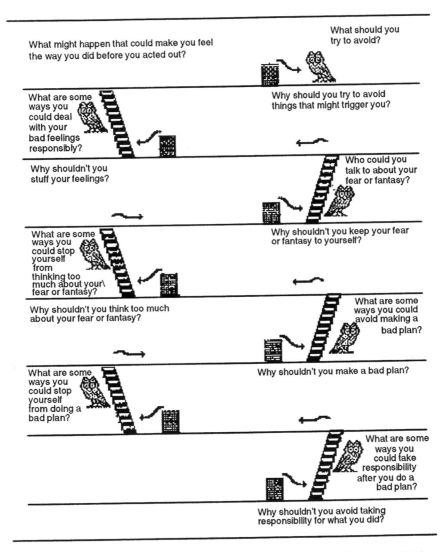

asked questions designed to help them explore the feelings and thoughts they experienced before, during, and after an offense they committed. For example, the first question, "What happened before you acted out?," refers to the child's trigger event. (The "Basket of Trigger Feelings" activity in Chapter 7 can help children identify their trigger events.) The second question, "What were your bad feelings?," asks children to list negative feelings they had in response to the trigger event. The answer to the third question, "How did you handle your bad feelings?," typically involves a description of "hiding," "avoiding," or "stuffing" one's feelings. For example, a child might respond, "I went to my room" or "I pretended to be happy." Next to each slide, children write the thinking errors they used. For instance, the child who stuffs his/her feelings by pretending to be happy would write "being phony" next to the second slide. The remaining questions help children examine each step of their abuse cycle.

The "Climbing Up" worksheet (see Figure 5.3) focuses on the staircases, or adaptive choices, and can help children understand how they might interrupt their abuse cycle. The question "What should you try to avoid?" refers to trigger events children can avoid by staying away from risky situations. Many trigger events are unavoidable; abusive children must learn to manage their reactions to events that provoke negative feelings, such as being rejected by peers. The fourth question, "What are some ways you can deal with your bad feelings responsibly?," elicits alternatives to stuffing feelings. These may include talking about feelings or distracting oneself when sexually aroused. The question, "Why shouldn't you do a bad plan?," requires the children to list reasons they should not engage in an abusive action, such as getting themselves in trouble or causing pain to their victims and others. The remaining questions can help children develop a plan to interrupt their maladaptive behavior at each step of their abuse cycle.

Process

Use of the Steps and Slides Abuse Cycle is ongoing. As children progress through therapy, they become increasingly familiar with this figure and more adept at using it to describe their own abusive behavior. Children should complete the "Sliding Down" and "Climbing Up" worksheets more than once during treatment. Each time they complete the worksheets, they may gain more skill in using the Steps and Slides Abuse Cycle to interrupt their abusive behaviors. Both worksheets can be filled out with the therapist's help or assigned as homework, depending on children's reading abilities and levels of insight about their thoughts and feelings.

Sliding Down Worksheet

When sexually abusive children are beginning treatment, they may use the "Sliding Down" worksheet to examine abusive behaviors that are nonsexual, such as bullying or teasing other children. By beginning with nonsexual abusive behavior, even children who deny having engaged in sexually abusive behavior can begin to understand their abuse cycle. Nonetheless, it may take children several months of therapy to work through denial and gain enough insight to complete their first "Sliding Down" worksheet. They can then complete another worksheet to examine their sexually abusive behavior.

When children have completed a "Sliding Down" worksheet about their sexually abusive behavior, they are ready to "take the hot seat" in group (see the next activity, "The Hot Seat"). On the hot seat, children can take responsibility for their specific sex offenses and show what they have learned about their abuse cycle. They can use the Steps and Slides Abuse Cycle to describe their trigger events, feelings, thinking errors, setups, and coverups.

Climbing Up Worksheet

Children complete the "Climbing Up" worksheet after they have gained understanding of their abuse cycle and are ready to design their relapse prevention plan. This worksheet helps them identify specific strategies to interrupt their abuse cycle and prevent abusive behavior. After children complete a "Climbing Up" worksheet, they are ready to "take the hot seat" to present their relapse prevention plan.

Precautions

Therapists must be aware of individual differences in children's abilities to understand the Steps and Slides Abuse Cycle and make adjustments for children who have difficulty grasping abstract concepts. Applying the abstract sequence of the Steps and Slides Abuse Cycle to their individual experiences can be challenging to some children. The use of experiential therapeutic modalities, such as role-play or art therapy, may be necessary to help children with learning disabilities understand the Steps and Slides Abuse Cycle.

Additionally, therapists must be sensitive to individual differences in the thoughts and feelings involved in the children's abuse cycles. For example, a cycle initiated by feelings of arousal may involve excitement and approach behaviors, while a sequence initiated by feelings of powerlessness may involve fear and avoidance. Children may not understand the "fear or fantasy" question in the third and fourth levels of the Steps and Slides Abuse Cycle. Therapists must help children determine whether the sequence being considered involves a fear, a sexual fantasy, or both (e.g., when both powerlessness and arousal are present).

Efforts to understand the motivations involved in a particular child's sexually abusive behavior must be exploratory. Therapists should avoid using leading questions or telling a child what they believe the child was thinking or feeling. The Steps and Slides Abuse Cycle may not be an accurate reflection of the abusive sequence of all children with sexually abusive behavior problems; some children may have variations in their feelings, thoughts, and actions that do not correspond with the sequence described in this version of the sexual abuse cycle. The Steps and Slides Abuse Cycle is an intervention tool that therapists can use to help children understand and interrupt their abusive behavior, but it may not apply to all situations.

Adaptations

The Steps and Slides Abuse Cycle can be used effectively in individual therapy as well as in group and family sessions. It is too abstract to use with young children.

ACTIVITY: THE HOT SEAT

Target Group

Latency-age children.

Objectives

To help sexually abusive children:

1. take responsibility for their inappropriate sexual behaviors;
2. recognize and correct the thinking errors they used to justify their hurtful behaviors;
3. recognize the harmful impact of their inappropriate behaviors on their victims, and begin to develop empathy for their victims' feelings; and
4. develop and practice a workable and effective relapse prevention plan.

Materials

None needed.

Description

The "hot seat" is an experiential group activity often used with adult and adolescent sex offenders to help them take responsibility for their sex offenses. To "take the hot seat," an offender volunteers to talk about a sex offense he/she committed and receives confrontation and feedback from group therapists and other group members. This activity adapts the hot seat to the needs of latency-age sexually abusive children.

The Steps and Slides Abuse Cycle worksheets (see previous activity) help children understand the sequence of thoughts, feelings, and behaviors that led them to commit sexually abusive acts. Completing the worksheets helps prepare children to take the hot seat and discuss their inappropriate behavior with the group. Participation is voluntary. Children decide, in consultation with their parents and individual therapists, when they are ready for the hot seat experience.

On the hot seat, children discuss a specific incidence of their sexually abusive behavior. They can use their completed "Sliding Down" worksheet to identify the steps in their abuse cycle. Children describe their trigger events, feelings, thinking errors, setups, and coverups. They also talk about their victims' reactions and how they think their victims may have felt. Therapists and other group members ask questions, give feedback, and point out thinking errors.

Individual hot seat sessions can focus on only one or two steps of the abuse cycle. For example, a child may use a hot seat session to work only on identifying triggers. Setups and coverups may be addressed in subsequent sessions. Parents and therapists can help a child identify which steps of the abuse cycle are most problematic for him/her, and a hot seat session can be structured to address only those aspects.

Children may volunteer for the hot seat several times during the course of treatment. When children are first beginning treatment, the hot seat may focus on identifying their feelings and thinking errors prior to committing the offense. Later hot seats may deal with a description of the offense, including setups and coverups. Some children find it difficult to identify the triggers that began their abuse cycle. Identifying triggers may take place in later hot seats, after children have gained insight about their feelings and thinking errors.

The hot seat can also be used to address relapse prevention issues. Children can use the "Climbing Up" worksheet to begin writing a relapse prevention plan. They can then take the hot seat and present their plan to the group. Therapists and group members can give feedback about whether the plan seems adequate to help the children avoid high-risk situations and interrupt the abuse cycle.

Process

Clinicians who work with adult and adolescent sex offenders have traditionally used the power of the group milieu in the hot seat activity to confront offenders' denial, blaming, minimizing, and other thinking errors. The hot seat frequently becomes a confrontational process that holds offenders accountable for their behavior. Although a traditional use of the hot seat may be too harsh for many sexually abusive children, it is possible to adapt the hot seat to provide a balance of confrontation and empathic support.

Although it is important to confront obvious thinking errors, therapists should encourage group members to look for positive aspects and identify what the child in the hot seat does right. Therapists model this process by pointing out ways the child in the hot seat takes responsibility, corrects thinking errors, and tries to empathize with the victim. This modeling helps children learn to give each other positive feedback. Similarly, therapists model positive ways to point out problems and make suggestions. For example, a therapist might ask the group, "What could John do to improve this hot seat? What else does he need to talk about?" When used in this manner, the hot seat can become a learning experience that helps increase children's insight, accountability, and victim empathy.

The hot seat experience often helps children gain increased understanding about their sexual abuse cycle. Children may become more aware of the abusive aspects of their behavior. Some children do not realize the full extent of the abusiveness of their behaviors until they are confronted by other group members. For example, Kirk, age ten, showed almost no emotion as he told the group about inserting nails into his victim's rectum. He appeared surprised when several group members expressed disgust at his actions. Similarly, Tiffany, an eleven-year-old sexually abusive girl, was unaware of the effects of her nonverbal behaviors on her three-year-old victim. She could not identify any coverups because she did not say anything to her victim about not telling. Another group member pointed out that Tiffany had admitted giving her victim a "dirty look" after she fondled him. Her peer's confrontation helped Tiffany realize that the look was her way to ensure her victim's silence.

A critical component of the hot seat experience is becoming aware of the harmful impact of sexually abusive behavior on victims. As children on the hot seat talk about how they set up, carried out, and covered up their offenses, therapists may point out negative responses their victims made to the sexual behavior. Examining these responses may help the children gain increased awareness of their victims' feelings, as well as become more in touch with their feelings about their own abuse. For example, when twelve-year-old Charlotte described fondling a younger girl on her vagina, she told the group that her victim's eyes filled with tears when she touched her. She added that her victim then tried to touch her breasts, but "I wouldn't let her." When asked why, Charlotte expressed feeling "weird" and uncomfortable about letting the younger girl touch her body. She then admitted that these feelings reminded her of her own abuse when her uncle fondled her breasts. Through Charlotte's experience on the hot seat, she realized that her victim likely felt similar feelings (weird, uncomfortable) when she touched the girl's vagina.

Precautions

Although the hot seat can be a powerful and effective way to help sexually abusive children become more accountable and empathic, therapists must use it carefully. Many children are not comfortable being the focus of a group discussion. When that discussion requires children to disclose shameful information, their fears of rejection and criticism can seem overwhelming. To alleviate these fears, taking the hot seat must always be voluntary.

It is also important to ensure that children do not use hot seat sessions to criticize each other, or build themselves up at the expense of other group members. Therapists must help establish a caring, supportive atmosphere in the group milieu. Hot seat sessions should not be undertaken until trust and group cohesiveness have been established. A supportive milieu facilitates hot seat sessions that balance confrontation with empathic support.

Therapists must also be careful to monitor group members for signs of sexual arousal during hot seat sessions. When children discuss their sex offenses in group, other group members may become sexually aroused. Therapists can reduce this possibility by limiting disclosures of the actual details of the offending behavior. However, it may be necessary for some children to describe their sexually abusive behavior before they can be fully accountable or begin to have empathy for their victims. Some discussion of details of the offense is therefore unavoidable but must be carefully monitored. Sexual arousal in the session may be decreased by moving the discussion to less sexually laden or more intellectual topics following the hot seat activity.

Children can learn to manage sexual feelings through group discussions that focus on what the children can do if they become sexually aroused or have sexual fantasies following a hot seat session. Therapists may want to caution the children to implement their relapse prevention plans if they have any sexual fantasies following the session. Children should be encouraged to inform their parents or another trusted adult and talk about their feelings. If therapists have concerns that a particular child may have become sexually aroused during a hot seat session, it is wise to inform the parents following group.

Adaptations

This exercise is appropriate for latency-age children only. It is not appropriate for younger children. With younger children's groups, it is best if therapists keep discussion of sexually abusive behavior more general.

ACTIVITY: CATCH THAT THINKING ERROR!

Target Group

Parents/children combined.

Objective

To help parents and children understand, identify, and correct thinking errors.

Materials

"List of Thinking Errors and Corrections" (see Figure 5.4) as a handout or printed on large poster board, chips for points, and "Catch That Thinking Error Game Cards" (see Figure 5.5).

Description

Players are asked to identify and correct thinking errors in hypothetical situations. For example, one game card presents the following situation: "Tom and Jimmy got caught stealing candy from the store. Tom said it was Jimmy's idea. What thinking error did Tom use? (blaming). What is the correction for blaming? (admit you did it). What could Tom say to admit he did it? (e.g., 'I stole the candy')."

The activity uses a TV game show format in which parents and children compete in teams. The rules of the game are as follows:

1. Each game card is worth two points; one chip marker is awarded for identifying the thinking error and one chip for giving an example of how to correct the thinking error.
2. The chance to respond rotates within teams so that every player has an opportunity to earn points for the team. One player is "up" at a time.
3. To begin play, the "game show host" (therapist) reads a game card, and the first player up for the first team is asked to identify the thinking error. If the player identifies the thinking

error, he/she earns one chip for the team and the chance to earn a second chip by providing an example of the correction for that thinking error. If the first player earns both points, the chance to respond to a new game card passes to the player who is up for the opposing team.

4. When an incorrect response is given, the player who is up on the opposing team has the opportunity to earn the remaining points for that game card. For each game card, the play continues to alternate between teams until both points for that card have been earned. Teams take turns beginning play on a new game card, regardless of which team earned points from the previous card.

5. Players may refer to the "List of Thinking Errors and Corrections" (see Figure 5.4).

6. Throughout the game, behavior on the part of *any* player that would normally result in a time-out will instead result in a two-point penalty for that player's team.

The team with the most chips at the end of the session wins a stuffed "Oscar the Owl" trophy for catching and correcting the most thinking errors. The losing group gets a trophy of "Stinky the Skunk." These traveling trophies become group mascots until the next time the game is played.

Process

To ensure that the game functions as a learning process, correct answers are always followed by a brief explanation. Ideally, this explanation is provided by the player who gave the correct answer. For example, after a player has identified the thinking error, a therapist can ask, "How did you know Tom was using blaming?" The player might then explain, "Because it doesn't matter who thought of stealing the candy. Tom was the one who took it. Tom was just trying to get out of being punished for what he did." If the player is unable to provide an explanation, or the explanation is incomplete, therapists can ask for a volunteer to explain the answer. If none of the players can do so, a therapist provides the explanation. Players who are unfamiliar with thinking errors often attempt to guess the correct answer by randomly selecting one of the thinking errors

FIGURE 5.4. List of Thinking Errors and Corrections

THINKING ERRORS	CORRECTIONS

"Stinky Thinking"   "Oscar Thinking"

THINKING ERRORS

1. Blaming
2. Excuse making
3. Victim playing
4. Avoiding
5. Being phony
6. Changing the Subject
7. Minimizing (Make it seem smaller)
8. Assuming
9. Anger (Make others do what you want)
10. Lying:
    - Make up a story
    - Leave something out

("Yes, I went to school"–but I didn't stay there)

    - Don't correct someone

("Great bike!" It's not yours, but you say "thanks")

CORRECTIONS

1. Admit you did it
2. Admit you had a choice
3. Try to change it
4. Deal with it
5. Be real
6. Stay on the subject
7. Tell it like it is
8. Check it out
9. Take "no" for an answer
10. Be honest:
    - Tell the truth
    - Tell everything

("I went to school, but then I left")

    - Correct someone

("I know, but it's not mine")

FIGURE 5.5. Catch That Thinking Error Game Cards

Tom and Jimmy got caught stealing candy from the store. Tom said it was Jimmy's idea. What thinking error did Tom use?

(BLAMING)

When Dennis's dad asked him why he hadn't taken out the garbage, Dennis said he didn't have time. What thinking error did Dennis use?

(EXCUSE MAKING)

Lance got caught stealing candy. He said, "I only took one candy bar." What thinking error did Lance use?

(MINIMIZING)

Alan and Ron sexually abused a younger boy. Alan said Ron made him do it. What thinking error did Alan use?

(BLAMING)

Sara called Amy names until she cried. When Sara got in trouble for teasing Amy, Sarah said she couldn't help it. What thinking error did Sara use?

(EXCUSE MAKING)

When Conrad's therapist asked him what he did to his victim, he said, "All I did was touch her." What thinking error did Conrad use?

(MINIMIZING)

Jason accidentally broke John's model car. When John came home, Jason said the dog had stepped on John's car. What thinking error did Jason use?

(LYING)

Jane's friend, Susie, did not come to Jane's slumber party. Jane said to herself, "Susie didn't come because she knows I was sexually abused and she doesn't like me anymore." What thinking error did Jane use?

(ASSUMING)

Scott cheated on a math test. He told his friends about it because he thought they'd think it was cool. They turned him in for cheating. What thinking error did Scott use?

(ASSUMING)

*These cards apply to children under eight.

Jill pushed Ann out of line so she could get her lunch first. She told her friends that Ann let her cut in. What thinking error did Jill use?

(LYING)

Andy's mom asked him if he was planning on doing his chores tonight. Andy said, "Maybe." What thinking error did Andy use?

(AVOIDING)

Alice tried out for a part in the school play and didn't get it. She said she didn't really want the part anyway. What thinking error did Alice use?

(BEING PHONY)

John's mom asked him if he got his homework done and he told her, "I finished my math." He didn't tell her he still had some English homework to do. What thinking error did John use?

(LYING BY OMISSION)

Jeff decided to have a temper tantrum in the store when his mom said she wouldn't buy him what he wanted. What thinking error did Jeff use?

(ANGER)

Sandy got mad at Bill and said she didn't want to be his friend anymore. Bill told her, "I don't care," but he was sad to lose his friend. What thinking error did Bill use?

(BEING PHONY)

Lucy took money out of her mom's purse without asking. Her mom said, "I must have spent it at the store." Lucy was glad she didn't get caught. What thinking error did Lucy use?

(LYING BY ASSENT)

Brian's teacher asked him for his homework on the history of flight. He hadn't finished it, so he told her that his neighbor was a pilot. What thinking error did Brian use?

(CHANGING THE SUBJECT)

A mom said she can't get her kids involved in social activities because they have to come to too many therapy appointments. What thinking error did she use?

(VICTIM PLAYING OR EXCUSE MAKING)

FIGURE 5.5 *(continued)*

Cheryl told Susan that the cookies Susan made were great. Susan had bought the cookies at the bakery, but didn't tell that to Cheryl. What thinking error did Susan use? (LYING BY ASSENT)	When Jeff's mom asked him why he didn't do his chores, Jeff asked her if she had a good day at work. What thinking error did Jeff use? (CHANGING THE SUBJECT)	Todd got a "D" on a report he worked hard on for two weeks. He tore up the report and said, "I don't know why I even try." What thinking error did Todd use? (VICTIM PLAYING)

from the list. When the correct answer is guessed in this manner, it is particularly important that the answer be explained.

Precautions

The power and control issues of sexually abusive children can make competitive game activities problematic. If this game is not carefully monitored, negative group interactions may take place. Some children may become impatient with teammates who fail to earn points for their team and react by making critical and demeaning comments. It is therefore important to require players to be patient and respectful of one another. Therapists can prevent disrespectful comments through consistent use of rule number 6 (i.e., loss of two points for any disrespectful utterance). As therapists monitor group interaction and confront disrespectful statements, they can help the children become more responsible in how they treat one another.

Because the game requires children to think abstractly, children with below average intellectual skills may find the game frustrating. When children are intimidated by the cognitive demands of the game, they may resist participating by becoming distracting, disruptive, or withdrawn. Therapists should try to identify these children in advance so they can help them adapt to the game.

Adaptations

This game can be played within any of the groups as well as family therapy sessions. When playing within groups, group members are treated as a single team. Instead of competing against one another, group members pool their chips to earn a reward for the group, such as extended social time or a special treat. (The mascot prize should be reserved for intergroup competition.).

This game may be played with young children, using only the game cards that give examples of blaming, lying, and excuse making. To facilitate use of the game with younger children, this subset of game cards has been marked with an asterisk in the upper right-hand corner.

A variation of this game is "Thinking Error Charades." Each of the two teams is asked to plan a role-play demonstrating an interaction that includes a thinking error. One team presents the thinking error role-play as a "charade." The other team is asked to guess which thinking error is being acted out. After a number of charades, the role-plays are repeated; only this time the players are asked to show the same interactions without the use of thinking errors. Players can refer to the corrections ("Oscar Thinking") on the "List of Thinking Errors and Corrections" for help in planning interactions that do not include thinking errors.

"Thinking Error Charades" can be played in the children's groups, parent groups, or combined groups. When parents and children are on the same team, they have an opportunity to practice identifying and correcting thinking errors with members of their own family. After the game, the therapists can ask participants to express their feelings about the role-plays. Questions may include: Which thinking errors were the hardest to identify? How did you feel when you were using the thinking error in the role-play? How did you feel when the thinking error was being used on you in the role-play? Which thinking errors are most commonly used in your family?

Chapter 6

Empathy

ACTIVITY: "CONVERSATION" WITH THE VICTIM

Target Group

Latency-age children.

Objective

To help sexually abusive children identify their victims' feelings about being sexually abused.

Materials

Two chairs placed facing each other within the circle of group members.

Description

Children use the double-chair technique (Perls, 1969) to role-play a conversation with one of their victims. A child acts out both parts and switches chairs as he/she speaks for each character. The child's questions to his/her victim must stay focused on the victim's feelings. When the child role-plays the victim, he/she speaks as if the victim were expressing feelings about the abuse to the abusive child.

The authors wish to thank Denzil Grimshaw, LCSW, for his collaboration in the development of this activity.

Therapists instruct the children to perform a "one-person show" and "make up lines for both characters." The therapist may say, "Try to make us believe the conversation is really happening here in this room. One thing actors do to make their performances seem real is called 'staying in character.' Begin by describing your victim; taking the role of your victim, tell everybody your name, your age, what you look like, and what you like to do."

Process

Therapists help a child remain in character by directing all comments and suggestions to specific characters. For example, if a child does not know how to begin, a therapist might suggest, "Ask her [or him] to tell you about the way she [or he] was feeling." The child would then repeat the question and move to the "victim's" chair to answer. Alternatively, the therapist could role-play the therapist as a participant in this "session" and say to the "victim," "Tell him [or her] about the way you were feeling when he [or she] molested you."

In addition to exploring victims' feelings during abuse, the children can also ask about their victim's reaction to the events that followed the abuse (e.g., disclosure, investigation, talking to a juvenile court worker). If a child does not introduce these topics spontaneously, therapists may prompt discussion of these experiences.

Precautions

Children may avoid experiencing feelings by keeping their role-play focused on circumstantial details. When this occurs, therapists can redirect the "conversation" to a discussion of feelings. Therapists must be careful not to let their feelings interfere with a child's exploration of the victim's feelings. When this process becomes emotionally intense for a child, a therapist may be tempted to "rescue" the child from the experience. Similarly, discomfort with silence might lead a therapist to unintentionally distract a child from an emotional experience by asking another question.

Adaptations

The double-chair technique can also be used in individual or family therapy or in group therapy with parents. Parents may role-play a conversation with the victim and/or the victim's parents to explore the emotional impact of their child's perpetration on the victim and his/her family. In addition, parents can role-play a conversation with their child to explore the child's feelings about their response to his/her perpetration.

ACTIVITY: LETTER TO THE VICTIM

Target Group

Latency-age children.

Objectives

To assist sexually abusive children demonstrating empathy for the feelings of their victims and communicating responsibility for their harmful behaviors to their victims.

Materials

Paper and pens or pencils.

Description

The sexually abusive child prepares a letter of apology. This letter will not necessarily be sent to the victim, but is written as if it were to be sent. If the child has more than one victim, separate letters should be written to each one. The child should tailor the letters to meet the specific needs of each victim.

Children must have progressed sufficiently in therapy to begin to accept accountability for their offending behavior and to identify feelings their victims might have had about their abuse. Writing the letter may require several sessions and involve several revisions. The children begin their letters with their individual therapists. They read them in group and request feedback from group members as well as therapists. More advanced group members may present their own letters as models for the newer group members who are beginning to write letters. After receiving the group feedback, children take their letters back to their individual therapists and continue to revise them until the individual and group therapists agree the letters are acceptable.

Therapists evaluate the quality of apology letters by assessing whether the children have clearly expressed empathy and accountability. To be considered acceptable and complete, apology letters should contain the following elements:

1. A statement of apology to the victim (e.g., "I am sorry for sexually abusing you.").
2. A clear statement acknowledging responsibility for the offending behavior (e.g., "What I did to you was wrong." "I wanted to touch you, and I wasn't thinking about your feelings. I was only thinking of myself."). Sexually abusive children must be accountable for behavior and not give excuses. For example, statements such as "I was having a bad time," "I was depressed," or "I did it because I was abused" rationalize the abusive behavior and are not appropriate for an apology letter.
3. A clear statement alleviating the victim from any responsibility for the sexually offending behavior (e.g., "What happened was *not* your fault. It was my fault.").
4. An expression of empathy for the feelings of the victim, which validates the victim's right to have such feelings (e.g., "I think you were probably pretty scared and sad about what I did to you." "You really trusted me, and I hurt you, so it may be hard for you to trust me." "You might be mad at me because of what I did."). The sexually abusive child must be careful to only state what the victim *might* have felt. He/she should never presume to *know* what the victim felt or tell the victim what to feel.
5. A description of the setup and coverup used to get the victim to go along and/or not tell about the abuse (e.g., "I gave you cookies and candy to get you to let me touch you." "I tried to scare you by saying I'd kill you if you told."). Care must be taken to validate feelings of confusion and betrayal the victim may feel toward the sexually abusive child. This can be done by including statements to indicate the type of relationship the sexually abusive child had with the victim (e.g., "Because you are my sister, you should have been able to count on me.").
6. A description of what the sexually abusive child has learned in therapy (e.g., "I'm learning how to express my feelings. I'm going to try my best to never molest again."). This description should communicate to the victim that the sexually abusive child is receiving help and affirm that it was important for the victim to tell. It is not appropriate for sexually abusive children to discuss their treatment progress in an attempt to "look

good" or to imply that their victims should be making similar efforts.

It is critical that therapists first ask the children to write an apology without providing them with the previous specific guidelines. This way they must struggle with creating an apology letter on their own. If the children are handed these guidelines, this exercise loses meaning, as they merely copy the suggestions.

Process

When writing apology letters, sexually abusive children must be aware of the developmental level of their victims and adjust the wording in the letters accordingly. Letters must be written in a way that young children can understand.

Apology letters can be an important part of therapeutic recontact when sexually abusive children are likely to have ongoing contact with their victims. When the victim is a family member or close friend, writing and sending an apology letter can help prepare both the sexually abusive child and the victim for family therapy sessions or other recontact. If the sexually abusive child is not likely to have any more contact with the victim(s), the letter serves as a tool to work on empathy and accountability.

Precautions

The sexually abusive child and his/her therapist must consider the feelings of the victim when determining whether to send an apology letter. The decision to send a letter must be carefully coordinated among the parents and therapists of both the victim and the sexually abusive child. All involved must ensure that the apology letter will be beneficial to the victim and will not cause any further harm. Approval of the victim's parents and therapist is necessary before the letter can be sent.

Therapists should be careful to emphasize that sexually abusive children should not independently contact their victims to apologize. Attempting to communicate with the victim's family without therapeutic mediation may exacerbate problems. When intense interpersonal conflict exists between the victim's parents and the perpetrator's parents, sending an apology letter may further inflame an already volatile situation.

Other cautions to be communicated to the sexually abusive child are:

- Don't make excuses for your behavior.
- Don't ask for forgiveness.
- Don't talk about your own progress.
- Don't give your victim(s) advice.
- Don't tell your victim(s) what to feel.
- Don't assume your victim(s) want to see you again or have an ongoing relationship with you.
- Don't write the letter to meet your needs; write it to meet the needs of your victim(s).

Figures 6.1, 6.2, and 6.3 present a case example of the apology letter process. Ronald, age eleven, sexually abused Matthew, a seven-year-old boy in his neighborhood. Ronald helped coach Matthew's soccer team and used their association on the team to cultivate a relationship. He spent extra time with Matthew practicing soccer plays and helping him with homework. After he began sexually abusing Matthew, Ronald gave him gifts and made him promise to keep their sexual contact secret. Figures 6.1 and 6.2 show the first two drafts of Ronald's apology letter to Matthew. The completed apology letter draft is presented in Figure 6.3.

Adaptations

Although primarily an activity for latency-age children, young children can also write apology letters to their victims. The letters they write will understandably be less complex than those of older children. However, young children's letters should contain statements in each of the six areas outlined previously.

This activity can be used in a combined group in which the children read and discuss their letters with their parents. Parents can give feedback to the children about their letters and assist them in revising them. This process of collaboration between parent and child can also take place in family therapy.

FIGURE 6.1. Letter to Victim—Draft 1

Ronald,
   You need to take responsibility. Think about how
Matthew might feel about what you did.

Dear Matthew,

   I'm sorry for sexually abusing you. I promise I

won't ever do it again. I hope you're doing alright.

I didn't want to hurt you. ~~I did it because I got~~   *Excuse*
                                                          making

~~abused too.~~

   I'm going to a group about touching, and ~~I had~~

~~to go to court 3 times.~~ ← He doesn't Need to Know that.

What does this   Don't
have to do with ~~Are you still playing soccer? My team's doing~~ *assume*
the goals of   *he still*
the letter? ~~pretty good. We've won 4 of our last 5 games. I'd~~ *wants to*
                                                          be friends
~~still like to play soccer with you when you want to.~~

   Again, I'm sorry for what I did, so ~~please forgive~~

~~me. I hope we can still be friends.~~   *Don't ask him*
                                                      to forgive you.
   Sincerely,
                                         Don't put pressure
                                              on him

Ronald

The comments in italics were made by Ronald's individual therapist to assist
Ronald in revising the letter.

   It also may be helpful to use this activity in the parent group. The
parents may choose to write letters to the victims or to the victims'
parents. All the precautions mentioned earlier also apply to letters
written by parents. Parents should include the following elements in
their letters:

FIGURE 6.2. Letter to Victim—Draft 2

Ronald, this is better, but it still needs work!

Dear Matthew,

I'm sorry for touching you in your private parts. It was wrong of me to do that. It wasn't your fault at all; it was all my fault. Maybe you feel sad and mad at me and if you do, that's alright cause I understand. I was abused too and that's how I felt. I was pretty sad when I sexually abused you cause my dad and I were fighting a lot. But don't worry, I won't ever do it again. I'm going to therapy now and my therapist says I'm doing real good. I've got a prevention plan now.

I hope you're having fun playing soccer. If you want me to help you with your math like I used to, I'd really like to. Again, I'm sorry for what happened between us.

Your friend,

Ronald

Good Accountability!

Don't give him permission to Feel.

Excuse making

Don't tell him what to Feel.

Don't talk About your own progress

← SAY MORE!

STOP TRYING TO BE FRIENDS!

You are blaming him. You Need to take All the Responsibility. How did you set him up?

The comments in italics were made by Ronald's individual therapist to assist Ronald in revising the letter.

FIGURE 6.3. Letter to Victim—Final Draft

Dear Matthew,

I'm sorry for touching you in your private parts. It was wrong of me to do that. It wasn't your fault at all; it was all my fault. I was thinking of myself when I touched you—I didn't think about you at all. I don't know how you feel about what I did, but I'm guessing you feel sad, mad, and confused. You should have been able to trust me since I helped coach your soccer team. I gave you presents and spent extra time with you so I could get to let me touch you. That was wrong and I'm sorry. I told you not to tell cause I didn't want to get in trouble.

I'm really glad you told on me so I could get help. Everything I did to you was my fault.

Sincerely,

Ronald

1. An acknowledgment that their child committed a sex offense, ("I'm writing to let you know how sorry I am that Kenny sexually abused Amy." "We regret that Ronald took advantage of Matthew by molesting him.").
2. A statement indicating recognition of the harm resulting from their child's actions ("I know Kenny really hurt Amy when he did what he did." "We know Ronald's actions have caused you a lot of pain.").
3. Statements communicating concern and empathy for the feelings of the victim and his/her parents ("I'm concerned about Amy and hope she will be okay." "Ronald really betrayed your trust. It must have been very frightening for Matthew.").

ACTIVITY: THE GIVING TREE

Target Groups

Latency-age and young children.

Objective

To help sexually abusive children develop empathy for the feelings of victims.

Materials

A copy of the book *The Giving Tree,* by Shel Silverstein (1964).

Description

The story, *The Giving Tree,* is about a tree who loves a little boy and wants to give to him. At first, the relationship between the boy and the tree is a mutual friendship, and both give to each other. However, as the boy grows older, he focuses primarily on his own needs and ignores the needs of the tree. He takes more and more from the tree until the tree is nothing more than a stump.

To use this book in group treatment, a therapist first reads the story and then discusses with the children their impressions of the characters. Questions asked may include the following: "How do you think the tree felt about the way the boy treated her?" "How is the tree like the person you touched?" "How are you like the boy?" If children are victims of prior abuse themselves, a therapist can ask, "How is the boy like the person who abused you?" and "Did you feel the way the tree felt?" In addition to discussing the feelings of the characters in the story, the therapist can ask the children to identify thinking errors used by the boy to justify his treatment of the tree.

Process

The theme of exploitation in *The Giving Tree* can be related to sexual abuse. The metaphor helps children understand the impact of abusive behaviors on others. By examining the actions of the boy, children can become more aware of their own hurtful behaviors. Talking about the feelings of the tree can help them begin to develop empathy for the feelings of victims. For example, Todd, age nine, compared the boy's actions to his own offense when he said, "The boy isn't thinking of the tree at all. He just wants what he wants. When I touched my sister, I didn't think about how she felt."

Children's literature can be a valuable aid to therapy when the books used focus on feelings. Examples of books that discuss feelings often experienced by abuse victims include: *The Hurt* (Doleski, 1983), *Mean Soup* (Everitt, 1992), *The Man Who Kept His Heart in a Bucket* (Levitan, 1991), and *There's a Nightmare in My Closet* (Mayer, 1968). Books or stories that deal with general themes of taking responsibility for one's behavior, understanding and being sensitive to the feelings of others, and developing friendships can also be used therapeutically with sexually abusive children. In addition, there are a number of children's books that focus specifically on abuse issues: *The Knight Who Was Afraid of the Dark* (Hazen, 1987), *Alice Doesn't Babysit Anymore* (McGovern, 1985), and *Secret Feelings and Thoughts* (Narimanian, 1990). Using children's literature in therapy can be an effective strategy to help children address feelings associated with trauma, separation, and loss (Berstein, 1983; Rasmussen and Cunningham, 1995).

Precautions

Discussion of stories and books should always be sensitive to the developmental level and cognitive maturity of the group members. Young children may have difficulty attending to a long discussion. It may be most effective to allow them to role-play the story, or draw the characters.

Therapists should also remember that young children may not always understand the analogies presented in stories. Often children conclude the boy loved the giving tree, although they can understand he did not treat the tree well. It is not helpful to convince them to see a story as analogous to abuse. To teach empathy, it is best to talk to children from the point of their own understanding. They may then find it easier to identify with the characters in the story and apply the lessons learned by the characters to their own relationships.

When using books and stories in therapy, therapists should carefully monitor the emotional responses of the children. A well-written story dealing with themes related to abuse may provoke intense emotional responses or anxiety. If stories provoke unresolved feelings, children must have adequate support in group and individual therapy to talk about and work through these feelings.

Adaptations

When presenting stories to children, it is helpful to read or describe the story in parent group as well. Parents are then prepared to discuss the story with their children at home. In the combined group, children and parents can ask each other questions about the stories or participate together in acting out the story.

ACTIVITY: DRAW VICTIM/OWN FACE

Target Groups

Latency-age and young children.

Objective

To help children learn empathy by "seeing" the feelings of their victims.

Materials

Paper, pencils, crayons, and markers.

Description

Children are each given paper and asked to fold the paper in half horizontally. At the top of one side the children write "victim." A therapist asks the children to draw the face of their victim during the sexual offense on that side of the paper. They may use any art medium available. When that drawing is complete, a therapist instructs the children to write "me" at the top of the other side of the paper. They are then asked to draw what their face looked like while they molested their victim.

Process

Children should be encouraged to draw whatever they remember. It is usual for the children to see the victim's face as somewhat blank or similar to their own face. They are often able to impart more feeling to their own facial expression. Other children draw their victim smiling, as if he/she is enjoying the offense.

When both drawings are complete, the therapists ask volunteers from the group to describe their drawings and state what they might have learned from this activity. Identification of the feelings of the victim as well as one's own feelings at the time of the offense are emphasized. Any similarities in the drawings should be noted.

Some children need considerable encouragement to share their work with others. In addition, the other group members are encouraged to give feedback about what the faces look like to them. Everyone is reinforced verbally for any empathy demonstrated during this group process.

Precautions

This activity can elicit strong emotions from the children, particularly if they relate their own prior trauma to the victim face they have drawn. Therapists should allow adequate processing time for anyone who becomes upset. Children may become defensive and maintain that the victim liked the sexual offense because he/she smiled. Therapists need to confront this misperception and discuss possible reasons a victim might smile or laugh during an offense (e.g., some children smile when scared or embarrassed). As the children become aware of the feelings their victims may have felt, they are usually better able to admit that their behavior was hurtful.

Adaptations

Young children can be asked to draw how their face looked when they were being molested, as well as how they felt. If a child has not been molested, they are helped to identify a time they were hurt by someone. They then present both pictures to the group, and the group leaders point out how these two pictures often look different. The children tend to draw themselves looking normal or staring blankly, when they actually felt like crying or screaming.

The two pictures may be drawn on paper plates, on either side, or on separate plates. Then the plates can be used to demonstrate more clearly how expressions may mask real feelings. The children may use the "mask" to cover their actual feelings. They may even want to cut out eyes and tie strings to their plates so they can wear these faces.

The children are asked to think about why they did not necessarily show their true feelings when they were molested. Most children readily understand that they don't always show how they feel. If they do not at first grasp this concept, they can be asked to remember a time when they lied and looked innocent (or acted like they didn't do anything wrong) to get out of trouble.

ACTIVITY: HOW WOULD YOU FEEL IF ...?

Target Groups

Young and latency-age children.

Objective

To teach children empathy by asking them to put themselves in others' situations.

Material

A list of twenty situations in which children can empathize with others (see Table 6.1), a "big cookie" or other reward for the winner or winning team.

Description

If the children are evenly matched in terms of cognitive ability, they may play this game as individuals. If not, it is suggested the therapists divide the group into two matched teams. The situations are read, and each child (or each team) is asked to guess how the main character would likely feel. After each response is recorded, the other group members evaluate whether the main character might *really* feel that way. If the response appears to be a likely possibility, the person or team providing that answer earns a point. The winner or winning team at the end of the game gets the "big cookie."

Process

Some suggestions for situations are presented in Table 6.1. It is always best to include incidents that have occurred in group as well. Therapists can create situations that are appropriate for their treatment population.

Precautions

It is important to ensure that all children have opportunities to earn points. At times, a therapist may team up with a child who has

TABLE 6.1. Situations for How Would You Feel If . . .?

1. Joey has not been invited to a friend's house, although most of the other children in the neighborhood are going to be there.

2. Mary notices her mother has been hugging and kissing her little brother a lot lately, and Mary is afraid she likes him better.

3. A friend insults Rebecca in front of other people.

4. John's favorite aunt comes over and does not seem to notice him.

5. Georgia has a big bruise on her face, and her enemy tells her how nice she looks.

6. Jared tells the teacher that Sam did not ask to borrow a pencil, when Jared really refused to lend him one. Sam is in trouble for not completing his work because he did not have a pencil.

7. Rickie trips and falls, and the class laughs.

8. Travis overhears his father say he does not want to take him camping.

9. Jennifer overhears her parents talking about getting a divorce.

10. A teacher calls a child stupid in front of the class.

11. Susan has just learned she may be held back in the same grade in school.

12. Duane takes away a boy's school lunch money.

13. A group of bullies tell Melanie they will not allow her to leave the playground until she fights each one of them.

14. A child is caught stealing money from her mother's purse.

15. Carrie's best friend tries to talk her into skipping school.

developmental delays or is the youngest in group. At other times, older children in the group can help out by giving a younger child ideas for responses. The purpose of the game is to look at how other people might feel in various situations and to practice empathy. At times it may be decided that both teams win.

Adaptations

This exercise may be utilized in a combined group. Parents and children may either work together as family groups, or parents may be coupled with children other than their own. With latency-age children, parents and children may work as two opposing teams. Similarly, this game may be introduced in family therapy.

In a further adaptation, children may want to act out situations in a "feeling charade." The group can opt for made-up situations, or individuals may act out past experiences in which they had strong feelings. Therapists may occasionally suggest situations in which children have had thoughts of sexual touching.

ACTIVITY: WHY MY CHILD DIDN'T TELL ME

Target Group

Parents.

Objective

To enhance parents' empathy for their children.

Materials

Paper, pens, and pencils.

Description

Parents are asked to write down three reasons why it may have been difficult for their children to tell them when they were molested. All parents can participate in this exercise. If their children were not molested, parents can usually think of other circumstances in which it was difficult for their children to tell them about being victimized (e.g., being bullied by another child). After the parents are given sufficient time to complete their lists, they discuss which reasons seem most closely related to why their children did not tell.

As a separate step, parents may be asked to think of three reasons why it is difficult for their children to talk to them about their (children's) own sexually abusive behavior.

Process

Parents discuss how difficult it is to share very personal information. Those parents whose children first told a person outside the immediate family about their victimization may relate why they perceive it was easier for their child to tell that person. Individual characteristics of each child may be explored, particularly in cases in which children did not willingly disclose information. Characteristics of the perpetrator also need to be considered as a factor that may have inhibited disclosure, particularly when the perpetrator has been emotionally close to either the parents or child.

When parents discuss barriers to disclosure, they often mention similar reasons. Often, some children and/or parents have significant difficulty communicating any feelings to one another. Parents are encouraged to identify their part in problems with communication, such as being rigid or highly motivated to achieve or feeling guilty, angry, etc.

The goal of the session is for each parent to develop an understanding of influences affecting their children. Differences between individual children and family circumstances are emphasized. The potential for positively altering communication patterns in each family is a focus throughout this exercise.

Precautions

It is sometimes extremely hard for parents to accept that their children did not come to them with a serious problem. They may think that they have failed or that their child prefers other people. It is important to remind parents how they did not always tell their own parents about problems. Sometimes children are afraid of getting in trouble. At some developmental stages it is easier to talk to peers. It is important to diffuse anger that may be directed toward children who did not tell their parents about their abuse. Children can be inhibited by their parents' anger, and it then becomes increasingly difficult for them to communicate. Occasionally, a parent in group perceives the other children were better able to talk to their parents than his/her own child and becomes resentful and/or exhibits defensive anger. This anger is discussed so parents may support and reassure each other and so that they can learn to facilitate more open communication with their children.

Adaptations

Children also benefit by understanding why they did not tell their parents or why they waited to tell. Therefore, these same issues may be presented in the children's groups. After there has been discussion in both the children's and parents' groups, family members may be prepared to share their ideas in a combined group or family session.

First, the parents can first share their ideas about possible barriers to communication in the combined group. The children may be asked if they think their parents understand them and whether they themselves can think of other barriers. These could all be listed on the chalkboard in a brainstorming manner. Parents and children can also be asked to discuss or list ways they can handle situations differently so that it will be easier to "tell" in the future.

ACTIVITY: EMPATHIC RESPONSES

Target Group

Parents.

Objectives

To help parents:

1. identify feelings their child may have, and
2. use "active listening" skills to communicate understanding of their child's feelings.

Materials

The handouts "Empathic Response Leads" (see Table 6.2) and "Empathic Response Vignettes" (see Table 6.3).

Description

This activity is intended to facilitate the acquisition of empathy. Parents first learn to identify their own and others' feelings. This activity focuses on how to *communicate* that understanding to another person.

Group members form triads. The therapists give the "Empathic Response Leads" handout to the person assuming the parent role in each triad. The person in the child role is given the list of vignettes. Each triad is to role-play the vignettes. The person in the child role decides how the child in the vignette is feeling and conveys those feelings in both verbal and nonverbal ways to the person in the parent role. The person in the parent role practices empathic responses to convey understanding of the feelings communicated by the "child." The third person acts as an observer to give feedback regarding body language, communication barriers, etc. He/she asks questions such as:

1. "Did you feel your 'parent' heard you correctly?"
2. "Did you feel your 'parent' understood how you felt?"

3. "How did you feel after your 'parent' responded?"
4. "What would have made it easier to tell your 'parent' your feelings?"

After three vignettes are role-played, everyone changes roles, until each person has played each part. The group then reconvenes and discusses this activity. Table 6.2 suggests empathic response leads, while Table 6.3 provides the list of suggested vignettes.

Process

Therapists should encourage group members to discuss what they learned from the role-plays. Feelings identified in different vignettes can be shared and discussed. The feelings of the "parent"

TABLE 6.2. Empathic Response Leads

The following list of phrases can be used by parents as a different lead-in to the empathic response: You feel _____ because _____. You want to _____.

You're kind of feeling . . .

So, you're sort of saying . . .

I'm picking up that you . . .

If I'm hearing you correctly . . .

To me it's almost like you are saying, "I . . ."

The thing you feel most right now is sort of like . . .

What I hear you saying is . . .

So, as you see it . . .

What I guess I'm hearing is . . .

I'm not sure I'm with you, but . . .

I somehow sense that maybe you feel . . .

I wonder if you're saying . . .

You appear to be feeling . . .

As I hear it, you . . .

Adapted from Hammond D.C., Hepworth, D.H., and Smith, V.G. (1977). *Improving therapeutic communication* (pp. 114-115). San Francisco: Jossey-Bass.

TABLE 6.3. Empathic Response Vignettes

1. You are nine years old and just failed a math test.

2. You are five years old and can't find anything to do.

3. You are eleven years old and just made a new friend.

4. You are ten years old and just had a fight with your best friend.

5. You are eight years old and can't figure out how to win the video game the kids are talking about.

6. You are six years old and wet your pants on the way home from school.

7. You are nine years old and are having thoughts about touching the three-year-old child next door.

8. You are ten years old and have fondled your brother's private parts.

9. You are eleven years old and want to tell your parents about when Uncle Bill molested you.

10. You are eleven years old and want to play video games at your friend's house. Your dad just told you to go clean the garage.

11. You are seven years old and just got told by your parents you can't go to your friend's sleepover because of your problem with touching privates.

should also be explored. The therapists can then help group members understand the importance of dealing with their own feelings separate from their responses to their children.

It is often useful to ask which role was the most difficult to assume. Some parents may have difficulty identifying with the feelings of the child, others with communicating their understanding of those feelings. Most parents will initially have trouble detaching from their internal thoughts and feelings and communicating understanding. Group members can explore reasons for these difficulties and practice additional vignettes.

Precaution

This activity requires communication skills and should not be attempted until parents are able to identify feelings.

Adaptations

This activity can be used in parent/child combined groups. It is recommended that individual children and their parents be separated into different triads to encourage more objective practicing.

Chapter 7

Coping with Trauma

ACTIVITY: BASKET OF TRIGGER FEELINGS*

Target Group

Latency-age children.

Objective

To help sexually abusive children identify feelings that initiate their abuse cycles.

Materials

Basket of at least fifty markers or crayons, two dozen sheets of blank paper.

Description

Therapists ask the group to brainstorm a list of feelings until the following words (or synonyms) have been mentioned: mad, sad, confused, uncomfortable, embarrassed, scared, powerless, helpless, frustrated, left out, disappointed, and lonely. Therapists help children identify complex feelings (e.g., powerlessness and helplessness) by describing situations that might provoke these feelings

---

*Adapted from James, B. (1989). *Treating traumatized children: New insights and creative interventions.* (p. 108). Lexington, MA: Lexington Books.

(e.g., "How might a boy feel if a person twice his size picked on him every day and no one would make him stop?"). As the feeling words are stated, therapists print each word in large letters on a separate sheet of paper and spread the pages on the floor or a large table. Children take turns using the feeling words to explore their reaction to some stressful event. Several sessions may be required to give each member an opportunity to complete this activity.

Process

The therapists ask a volunteer what he/she was doing before committing a sexual offense. They continue to ask "What happened before that?" until the child describes an event that appears to have provoked negative feelings. Once the child identifies such an event, he/she is asked to use the feeling words to describe his/her reaction to the event: "Use these words to help you think about the way you felt after _____. Choose all the words that describe how you felt. You might have had other feelings that we didn't write down yet. We can add more feelings as you think of them. Use the markers to show how strong a feeling was; the more markers you pile on a word, the stronger the feeling was."

The children may either discuss their feelings as they place the markers on the papers or wait until after they have finished. The therapists and other group members may ask questions about the feelings each child selects. The therapists ask the children to recall thoughts associated with each feeling. Children typically choose to explore their feelings in the order of strongest to weakest, but any sequence is permitted. Therapists prompt group members to empathize with each other in order to help them explore their feelings in greater depth.

Precautions

As they describe thoughts and feelings experienced in the past, the children may reexperience these same emotions. Sensitivity to each child's capacity to manage troubling emotions is necessary to ensure a child will not become overwhelmed. Following the session, parents should be informed of what transpired so they can be prepared to offer support.

Adaptations

James's "Basket of Trigger Feelings" is a versatile activity that can be used to explore any kind of emotional experience. It can be used by people of all ages, in groups, family sessions, and individual therapy, to explore reactions to diverse events, such as an interpersonal conflict, a divorce, the death of a loved one, or termination from therapy.

The "Basket of Trigger Feelings" can be used with children ages ten to twelve to facilitate discussion of sexual arousal. The therapists ask children to brainstorm a list of "feelings kids might have in their body before they molest." The children take turns describing what it is like for them to be aroused. They then explore thoughts they associate with their arousal. In our latency-aged group, the boys produced the following list: weird, nervous, horny, aroused, excited, confused, guilty, anxious, uncomfortable, uneasy, embarrassed, weak, hard, uptight, tingly, butterflies, and annoyed. It is interesting to note that most of the boys viewed arousal as a negative experience.

*ACTIVITY: WHAT HAPPENED AFTER YOU WERE ABUSED?**

Target Group

Latency-age children.

Objectives

To help abused children:

1. order the events they experienced from the time of disclosure of their abuse until the present, and
2. identify feelings related to these events.

Materials

Large sheets of paper (desk-pad size—16″ × 20″), pens or pencils, crayons or markers, chalk and chalkboard.

Description

In this activity, abused children review the events that took place after their abuse by drawing a "time line" beginning with the disclosure of their abuse and ending with the present. Therapists distribute large sheets of paper and pens or pencils. The concept of a time line is explained to the children, and examples are drawn on the chalkboard. Therapists then direct the children to "tell what happened after people found out you were abused."

Significant events are noted at different points on the time line. Below each event, the children record the age they were when the event took place. They also record significant people in their lives who were involved in the event. Above the event, the children record how they felt about what was happening.

The first point on the time line is the actual disclosure of the abuse by the child or by another person. The children write the

---

*Adapted from Cunningham, C. and MacFarlane, K. (1996). *When children abuse: Group treatment strategies for children with impulse control problems* (p. 152). Brandon, VT: Safer Society Press.

names of all the people involved at the time of the disclosure, including both those to whom they actually disclosed the abuse and those who were aware of this disclosure. For children whose abuse was reported to legal authorities, the next few points on the time line will likely describe the investigation process. For example, a child may write "talked with caseworker," "talked with police," and "started therapy" as separate points on the line. If a child was abused by someone in the home, another point on the time line might be the perpetrator leaving home. For children who were removed from their homes for protection purposes, placement in shelter or foster care can be a point on the time line.

The children are asked to think about how they felt at the time of each event and to write down their feelings. Older children can be asked to create a graph from their time line by entering a vertical scale ranging from -5 to $+5$ on the left-hand side of their paper. They can then examine each event and its accompanying feelings and rate their positive feelings on a scale of $+1$ to $+5$, and negative feelings on a scale of -1 to -5.

For example, if a child says he was sad when his uncle abused him, the therapist might ask, "How sad were you?" If the child responds that the abuse was the saddest time of his life, the event of being abused by his uncle would be rated as -5 on the scale. Similarly, the event of disclosing the abuse and being believed might be associated with positive feelings. If a child says he was happy when he told his mom and the abuse stopped, the therapist might ask, "How happy were you?" The child might then decide to score the event of disclosing the abuse to his mother as $+5$. Rating their feelings on the time line helps older children identify the relative intensity of their feelings. The resulting graph helps them see the high and low points they may have experienced. An example of a time line of an older child that includes a graph of feelings is presented in Figure 7.1.

To help the children place their abuse within the context of their entire life experiences, therapists should encourage them to add important events unrelated to the abuse that occurred during the same time frame. Significant losses, such as the death of a family member or the separation/divorce of parents should be noted. Positive events that took place (e.g., started softball, vacation to Disney-

FIGURE 7.1. Zachary's Time Line

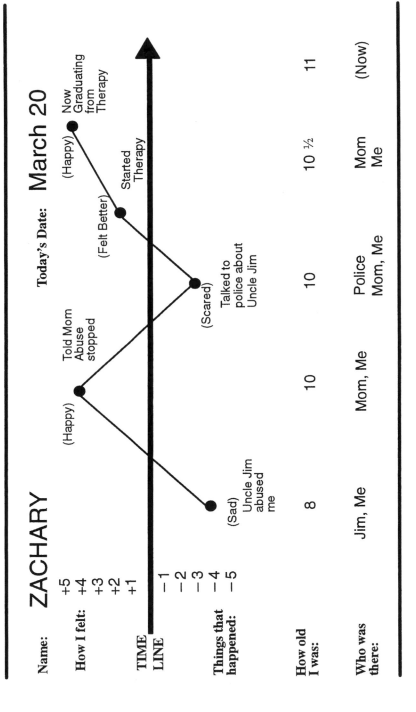

land) can be added as well as stressful experiences (e.g., broke arm, bike got stolen). Listing events unrelated to the abuse helps children view their lives as a balance of both positive and adverse events.

Process

When all time lines have been completed, the children can take turns sharing their time lines with each other. Discussion centers on "How did you feel when those things happened?" Discussing their time lines allows children to share their own feelings as well as to identify with the feelings of other group members. Sharing common experiences and feelings can help children develop empathy for others. The time line also provides abused children a means to put their trauma in perspective. When traumatic experiences are presented as a sequence of discrete events, they can appear less overwhelming and more manageable.

An example of a time line drawn by eight-year-old Jeff is presented in Figure 7.2. Jeff was sexually abused over a period of several months by his thirteen-year-old brother, Richard. He never disclosed the abuse to anyone until Bobby, a five-year-old neighbor boy, reported that Jeff had sucked his penis. When confronted with his sexually abusive behavior, Jeff told his mother that he had learned about oral sex from Richard. Bobby's mother reported Jeff's behavior to the legal authoritie so an investigation took place.

When Jeff presented his time line in group, he talked about how scared he felt when the police videotaped an interview with him. Jeff told the other boys, "I told the cop about what Richard did to me. He did it to me lots of times between Christmas and the summer. I didn't like being on TV, but the cop said he wouldn't show it to people." Jeff then expressed regret that the child protective services caseworker decided Jeff was not safe at home. Richard was removed and placed in a residential treatment center. Jeff told the group, "I really miss Richard. He's a pretty good brother even if he did do that to me." Jeff had good feelings about being in therapy because "sometimes Richard and his therapist come too, and we all get to talk." When the therapist asked Jeff if any good things had happened in his life since he told about the abuse, Jeff mentioned his soccer team taking first place in the league. He also talked about going camping with his cousins.

FIGURE 7.2. Jeff's Time Line

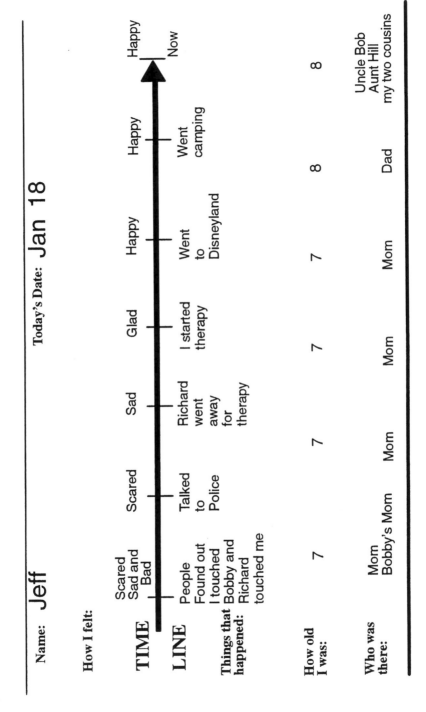

Name: **Jeff**

Today's Date: Jan 18

How I felt:

	Scared Sad and Bad	Scared	Sad	Glad	Happy	Happy	Happy

TIME LINE

Things that happened:

People Found out I touched Bobby and Richard touched me	Talked to Police	Richard went away for therapy	I started therapy	Went to Disneyland	Went camping	Now

How old I was:

7	7	7	7	7	8	8

Who was there:

Mom Bobby's Mom	Mom	Mom	Mom	Mom	Dad	Uncle Bob Aunt Hill my two cousins

Precautions

This activity is specifically designed for children who are documented victims of abuse. It may be difficult to use this activity in a mixed group with some children who report being victims of abuse and others who do not. Alternatively, children who have not been sexually abused might be asked to think of events in their lives where they felt scared or powerless and do a time line of those events.

As with all activities dealing with prior trauma, therapists need to be sure to provide children with adequate support in individual as well as group therapy. If this activity provokes a stressful response in a child, therapists should be sure to inform parents. They can then monitor their child for signs of excessive anxiety and help him/her verbalize feelings.

Adaptations

Young children may more readily understand this activity if they use "feeling faces" to draw rather than write their feelings. They can also draw pictures of the specific events on their time line.

Parents can complete time lines of the events that took place in their family following the disclosure of their child's abuse and/or their child's sexually abusive behavior. To help family members share learning experiences, this activity should be presented simultaneously in both children and parent groups. Therapists may wish to use the time line in family therapy as well.

The content of the time line can be changed to focus on other significant events in a child's life. For example, if parents divorce, the time line can reflect events following their breakup. If a child has experienced a severe loss such as a death, the time line can focus on events associated with the grieving process. The time line also makes an excellent activity when children are ready to terminate therapy. Drawing a time line of the events in their lives before and during the course of therapy or graphing their feelings about those events helps them to be aware of how their lives have changed. They can more easily see and acknowledge the benefits of therapy.

ACTIVITY: WHO IS RESPONSIBLE?*

Target Group

Young children.

Objectives

To help young children:

1. recognize abusive behavior when it occurs,
2. understand differences in power and authority between individuals, and
3. understand who is responsible for a sex offense.

Materials

Large and small puppets, paper, pencils, crayons or markers.

Description

Scenarios involving abusive actions are presented to the children. They are asked to evaluate the situation and determine which of the two individuals is the most responsible for what happened. The scenarios illustrate dimensions that need to be evaluated to assess responsibility. These dimensions include age and size differences, misuse of power and authority (intimidation), manipulative behaviors, and use of force and coercion. One therapist can draw illustrations while the other therapist is describing the situations.

Process

Therapists begin by describing situations that illustrate differences in age and size. For example, "Bonnie's dad touched her private parts. Who is responsible?" or "Tom's teenage brother Nick

---

*The authors acknowledge the collaboration of Machelle D.M. Thompson, LCSW, in the development of this exercise.

made him touch his (Nick's) penis. Tom is only eight years old. Who is responsible?" The therapists may also ask the children "Who started it?," "Whose idea was it?," or "Who is most at fault?" Most children readily understand that the person who is older or bigger is the most responsible.

Next, the children are given examples of how the use of authority (such as in a baby-sitting situation) makes the child with the authority the most responsible. The following is a situation describing misuse of authority (intimidation): "Aaron (age ten) is a crossing-guard at his school. He tells Jonathan (who is the same age and size) that if Jonathan doesn't touch his (Aaron's) penis, he will report him to the principal. Who is responsible?"

Other illustrations show how manipulating others or taking advantage of another's vulnerability make the offending person more responsible. For example, "Andrea (who is fourteen) was asleep when her brother Brandon (who is ten) came into her bedroom, reached under the blankets, and started touching her vagina. Who is responsible?"

Finally, the therapists describe situations involving the use of force or coercion. For example, "Jason (who is nine) and Scott (who is eight) are touching each other's private parts. Jason wouldn't do it until Scott threatened him with a stick. Who is responsible?" Children often struggle to understand that the person with the most power or force is more responsible, even if younger or smaller.

When all situations have been discussed, it is often helpful to give the children an opportunity to role-play with puppets. Large and small puppets can be used to represent the different characters. Obviously, role-plays must be limited to what the characters said to each other and should not include any touching. After each role-play, therapists can enhance learning through repetition by inquiring, "Who was responsible?"

To facilitate children's understanding, therapists should be familiar with the circumstances of each child's prior abuse and his/her sexually abusive behavior. Children can be helped to clarify differences in responsibility for their own victimization versus their offenses. It is important to help the children see how their perpetrators manipulated them. The children can then understand how they manipulated others through sexually abusive behavior.

Precautions

When creating situations to teach responsibility for abusive behavior, therapists should carefully consider the content. Children should not be given new ideas about how to threaten others. When children act out role-plays, therapists must always ensure that the focus of the role-play is on accountability for actions that are hurtful to others.

In presenting this exercise, therapists must be sensitive to the children's level of cognitive development. Young children may not be able to consider more than one dimension of responsibility, they may be confused by situations encompassing more than one dimension. Understanding who is responsible can be particularly difficult when young children were abused by others who were close to their same age or size.

Adaptations

Therapists can use the previous examples or create other situations to teach the concept of responsibility for abusive behavior. It is also helpful to use situations involving other kinds of abusive behavior (e.g., physical, verbal, or emotional abuse).

Although designed primarily for younger children, this activity can be adapted for use with latency-age children. Older children more readily understand differences in power/authority, manipulation, and coercion. They can be more focused in a discussion of these concepts.

This activity can be used in individual or family therapy to help clarify why one child is responsible for sexually abusive behavior and another is not.

ACTIVITY: HOW MY FAMILY HAS CHANGED

Target Group

Parents/children combined.

Objective

To help parents and abused children explore the impact of their abuse on themselves and their family.

Materials

Large sheets of paper (desk-pad size—16″ × 20″), pens, pencils, crayons, or markers.

Description

This exercise is primarily directed toward children who have experienced past abuse. A therapist instructs the group members to fold their papers in half. The group members are asked to write "before" at the top of one side of the paper and "after" on the other side. A therapist then instructs the group members to draw a picture of their families before and after their abuse. Children and parents should work independently. When everyone has finished, ask for volunteers to share their drawings with the group. Group members may then give feedback, sharing their impressions of the drawings. Empathic responses are modeled by the therapists. Positive feedback is given to group members whenever they make empathic responses.

Process

Children and parents will take considerable interest in what the other members of their family are drawing. Everyone should be encouraged to draw the family as he/she experienced it. Parents may need encouragement to draw if they have not previously used art to express themselves. Children may need some encouragement to share the meanings of their drawings with parents present. It is important to ask group members to explain any symbols present in the drawings.

Precautions

Parents may be surprised to learn that many children see their families as having more problems after disclosures about a trauma than before. For example, Lance drew his family before he disclosed he had been sexually abused as an apple tree. In his "after" picture, the apples had all fallen off the tree and were smashed at its base. Lance explained that he thought his family was ruined by the abuse.

It is important to explore all the feelings children have about the impact of trauma. The discussion may require follow-up in individual or family sessions. Children or parents who have not experienced abuse-related trauma may need assistance in identifying traumatic events (e.g., divorce, serious illness, etc.).

Adaptations

This activity can be used successfully in both younger and latency-age groups as well as in family therapy. It may also be modified to draw the family before and after the disclosure of the child's sexual offense. A follow-up activity might be to have parents and children work together drawing a picture of how they would like their family to change.

*ACTIVITY: THE FIRE**

Target Groups

Young children and latency-age children.

Objectives

To help sexually abusive children:

1. understand that they have choices when dealing with prior trauma, including (1) expressing and working through feelings (recovery), (2) hurting themselves (self-victimization), and (3) hurting others (assault);
2. recognize and correct thinking errors that support and maintain self-destructive and assaultive behaviors; and
3. express and work through feelings related to prior trauma.

Materials

A copy of the story, "The Fire" (included in this chapter), a boy doll, and the following puppets: three turtles, two owls, one skunk, and one rabbit. Other animal puppets may be substituted for two of the turtles (e.g., caterpillar, snake, dragonfly, or lizard). In addition, a red cape (to represent a fire) may be used.

Description

This activity uses bibliotherapy and role-play with puppets to help children identify with fictional characters and address abuse issues. A therapist reads the story, "The Fire." The children role-play the story using puppets and other props (see list of materials). Therapists can create interest and motivate the children to participate by telling them they have an opportunity to produce and act out a play. The therapists act as the directors of the play. If desired,

---

*The story, "The Fire," was written by Steven C. Huke, MS and Lucinda A. Rasmussen, PhD.

therapists can use a camcorder to videotape the role-play, and the children can create their own movie and watch it later.

After the role-play, the therapists encourage the children to discuss the thoughts, feelings, and behaviors shown by the characters. The therapists emphasize that the characters in the play showed three different responses (i.e., hurting themselves, hurting others, and expressing feelings) to a similar trauma. The thinking errors displayed by each of the three main characters (Tommy the Turtle, Stinky the Skunk, and Oscar the Owl) are pointed out and discussed.

The story, "The Fire," can be used with both sexually abused and sexually abusive children to illustrate the Trauma Outcome Process (Brown and Rasmussen, 1994; Rasmussen, Burton, and Christopherson, 1992):

Process

There are ten characters in the story. If the group is larger than ten members, therapists can create additional characters (e.g., additional friends for Tommy the Turtle, family members in the home that Stinky "visits," or other bunnies at the home of Roberta the Rabbit). One child can play the Fire, using the red cape. In addition, one of the children can be the narrator. If the group is smaller than ten, some children can be assigned more than one role.

It is best to allow the children to act out the story *as* it is read, rather than to read it aloud first. Therapists should encourage the children to stay in character as they act out their roles. The children can repeat each line of dialogue immediately after the therapist (or narrator) reads it. Alternatively, if they have copies of the story, the children can read along with the narrator and say their lines at the appropriate time. They may act out the story two or three times during the group session (perhaps have rehearsals first, and then the real play). After the children have practiced the story, therapists can encourage them to ad lib and add additional dialogue to the play.

Therapists should help children apply the story "The Fire," to their own situations as abused and/or sexually abusive children. The fire itself is symbolic of trauma. Therapists can emphasize that fires hurt a lot of animals, just as sexual abuse hurts a lot of people. Children can understand that the characters of Tommy the Turtle,

Stinky the Skunk, and Oscar the Owl symbolize three different responses to the same traumatic experience. These responses are self-victimization, abuse, and recovery.

As therapists point out the thinking errors displayed by Tommy, Stinky, and Oscar, they should help the children understand how the characters' thinking errors differ. Tommy engages in self-blame (e.g., "If I wasn't so slow, I could have gotten away."). Stinky blames others (e.g., "I hate people! They're all mean and stupid."). In contrast to Tommy and Stinky, Oscar corrects his thinking errors, has empathy for others, and chooses to talk about his feelings (e.g., "I don't really deserve that nest any more than the little owl. That's just a poor excuse to let myself steal"; "He'd [the little owl] probably feel mad and helpless, just like I did when the fire burned my tree"; "I'll go see my old friend, Roberta the rabbit. . . . She'll listen and help me figure out what to do."). Oscar's actions provide children with a model for a successful relapse prevention plan (i.e., correct thinking errors, have empathy for others, escape high-risk situations, and talk about troubling feelings).

Precautions

Therapists must ensure that children do not become so engrossed in the role-play that they do not see the metaphor. Particularly with younger children, therapists should clearly point out the choices that the characters are making to deal with their trauma. Children often want to play the character that shows the most dysfunctional coping (i.e., Stinky the Skunk). It is important to emphasize that Stinky uses many thinking errors and makes bad choices that hurt others. In contrast, Oscar the Owl thinks about others' feelings and deals appropriately with his own.

Adaptations

This activity can be used in conjoint groups or in family therapy. Children can act out the play for their parents. Parents and children can then discuss the meaning of the story with one another. This activity is also useful in individual therapy. A therapist can read the story and discuss the feelings, thoughts, and behaviors of the characters. As in group therapy, the three types of choices portrayed in the story should be emphasized. Children may also want to draw scenes from the story.

* * *

The Fire

Buddy was mad. As he walked through the woods, he thought, "It's unfair! Why should I have to stay home from the movie? My sister Sally dared me to break the window, and she didn't get in trouble at all!" Just then, he remembered the matches he had stolen from the house. "I'll bet this dry grass will really burn," thought Buddy. He lit a match and dropped it into the grass. Buddy smiled as he watched the fire burn. It spread really fast and began to catch some leaves on fire. "Uh-oh," said Buddy to himself. "I'd better get out of here!" He was scared now and ran away from the woods as fast as he could.

Buddy didn't know it, but the fire he started that day hurt a lot of animals living in the woods. Oscar, a very old and wise owl, smelled the smoke from his nest high up in the old oak tree. He flew high above the flames and saw a small boy running out of the burning forest. Oscar guessed correctly, "That boy just started this fire!" Feeling angry and helpless, Oscar watched the flames leap up the old tree and burn his nest into ashes.

Stinky the Skunk was sleeping in his den in a hollow log when the fire woke him up. He barely got out before the fire burned up his home. As Stinky ran to stay ahead of the flames he thought angrily to himself, "Just wait 'til I find out who started this fire. They're sure gonna know what it's like to smell bad!"

Tommy the Turtle was lying in the sun near the swamp when he saw the fire. Thinking quickly, Tommy told himself, "I'd better head for the swamp!" but the fire burned his feet as he crawled toward the water. The little turtle cried in pain, "Owwww! It hurts!" He soaked his injured feet in the cool water and watched the fire destroy the beautiful, green woods all around him.

When the fire finally stopped, the whole forest had been burned. Tommy crawled out of the swamp and walked through the ashes. He was very angry inside, but none of the other animals could tell how mad he was. Tommy sat down by the swamp and felt very sorry for himself. "I'm probably the only animal in this whole forest with burned feet. If I wasn't so slow, I could have gotten away," he thought. Now when his friends, Terrance and Timothy Turtle, asked him to play, Tommy just shouted, "Leave me alone!" The way he yelled surprised Tommy as much as it surprised the other turtles. "You don't have to snap at us, you stupid mudface," said Terrance. "Yeah, added Timothy, "Just see if we ever play with you again!"

Tommy didn't know why he yelled at the other turtles. "What's wrong with me?" he asked himself. "I must *really be* a stupid mudface. I don't think anybody likes me anymore." He thought about running away, but then he thought, "It won't do any good to go to a new swamp. No one will like me there, either." So Tommy just sat in the mud on the edge of the swamp and said to himself, "I just wish I was dead!" He started crying and crawled inside his shell. After a very long time, he didn't feel quite so bad, so he let himself fall asleep.

Stinky the Skunk stomped through the dirty, black ashes trying to figure out who started the fire. "It had to be a person," he thought angrily. "No animal could have done it. I hate people! They're all mean and stupid. They shouldn't be allowed in the forest."

By that night, Stinky had made a plan to get even. "They ruined my home, so I'm gonna ruin theirs," he thought as he came upon some houses at the edge of the town. Very quietly, Stinky climbed up to an open kitchen window. "Pssssst!" The sweet, cool breeze suddenly turned foul as Stinky raised his tail and sent his awful, smelly spray into the house. "Aaaaah, that feels better!" he sighed. Then he began to laugh, "By the time they figure out what happened, I'll be back in the woods and they'll never catch me."

As Stinky ran back to the woods, he thought about the family who lived in that house. At first, he just kept laughing and smiling, but then he started to feel bad for what he had done. Stinky got mad again as he stuffed those guilty feelings back inside. "So what if their house is a little stinky? They should be happy I didn't burn it down! Besides, I wouldn't have done it if they hadn't ruined my home first."

When Stinky got back to the burned forest, he sat down angrily in the ashes. He remembered how good it felt to get even, and right then he decided he would go do it again. "This time," he plotted,

"I'll go all the way inside a house, and spray the clothes in their closets!" Stinky grinned from ear to ear as he turned around and headed back to the town.

Oscar the Owl had found a new forest to live in, but he was still very angry. "I'll have to build my nest all over again," he thought as he flew above the woods. Just when he found the perfect tree, he noticed that a little owl already lived there. "But I want this tree!" Oscar thought. Right then, Oscar decided that he would just take over the little owl's nest. "After all, I'm bigger, older, and wiser. I deserve a fine home more than that little bug eater does," said Oscar to himself.

But as Oscar swooped down, he thought about what he was about to do. "I don't really deserve that nest any more than the little owl," he thought. "That's just a poor excuse to let myself steal." Then he thought about how the other owl would feel if he stole the nest, "He'd probably feel mad and helpless, just like I did when the fire burned my tree."

Suddenly, Oscar changed his mind, and he flew away from the little owl's tree. He thought, "I don't want to hurt that little owl. I need to build my own nest." But he was still very mad, and his anger didn't go away just because he decided to be nice. "Maybe I'd feel better if I talked about my bad feelings," thought Oscar. "I'll go see my old friend, Roberta the Rabbit. She's someone I can count on. She'll listen and help me figure out what to do."

Roberta the rabbit lived with lots of other rabbits in a field. Her big maze of underground tunnels didn't get burned by the fire, so Oscar found Roberta right at home where she usually was, taking care of all the little bunnies. It was warm and quiet in Roberta's home and Oscar always felt safe there. He told her, "I was so mad! I really wanted to hurt the boy who started the fire. Then I got really scared when I wanted to steal the little owl's nest." Roberta just listened and nodded. "What do you think you'll do now?" she asked. Oscar was thoughtful for a moment; then he said, "Well, the forest where the little owl lives is pretty big. I'm sure I can find another good tree for my nest. It'll be a new start, and maybe that's good." When Oscar had finished, Roberta gave him a big, soft hug, and he felt much better.

As for Tommy the Turtle, he spent a lot of time feeling sorry for himself and was hardly ever happy. It is true that Tommy never hurt anyone else, but he did hurt himself by holding his bad feelings inside.

Stinky the Skunk was really confused. Stinky knew one way to get his bad feelings out. What he didn't know was that he hurt others to make himself feel better.

Chapter 8

Relationship Skills

ACTIVITY: ANGER THERMOMETER

Target Group

Latency-age children.

Objective

To help children identify feelings and develop skills to manage their anger.

Materials

Paper, pencils, crayons or markers.

Description

The therapists begin this activity by having the group members brainstorm as many words for anger as possible and write them on the board. The word list should include a continuum of angry feelings from irritated to rage. Children are then instructed to draw a thermometer. Each child identifies his/her own range of angry feelings along their thermometer, with the most "explosive, out of control feeling" at the top of the thermometer, and "the feeling you have when a mosquito or fly buzzes around your ear" at the bottom. Next, the therapist asks them to identify angry feelings at midpoint and again between midpoint and the top, and midpoint and the bottom of the thermometer. Figure 8.1 illustrates the placement of feelings on the thermometer. The children may refer to the word list on the board for ideas.

When the children are satisfied that their angry feelings are placed at the right points, they are asked to identify how their body looks and feels at each point on the thermometer. Responses such as butterflies in my stomach, clenched teeth, tight fists, or a red face are common. Then they identify what they *do* at each point (e.g., withdraw, swear, hit, cry, stomp, or yell). Next, the children identify what kinds of thoughts they might have for each point on the thermometer. "I'd like to beat up somebody" or "I'm afraid my head will explode" are typical angry responses.

In the final step, the children identify anger management strategies for each point on the thermometer. Each step may require an entire session to complete and process. Figure 8.2 illustrates the completed thermometer.

Process

At each step, volunteers are asked to share their work with other group members. During the anger management step, therapists ask the children to talk about their feelings that are easiest to manage. They then learn to identify their body responses as cues to begin to use anger management techniques. The group brainstorms what would help a child stay in control of his/her own behavior (e.g., relaxation, distraction, deep breathing, counting to ten, etc.). The children identify strategies for managing their anger early on the continuum, before their feelings become out of control.

Adaptations

This exercise can be used in individual and family sessions, in combined groups with children and parents, and with young children. Young children can draw how they look and act rather than use verbal descriptions. Young children may only be able to identify a three-point continuum. They may need assistance identifying feeling words that describe different levels of anger. Terms such as "yelling mad" or "hitting mad" have been helpful with children as

FIGURE 8.1. Anger Thermometer

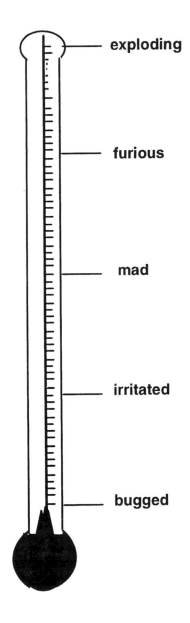

FIGURE 8.2. Brad's Anger Thermometer

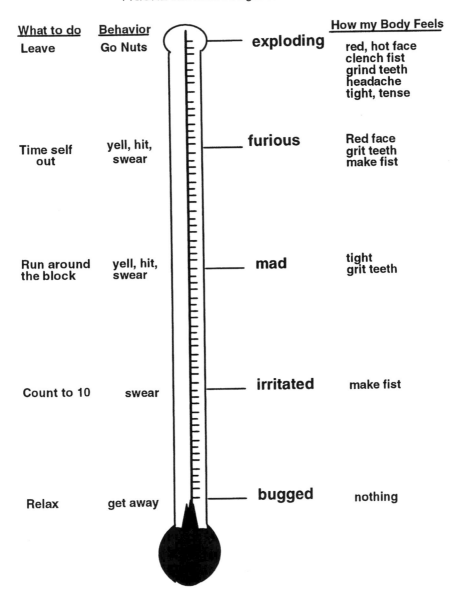

young as four years old. Anger management strategies for young children also should be simplified. Parents can be taught to recognize the early stages of their children's anger and help them implement strategies for dealing with this anger.

A similar exercise for use with young children is an "Anger Line." The children are asked to draw a line across a large blackboard to show how angry they feel. The children may draw how angry they were when they acted out sexually and compare the length of one another's lines. Some children may discover they were not angry when they offended. Then, therapists and the children try to identify feelings that led to the offense.

ACTIVITY: TRUST TARGET

Target Group

Latency-age children.

Objectives

To help children:

1. identify behaviors that increase or decrease the level of trust between two people, and
2. learn how to evaluate the trustworthiness of others and identify those to whom they can safely confide their feelings.

Materials

Chalkboard or flip chart, "Trust Target" handouts (See Figures 8.3, 8.4, and 8.5).

Description

Completion of this activity may require several sessions. Distribute "Trust Target" handouts and instruct the children to write the names of those people in whom they have "enough trust to tell my deepest secrets" in the center circle. In the second circle, they note those people in whom they have "enough trust to talk about personal things." In the third circle, they write the names of those people in whom they do "not have enough trust to feel safe." Outside of the three circles, group members write the names of people in whom they have "no trust at all." Figure 8.3 illustrates the trust circles.

Next, therapists ask the group members to explain what behaviors people in their center circle do that make them so trustworthy. These trust-building behaviors are listed on the chalkboard as "things that would make me gain trust in someone." Similarly, therapists ask the children to describe what behaviors people in their outer circles do that make them untrustworthy. These behaviors are listed as "things that would make me lose trust in someone."

FIGURE 8.3. Trust Target

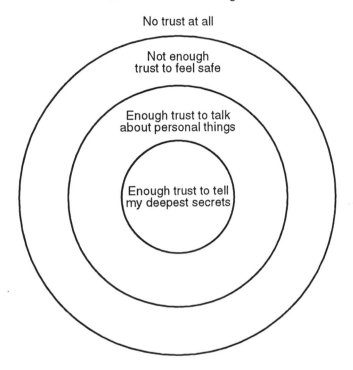

No trust at all

Not enough
trust to feel safe

Enough trust to talk
about personal things

Enough trust to tell
my deepest secrets

Children then rate each trust-building behavior on a scale ranging from +1 (minimal gain of trust) to +5 (great gain of trust). Behaviors that lose trust are rated from −1 (minimal loss of trust) to −5 (great loss of trust). To help group members arrive at these ratings, therapists ask them, "Which of these behaviors will lose the most trust?" The behavior they select is assigned a −5. Children assign a score of +5 to the behavior that would "gain the most trust." All the remaining behaviors listed are assigned scores between these two endpoints on the continuum. This scale of behaviors is then superimposed on a single "Trust Target" that can be referred to by the entire group. Figure 8.4 illustrates the trust target and behavior rating scale.

In the final part of the activity, group leaders present a series of case vignettes describing behaviors that build or take away trust. Group members are asked to rank the behaviors of the person described in the vignette on the trust continuum. Next, group mem-

FIGURE 8.4.Trust Target with Behavior Rating Scale

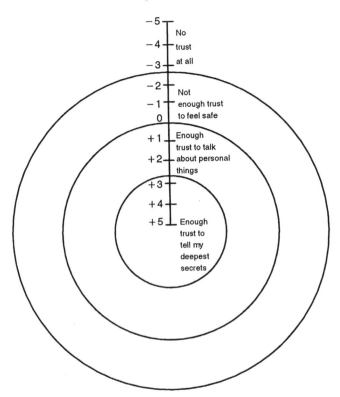

bers provide specific examples of how that person could gain trust or deepen the level of trust. A list of possible case vignettes is provided in Table 8.1.

Process

To facilitate the development of a trusting group milieu, therapists should encourage group members to include one another in their trust circles. Therapists can ask the children to decide if the people in their inner circles are those to whom they would disclose their sexual offenses. Group members may also identify to whom they could talk if they have thoughts and feelings about touching someone again.

TABLE 8.1. Sample Case Vignettes

- Brad was a nice guy, but he would never look you in the eye when you talked with him, and it sometimes seemed as if he wasn't listening.
- Chris's father sexually abused him and was arrested. He denied he did anything, but then admitted to the charge before the trial so Chris did not have to testify. His dad has been in a residential treatment program and is now ready for a recontact session to apologize for what he did to Chris.
- Jessica told her best friend Amy that she liked Bryan, but asked her to keep it a secret. The next day, all the girls in her class teased her about her new "boyfriend," Bryan.
- Kevin invited Jenny over to his house to jump on the trampoline. However, when she got there, he told her, "You can jump on it if you let me touch your privates."
- Mike's dad promised him for two weeks that he would take him fishing on the Fourth of July. On the morning of the Fourth of July, his dad called and said he had decided to attend an "important" social event with his friends from work.
- Travis invited his friend Jason to his house to play the new Nintendo game he got for Christmas. Right after Jason left, he noticed the game was missing. When he asked Jason about it the next day, Jason said, "I can't believe you'd think I'd steal from you. I don't want to be your friend anymore."
- James was feeling bad because their veterinarian had just informed his family that his dog had cancer. Chris came up to him and said, "Are you OK? You look kind of sad."
- Bill's boss asked him to prepare a proposal for an important contract for their company. Bill spent an entire weekend working on the proposal. When his boss presented it to the Board of Directors, he took all the credit himself and failed to mention Bill.
- Rebecca and Susan had been good friends for years and took turns babysitting each other's children. One night Rebecca's six-year-old daughter disclosed that she was molested by Susan's teenage son whenever Susan left him in charge while she went to the store.
- Nathan felt he could talk more easily to Paul because Paul had been sexually abused too.
- Jimmy was bigger than everyone on the bus. He was great to have as a friend because he could really protect you from bullies, but he was always beating up on kids who didn't want to be his friend.

Group discussions can focus on why changes in trust occur over time. Therapists can ask, "Have any of the people on your trust targets changed positions? Why? What did they do to change your trust in them?" When they discuss their trust targets, group members may begin to confide in one another. Discussions about trust help group members learn to identify trustworthy behavior in themselves and in others.

If any group members show disrespectful behavior during the activity, therapists can use the behaviors as examples of trust-losing actions. "When Kenny made fun of you earlier today, did your level of trust for him change?" "What would Kenny need to do to move into your inner circle?"

Precautions

Therapists must be sensitive to how a person might feel if he/she is placed in the outer circle of another's "Trust Target." Therapists can use this opportunity to help the two individuals discuss their relationship. For example, if a child is placed in the outer circle by another group member, he may feel hurt and frustrated by the other child's lack of trust. If the child wants to be trusted more, group members could suggest behaviors he might use to become more trustworthy.

Adaptations

The vignette portion of the "Trust Target" activity can be more enjoyable if structured in a game format. Group members can be divided into teams and earn points for giving examples of ways to increase trust.

"Trust Targets" can be used with young children (ages four to eight) to complement the "Wheels of Intimacy" exercise described later in this chapter. Simplifying the instructions may be necessary. For instance, young children can be asked to write names of people they "can tell anything to" in the center circle or "bull's-eye." The middle circle can include names of people they can "tell about most things, but *not* about my touching problem." In the third circle and outside the circles, young children can place the names of those people with whom they "don't feel safe." Therapists can help young children make a list of behaviors that "win trust" and "lose trust," but they do not assign points to the behaviors.

Trust targets are saved and can be referred to when issues about trust arise during later group sessions. Similarly, a blank "Trust

Target" diagram can be used spontaneously to facilitate discussions as they occur.

The "Trust Target" activity can also be used effectively in family therapy. Parents can rate their children using the "Parents' Trust Target" presented in Figure 8.5. Family members can identify ways a child can gain more trust, and eventually be allowed more choices. This adaptation clarifies the need for supervision of the sexually abusive child to all family members.

FIGURE 8.5. Parents' Trust Target

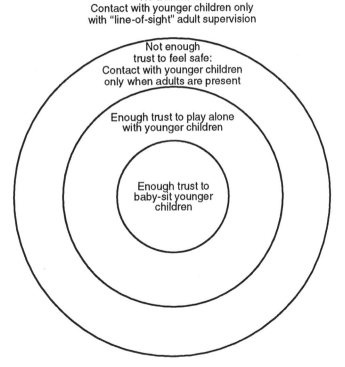

No trust at all:
Contact with younger children only
with "line-of-sight" adult supervision

Not enough
trust to feel safe:
Contact with younger children
only when adults are present

Enough trust to play alone
with younger children

Enough trust to
baby-sit younger
children

*ACTIVITY: TRUST EXERCISES**

Target Group

Latency-age children.

Objectives

To help sexually abusive children:

1. develop a supportive group milieu,
2. practice behaviors that will help them be viewed as trustworthy, and
3. practice entrusting themselves to the care of others.

Materials

An experiential education game book, such as *Silver Bullets* (Rohnke, 1984), that contains a complete description of the various "Trust Exercises."

Description

Group members take turns entrusting their physical safety to other group members through a series of progressively more challenging exercises. The first exercise is conducted in dyads in which the children press their hands together and support each other's weight. The second exercise involves trios in which one child falls forward and back into the arms of two supporters. The final exercise involves the entire group. One child stands in the center of a circle of "catchers" and falls in any direction he/she chooses. At least two sessions are required to complete the exercises.

Process

The children are informed that the group cannot advance to the next exercise in the sequence until they have gained the trust of the

---

*Rohnke, K. (1984). *Silver bullets.* Hamilton, MA: Project Adventure.

therapists. Group members earn the trust of the therapists by demonstrating that they are ready to complete the next exercise safely. Therapists clearly establish expectations from the outset. The children are expected to begin each fall with the following verbal preparation: the individual about to fall asks his supporters,"Ready?" The supporters respond in unison, "Ready!" The "faller" then declares, "Falling!" but does not fall until he hears his supporters respond, "Fall!" Whenever this verbal preparation is not done cleanly or is omitted, the facilitator says, "Stop!" and directs the group to start again.

This activity is presented to help group members unite as a group. Any behavior that interferes with the group's success, such as "goofing off" or lack of concentration, results in an interruption of the activity in order to deal with the "group's problem." Positive peer pressure and feedback is used to get group members to work together to complete each exercise. Because these exercises require children to take personal risks, taking a turn as the "faller" must be voluntary. However, a child who is hesitant to entrust his/her safety to the other group members should be encouraged to identify what he/she would need from the group before he/she would be willing to fall. Quite often, group members will comply with the child's expectations, and the child will agree to try a fall.

Overcoming the perceived risk involved in the exercises facilitates the development of trust among group members. Group members give one another feedback regarding which of their behaviors facilitate trust and which interfere with the development of a trusting relationship. For example, when beginning trust falls, individuals responsible for doing the catching may sometimes make jokes and may not necessarily seem to be taking their task very seriously. When such behaviors are present, it is likely that the child who is about to take the risk of falling will hesitate or refuse to continue. (If the child fails to note the danger, the therapist interrupts the activity.) The child is asked to state what he/she needs from those providing support in order to trust them (e.g., "pay attention and take this seriously"). In this way, the "catchers" learn to improve their behavior to gain the trust of other group members. At the same time, those entrusting themselves to the care of others gain practical experience in evaluating the trustworthiness of others.

The interpersonal closeness experienced as a result of the trust falls may create a therapeutic milieu that facilitates discussion of the children's offenses. When group members are called upon to share embarrassing information about their sexually abusive behavior, they can use what they learned from the trust falls to meet the challenge of self-disclosure. For example, a child might say to the group, "I need you guys to pay attention and promise you won't laugh so I can trust you."

Precautions

To avoid injury, therapists should exercise caution when employing trust falls. It is important to ensure participants pay attention and take these exercises seriously. There is a perceived risk of injury involved in trust falls that contributes to their experiential impact.

Adaptations

Trust falls could be used in family therapy to facilitate increased trust among family members.

ACTIVITY: WHAT MAKES A FRIEND

Target Group

Young children.

Objective

To assist children to identify aspects of friendship that are important to them.

Materials

Paper, pencils, crayons, markers, and a list of questions about friendship.

Description

The paper and pencils are distributed, and the children are asked to spend a couple of minutes thinking about one of their friends. Then they are asked to draw this friend. Each person takes time to introduce his/her friend to the group. The group members then follow the same order in answering the following questions:

1. What do you like to do with your friend?
2. What do you like about your friend?
3. What does a good friend do for you?
4. What do you wish your friend would do?
5. What are you glad your friend does not do?
6. What can you tell your friend?
7. What don't you tell your friend?
8. Why would someone want to be your friend?
9. What do you think you could change in order to be a better friend?
10. What would you like to do differently?

Process

An effort is made to elicit personal qualities that would make a good friend. Generally young children focus on activities they do with their friends (e.g., "we play cars"). Therefore, the first question deals with the activity component of friendship. The therapist then leads the children to think about friendship in a more abstract fashion. Questions two through four help to focus on the importance of the quality of the relationship. As children bring up aspects of friendship (e.g., "he/she likes me"), they are encouraged to explore further and assess why their friends like them. In addition, they are directed to question whether they tend to like friends with similar qualities as do others in group. During this discussion, the therapists point out similarities and differences in what people like. For example, while most children like others to share, they may not all appreciate friends who are good at sports (if they are not interested in those sports).

Finally, group members are asked to look at trust issues. They explore how they themselves compare to their friends in trustworthiness. Although they may identify ways in which they could be better friends, they may not always want to do these things; for example, a child may be tired of trying to help a particular friend. Identifying one's own needs and setting boundaries are important aspects of friendship.

Precautions

This exercise does not usually present many problems. Occasionally children have difficulty thinking of more abstract friendship qualities, but the brainstorming aspect of this exercise tends to help group members identify characteristics of their friends. When a particular child cannot think of any reason a person would want to be his/her friend, the leaders of the group can encourage the other children to think of ways in which that child has been a help to other children in the group. Although the therapists can usually identify positive qualities about each child, the comments of their peers are more effective. This type of interaction among group members facilitates the development of close relationships in group. Learning to be a friend in group may then generalize to peers outside of group.

If a child is very socially isolated, he/she may be encouraged to "imagine" what is important in friendship. As with all exercises, therapists need to be patient and allow the children sufficient time to develop and express their own ideas. They will more likely generalize their group experiences to other aspects of their lives if they reach conclusions for themselves versus being "instructed" by therapists.

Adaptations

Latency-age children might be asked to list both qualities they admire in their friends, and how they themselves are good friends to others. It is best to ask children to make these two lists in separate steps so they are not preoccupied with whether they and their friends have the same qualities. They are then able to concentrate on their own positive attributes, without making comparisons.

During one of the combined groups, the children and their parents may choose to role-play assertiveness with friends. In this way, identifying one's needs and setting boundaries can be clarified within the context of being a friend. Suggestions for role-plays are presented below in Table 8.2.

TABLE 8.2. Suggestions for Role-Plays

1. Your friend pushes ahead of you in line.
2. Your teacher blames you for allowing your friend to copy your paper, which you did not do.
3. Your friend's mother tells you to go home because she believes you previously stole a toy from her younger child.
4. A storekeeper keeps waiting on adults and ignores your friend.
5. A baby-sitter (older child) asks you to play strip poker.
6. Your friend steals from a store and asks you to promise not to tell.
7. You are teased and bullied on the playground when an adult is not present.
8. An older friend asks you to touch his privates.

ACTIVITY: WHEELS OF INTIMACY

Target Group

Young children.

Objective

To assist children in identifying people with whom they can share very personal information.

Materials

Construction paper, markers, two jars of different sizes, and scissors.

Description

Two sizes of "wheels" are made by each child. The children use the jars to make circles and then cut out the circles. The group is then asked to use the larger circle and a marker to write down people to whom they can go for help if someone approaches them in a threatening manner. They can include both people in specific roles (e.g., teacher, neighbor) and the names of people they know. Following completion of this task, the children are asked to use the smaller circle to write down those to whom they could talk to if they themselves were tempted to touch another's private parts. The two circles are compared and may be attached at the centers so they display names on either side.

Process

Young children can be helped to print or make drawings on their paper. The children typically understand that they would not share both types of information with everyone listed on their first wheel. Occasionally, a child will misunderstand the directions and begin putting a policeman or other relatively unfamiliar person on their smaller wheel. When asked whether they would really tell a policeman if they felt like touching someone, they typically change their response.

Precautions

In most circumstances, it is helpful to emphasize the importance of being able to communicate with primary caretakers to get help with problems. However, it is important to recognize when children are not living in homes in which this open communication is possible. Family therapy sessions may be used to facilitate open communication.

Adaptations

The wheels may be shared with parents in a combined group. Parents need to understand that a major goal of therapy is for their children to talk to them about their thoughts/feelings regarding sexual abuse. Parents must help with relapse prevention. If a child discloses thinking about touching another child's private parts, parents need to be prepared to accept this disclosure in a way that facilitates future communication.

ACTIVITY: FLIGHT PLAN
FOR EFFECTIVE COMMUNICATION

Target Group

Parents.

Objectives

To help parents:

1. learn elements of effective communication,
2. increase openness to feedback from their children, and
3. identify gaps in their communication skills and develop a plan for enhancing their skills.

Materials

"Flight Manual for Effective Communication" handout (at the end of this chapter).

Description

This activity introduces a metaphor for the knowledge and skills parents need in order to have clear and effective communication with their children. Talking with children is compared to a pilot's discussion with air traffic control. This includes following established protocols for flight preparation, filing a flight plan, takeoff, flight, and landing.

Therapists introduce the metaphor by telling parents that during this group session being a parent will be compared to being the pilot of an airplane. Parents are asked to imagine entering the cabin of the plane, fastening their seat belts, and waiting for "flight instructions." The handout "Flight Manual for Effective Communication" is distributed. Therapists then ask for volunteers to role-play. The chairs are arranged to form a "cockpit" where the parent who role-plays the pilot can sit. Another parent is asked to role-play the air traffic controller ("pilot's child"). The other parents are lined up in the passenger seats. The therapists act as "ground control" to provide specialized guidance through "turbulent parenting."

The therapists lead a discussion that follows the handout. They ask the parents to think of recent interactions with their children. Parents identify ways their interactions have involved "safe flying," times they have been guilty of "pilot error," and how they encountered "turbulent air currents." The therapists and parents then brainstorm ways to correct problematic situations.

Process

The parents are led through each part of the handout. Parallels are drawn between parenting and the metaphor of piloting an aircraft. The importance of following established protocols in both situations is stressed. Therapists can assist parents in their discussion of the dangers of taking shortcuts in parenting and in managing day-to-day interactions. Parents are encouraged to identify what happens when they don't take time to clearly understand their children's concerns. Therapists can point out some of the requirements of aircraft upkeep, pilot licensing, and aircraft inspection and relate that to how parents need to update their skills periodically. Just as pilots need to be certified in each type of aircraft they fly, parents need to learn how to relate to their children's individual uniqueness.

Precautions

Therapists should ensure that parents understand the metaphor.

Adaptations

The metaphor can be applied in various ways. The therapists can be the flight instructors who certify parents to fly this particular aircraft, or "give them their wings." Therapists could also be insurance agents who determine if parents are flight-worthy enough to insure. Finally, therapists could represent officials from the Department of Business Regulations who renew flight licenses of parents. Ongoing training and recertification is encouraged.

The "Trust Target" activity can complement this exercise. Therapists can ask parents if others would trust "flying" (i.e., communicating) with them. Parents can speculate where their children would place them on the trust target. A therapist might ask "Do you think your child's trust target shows whether he/she feels safe with you as "the pilot?"

Parents also may be encouraged to develop their own metaphors involving parenting. Each parent could describe how developing relationship skills with their children may be analogous to learning a job or occupation. Proficiency in any area (including parenting) does not come without study and practice; it is acquired.

FLIGHT MANUAL
FOR EFFECTIVE COMMUNICATION

Safely reaching your destination (listening, understanding, and helping your child) requires knowledge of flight protocol. To avoid pilot error you must be skilled.

Key Aircraft Terminology

- **Pilot:** *You, the parent*
- **Air traffic controller or "the tower":** *Your child*
- **Aircraft passengers:** *Others in your family*
- **Ground school:** *Books on parenting, parent skills training classes preparing you for "flight"*
- **Radio Frequency:** *Getting on the same wavelength. (Clarity in communication between yourself and your child.)*
- **Ground Control (Flight Instructors):** *Your therapists*

Visual Flight Rules: Following established procedures (*parenting skills*), checking in as needed to report position (*awareness of thoughts and feelings*), and obtaining clearances to take off and land, etc. (*clarification of issues*).

Instrument Flight Rules: Additional help needed for guidance through cloudy areas, inclement weather, night flights (*any time you can't see clearly*). The instructors (*therapists*) are there to help you and are readily available through radio contact. You are to check in with them regularly.

Preflight Check

Are things in order for a safe flight?

1. **Do you have the proper equipment on board?** *(Interest, respect, warmth, acceptance, and the desire to be a good parent.)*
2. **Is your aircraft in order? Check fuel and fluid levels.** *(Do you have the time and energy to spend with your child to adequately hear and understand him/her?)*
3. **Have you removed unnecessary items** *(such as your own emotional baggage)* **to the baggage compartment?**
4. **Have you made sure others are "clear" of the propeller before starting the engine?** *(Have you removed distractions and gotten other business out of the way?)*
5. **Are all passengers in their assigned seats?** *(Do family members know their role in this situation? Are they part of the "flight crew"? Do they need to be involved in this discussion? Do they need to be in their assigned seats and not interfere with the flight operations on this particular flight?)*
6. **Is your seat belt on?** *(Have you taken a deep breath and emotionally prepared yourself for whatever your child throws your way?)*
7. **Have you tuned into your child's radio frequency to ensure clear and accurate communication?** *(Are you sensitive to your child's unique ways of communicating?)*

Activate Flight Plan

When, where, how?

1. **What is your destination?** *(Do you know where your child is headed with this conversation? What are the issues to be addressed? Does he/she need you just to listen or offer suggestions about how to solve a problem?)*
2. **What is your estimated time of departure?** *(If you can't listen to your child now, when can you? Have you communicated your time line to him/her?)*
3. **What is the anticipated length of your flight?** *(Have you let your child know how much time you have available? "I only have a few minutes, we will have to talk fast." or "I have as much time as you need.")*

4. **What is your estimated time of arrival?** *(Do others know when to come looking for you if you do not arrive on time? Is your spouse prepared to assist in rescue or relief operations if you run into trouble?)*
5. **Do you know how to get to your destination?** *(Are you likely to need additional direction from "ground control"?)*

Taxi to Runway

Get to the topic.

1. **Have you contacted your traffic controller for directions to the right runway and permission to enter the traffic pattern?** *(Are you letting your child guide you to the topic he/she wants to address?)*
2. **Ask permission from the "tower" for "take off."** *(Does your child feel totally ready to proceed?)*

Takeoff

Get to the "real" issue.

1. **Are you alert and positioned correctly?** *(Does your eye contact and posture indicate you are paying attention and showing interest in what he/she has to say.)*
2. **Are you maintaining proper speed for liftoff? Increase throttle steadily and gradually. Avoid hesitating or rushing the process; it may result in a "stall out."** *(Are you allowing your child to set the pace? Has he/she broached the "real" issue? Be careful not to interrupt and interpret; let your child guide you.)*
3. **Are you watching for incoming aircraft? Are you careful to not veer off the runway?** *(Are you sticking with the topic and alert to possible distractions or diversions?)*
4. **Do you feel the liftoff?** *(Does it feel as though you are on the right track with your child? Does he say, "Yes, that's how I feel!"?)*
5. **Are you careful to gain the appropriate altitude, maintain air speed, and fit into the traffic pattern in order to avoid collision?** *(Can you keep focused despite daily stress?)*

Flight

Get it all said.

1. **Now that you are in flight, are you sure you are tuned in to the appropriate radio frequency?** *(Are you hearing your child accurately?)* **Are you checking regularly to report your position and be sure you are remaining on course?** *(Are you checking with your child to ensure you understand his/her concern and how he/she wishes you to assist him/her?)*
2. **Are you surveying the environment to watch for obstacles such as towers, power lines, tall buildings, and mountains?** *(Are you paying attention to both verbal and nonverbal communication?)*
3. **Are you attending to navigational issues? Are you clear about where you are going, and do you know how to get there?** *(Are you remembering your goals to hear and understand your child's concerns and assist if he/she requests help?)*
4. **Do you need additional "Instrument Flight" assistance?** *(Are you relying on resources such as therapists, books, and classes to guide you? Do you need basic skills or more specific directions to get through this situation?)*
5. **Are you prepared to maneuver in changing air currents or in case of inclement weather?** *(Are you flexible enough to avoid being rigid in your response? Can you make necessary adjustments in your interventions?)*
6. **Can you use your "ailerons" to bank and turn your aircraft as needed?** *(Can you be flexible enough to change directions as your child needs, without allowing him/her to avoid dealing with issues?)*
7. **Can you deal with air turbulence without becoming alarmed or overreacting?** *(Can you remain unruffled enough to clarify misunderstandings or inaccurate assumptions? Can you use your "flaps" to slow escalations in emotional intensity and anger?)*
8. **Do you have the patience to stick with a procedure and avoid shortcuts that might endanger your aircraft?** *(Do you have the patience to stick with your child while he/she*

struggles with identifying and expressing a feeling or a concern? Can you avoid telling him/her how he/she feels?)

9. **Are you maintaining FAA regulations for proper altitudes to avoid collision with other aircraft?** *(Are you actively avoiding collision with irrelevant issues?)* **If you get into incorrect airspace, how quickly can you get back on track?** *(If you get sidetracked, how quickly can you recognize and return to the topic being addressed?)*

10. **Is your cabin pressure consistent to avoid the need for oxygen?** *(Are you afraid of losing control? Are you able to keep the conversation within an emotionally tolerable range?)*

11. **Are you enjoying the flight?** *(Are you using this opportunity to further your understanding and to deepen your relationship with your child?)*

Landing

Reach a resolution.

1. **Are you ready to land? Landing gear down and landing lights on if necessary?** *(Are you and your child ready to bring the discussion to a close?)*

2. **Have you checked with your air traffic controller to request clearance to land? If all issues have not been adequately addressed, you may be asked to circle the airfield a time or two. If you have clear radio communication, the "tower" will let you know when you may reenter the traffic pattern. The "tower" will direct you when to begin your descent and tell you which runway to use.** *(Are you able to recognize when your child feels issues are adequately addressed as opposed to responding to your own sense of resolution?)*

3. **Do you know how to balance airspeed and altitude for a successful descent, which brings you in line with the runway?** *(Do you know how to begin to diffuse the intensity, clarify the issues, review any resolution decided upon, and provide your child with encouragement and confidence so he can now handle his concern?)*

4. **Are you able to bring the aircraft in as smoothly as possible so that there is confidence by all on board that they**

have arrived in safety? *(Are you able to end discussions in a way that leaves all involved feeling heard and understood? Are issues resolved to the point at which others would be encouraged to engage in this process again?)*

Postflight Review

What happened?

1. **Was your flight enjoyable?** *(Did you enjoy talking with your child?)*
2. **Did you feel in control?** *(Did you feel prepared to help your child express his/her feelings and concerns? Did you feel you heard clearly what he/she was trying to communicate? Were there times you felt uncertain about what the issue was or how to help your child?)*
3. **Do you feel your child will be eager to "fly" with you again?** *(How did your child react?)*
4. **Do you feel a need for more consultation from your flight instructor to help you through difficult interventions? Do you feel a return to "Ground School"** *(to increase knowledge or skills)* **would be helpful in any area?**

ACTIVITY: BLUEPRINT FOR BOUNDARIES

Target Group

Parents.

Objectives

To help parents:

1. understand the need for appropriate boundaries to ensure personal space and privacy,
2. iIdentify boundary problems in their own home environment and formulate plans for correction, and
3. develop adequate supervision to ensure family members respect boundaries.

Materials

"Blueprint for Appropriate Boundaries" worksheet (at the end of this chapter), large sheets of paper, pencils, erasers, markers, and rulers.

Description

Therapists distribute the "Blueprint for Appropriate Boundaries" worksheet and give a large sheet of paper to each parent. Parents are asked to draw a blueprint of their home environment on the paper, including both a floor plan of their house and a map of their yard. They then respond to all items on the "Blueprint for Appropriate Boundaries" worksheet. The questions on the worksheet address four aspects of boundaries: (1) structural problems in the house (e.g., arrangement of rooms, missing doors, holes in walls); (2) norms for personal space and privacy of family members (sleeping arrangements, changing clothes, bathing, and using the toilet); (3) family interactive behavior (parent/child roles and respect for each other); and (4) supervision of children (in the home, yard, neighborhood and community). Parents discuss their responses.

Process

Two or three sessions may be needed to complete this activity. Therapists encourage parents to talk about why individual items on the worksheet are important to their own situations. Therapists may refer parents to the suggested guidelines presented in Table 3.4 in Chapter 3. These guidelines may be helpful to parents as they evaluate the boundaries in their home and discuss family rules pertaining to personal space, privacy, generational roles, family interaction, and supervision.

Structural Problems

Group members may help one another identify problems and work out solutions. For example, in one parent group, Ann disclosed that her four-year-old daughter, Mary, was sleeping across the hall from ten-year-old Jared, who sexually abused her. Ellen suggested that Mary might feel safer if her bedroom were upstairs by Ann. Ann responded that if she moved Mary, she would need to place her other daughter in the bedroom across from Jared's room. Another mother in the group, Sheila, suggested that Ann move Jared to the bedroom next to hers so she could better supervise him and move both girls downstairs. Ann agreed it was a workable solution and carried out the changes that next week.

Group discussions also help parents understand why setting appropriate boundaries in the home is essential to interrupt their children's sexually abusive behaviors. The floor plan of their home and yard can help parents identify problematic areas in their houses that may contribute to violations of privacy (e.g., missing doors, holes in walls, or hiding places). Scrutiny of the floor plan can ensure family members have adequate personal space for their personal belongings.

Norms for Personal Space and Privacy

Privacy rules are particularly important to maintain good boundaries. Group discussions of privacy rules assist parents to identify privacy violations and to make corrections. For example, Terri admitted to the group that she had always allowed her two sons,

Brandon (age seven) and Trevor (age five), to bathe together. She resisted discontinuing the practice, although her sons had sexually touched each other. Other group members helped Terri understand that having the boys take separate baths could eliminate a high-risk situation and help prevent further sexual acting-out behavior.

Family Interactive Behavior

Family interaction questions on the worksheet refer to parent/ child roles and respectful communication between family members. Group discussions can help parents identify ways to meet their own emotional needs without placing undue responsibilities on their children or expecting their children to be confidantes. Group members also can talk about how to help their children learn to treat each other with respect. Parents can identify disrespectful interactions in their families (e.g., interrupting others, name-calling, yelling, hitting others, taking another family member's belongings without permission, or destroying other family members' belongings). Group members can brainstorm strategies for interrupting disrespectful interactions and encouraging respectful communication.

Supervision

The final section of the "Blueprint for Appropriate Boundaries" worksheet addresses supervision issues. Parents identify which of their children require supervision and specify a level of supervision for each of these children (e.g., direct line of sight, check every few minutes, unsupervised for a few minutes, unsupervised for a longer period). Parents discuss times when it is difficult to provide adequate supervision, such as mealtimes and bedtimes. They assess whether locations of play areas and sleeping arrangements permit adequate supervision. They discuss restrictions to place on their sexually abusive children's interactions with other peers, such as whether to allow their children to play at friends' houses or have sleepovers. Finally, parents discuss what information they should share about their sexually abusive children with other adults in the community (e.g., baby-sitters, teachers, principals, church leaders, relatives, and neighbors). They discuss how to balance their child's need for confidentiality with their responsibility to ensure community safety.

As they discuss the questions on the worksheet, group members can help each other identify feasible alternatives to problematic arrangements. Therapists should encourage parents to collaborate with their individual/family therapists to adapt workable solutions to their unique family situations.

Precautions

When problems are identified, suggestions for improvement must be feasible. For example, parents often have trouble deciding where a sexually abusive child should sleep. Ideally, a sexually abusive child should not sleep in the same room as another child. However, many houses are small, and there may not be enough bedrooms to adequately accommodate all family members. A small house with few bedrooms may mean that a sexually abusive child must share a bedroom with a sibling. Parents may need to take other steps to reduce risk. Ensuring that children each have their own beds, dividing the bedroom with curtains, and stressing assertiveness and self-protection skills to all family members may be workable alternatives for creating a safe environment.

Adaptations

This activity is useful in both the combined group and family therapy. Children and parents can talk directly with each other about how best to arrange their living situation, set rules to enhance boundaries, and provide adequate supervision. Family members can learn skills to communicate respectfully with one another and enforce safety in the home environment. Therapists and parents may encourage children to identify their needs for privacy. When family members communicate directly about privacy issues, they may validate each other's needs and develop a plan to ensure individual privacy within the family.

BLUEPRINT FOR APPROPRIATE BOUNDARIES

Boundaries help us respect the personal space of others and keep others from invading our space. You can be more effective in helping your sexually abusive child when you have appropriate boundaries in your home. This exercise is designed to help you:

1. understand the need for appropriate boundaries to ensure personal space and privacy,
2. identify boundary problems in your home environment and formulate plans for correction, and
3. develop adequate supervision to ensure that the members of your family respect boundaries.

Completion of this exercise can help you recognize areas of potential risk for boundary violation and initiate a corrective plan of action. Parental guidance and supervision is crucial to your family's success in establishing sound boundaries.

Instructions

On a separate piece of paper draw a blueprint of your home environment by making a floor plan of your house and a map of your yard. Note doors, windows, closets, laundry areas, play areas, telephones, etc.

Now respond as completely as possible to the following items. Write responses next to the questions or on the blueprint as indicated.

Home Physical Structure

1. Are there hiding places?

2. Are there peek holes? Where?

3. Are there areas lacking doors? Door knobs? Where?

4. Are there areas lacking curtains (especially where people sleep, shower, or change clothes)?

5. Do you need to go through any room (or a personal space area) to get to another room? For example, do you need to go through a bedroom to get to a bathroom or a laundry area?

6. How long are phone cords? What is the range of cordless phones? Are there areas out of your view for supervision while on the phone? Do phone calls ever distract you from paying attention to your children?

Personal Space and Privacy

7. List all persons residing in your home; make a symbol to represent each person. Write the age of each child inside the symbol; write SA under the symbol for your sexually abusive child.

8. Does each person have a place designated to keep his/her personal belongings? Show these areas by noting family members' symbols on the blueprint. Also note where personal belongings are kept (e.g., toy chest, chest of drawers, closet, etc.).

9. Does each person have a designated bed or sleeping area? Place each family member's symbol at his/her sleeping area.

10. Do any family members change sleeping arrangements during the night or at other times? Place their symbols where they might sleep instead and explain.

11. Identify areas of multiple use—where more than one person uses the same space (e.g., bathrooms, kitchen area, closets, hampers, etc.) Place the symbols of all family members who share the area on the blueprint.

12. Do family members get time to themselves? What activities do family members enjoy? For each family member, note the following:

Family Member	Type of Activities	Average Frequency and Duration of Activities

13. What are your family's rules for changing clothes, bathing, and using the toilet?

14. What are your family's rules for modesty (sleepwear, robes, etc.)?

Family Interaction

15. Who seems to be the "boss" in your family?

16. Who seems to always get their own way?

17. Who seems to give up what they want to do in order to please other family members?

18. Which family members get along best in the family?

19. Which family members have the most conflict?

20. How are disagreements between family members usually handled?

21. List the household responsibilities of all family members. Are their responsibilities appropriate for their age?

Family Member	Household Responsibility	Appropriate for Age?

22. Estimate the frequency of the following interactions between family members:

Respectful Interactions	Seldom	Frequently
Say "May I . . ." Say "Please." Say "Thank you." Ask before borrowing another family member's belongings. Share with one another. Listen to one another. Compliment/praise one another. Respect other family members' need for privacy. Grab things. Borrow things without permission. Destroy another person's belongings. Interrupt to get one's own point across. Demand time. Call other family members names. Use sarcasm and put-downs. Disrespectful of others' need for privacy Hit or kick one another. Hug or kiss without permission. Expose themselves.		

Supervision

23. Does anyone need supervision to ensure boundaries are respected? Who?

24. Indicate type of supervision required for the family members listed in Question 23.

    a. Keep in sight (i.e., direct observation of the person's behavior at all times).
    b. Check every few minutes.
    c. May leave for a few minutes to go to the store.
    d. May leave the person unsupervised for a few hours and check with persons left at home to see if problems develop.
    e. None. The person does not require supervision by others.

25. Who supervises? List names.

26. How are children supervised when parents are busy preparing meals, getting ready in the morning, getting everyone to bed at night, etc.?

27. Write the instructions you give to others who are involved in your sexually abusive child's life:

    a. baby-sitters:

    b. teachers and principals:

    c. church teachers and leaders:

    d. relatives or neighbors, if the child visits their houses:

28. How is your sexually abusive child supervised when other children come into your house or yard?

29. Are sleepovers allowed? At other people's homes? At your own home? If so, what are the supervision arrangements for your sexually abusive child?

30. Who helps with diapering, dressing, or bathing younger children? What kind of supervision is provided?

Plan for Corrective Action

31. Please list areas of concern you previously noted or have discovered during this exercise.

32. List ideas to correct any identified problems. How will you help your children to respect the personal space of others? How will you help them to establish boundaries for themselves?

Chapter 9
Sexuality

*ACTIVITY: BODY RESPECT**

Target Group

Young children.

Objectives

To help young children:

1. develop acceptance and respect for their own and others' bodies, and
2. protect themselves from further victimization.

Materials

Copies of the "body" pictures (see Figures 9.1 and 9.2), paper, crayons or markers.

Description

This exercise acknowledges that all body parts are good. The children talk about the unique and positive aspects of each body part, as well as differences between boys and girls, self and others. Beginning with hair and moving down the body, a therapist asks the children questions about each body part and its function. The therapist emphasizes that each body part is beneficial.

Children must learn to recognize when their bodies are treated inappropriately by others. Therapists present examples of inappropriate

---

*The authors acknowledge Machelle D. M. Thompson, LCSW, for developing this exercise.

FIGURE 9.1. My Body

FIGURE 9.2. My Body

treatment of body parts. The children are encouraged to protect every portion of their bodies by asserting themselves. Therapists help the children practice saying "No!" to situations involving inappropriate or intrusive touch. For example, a therapist might ask, "What would you say if someone asked you to take off your clothes?" The children are taught that each part of the body is good even if that part has been hurt in some way. The same method is used for each body part. The human body is addressed as a whole; private areas are a positive part of that whole. Figures 9.1 and 9.2 help illustrate the discussion.

Process

It is more interesting to the children if a therapist draws each body part as he/she discusses it, even if the group leader's drawing abilities are limited. First, a picture of different styles of hair is drawn or displayed (see Figure 9.1). The children are asked "What is this?" They will usually guess, "Hair!" Children typically have fun guessing the body part as it is being drawn. "Good guessing," says a group leader. A therapist then discusses everyone's hair in the room, asking questions such as "How many different colors of hair do you see in the room? Who has the curliest hair? Who has the longest (shortest) hair?" The therapist then asks, "Why do we have hair? What is hair good for?" It is important to allow the children to come up with their own answers. The group leader encourages the children to treat hair with respect by asking, "Is it okay to brush hair? Is it okay to pull hair?," meanwhile prompting children to give answers that demonstrate appreciation of hair. When presenting negative scenarios, therapists should continue, "What would you say if someone tried to pull your hair?" At this point it is essential to help the children find ways to say "No!" to harmful touch. Very young children can all shout, "No! I don't like that!" The therapists continue with follow-up questions such as, "Would your hair still be good hair if someone pulled it?" The therapists help the children understand that their hair would still be good hair even if someone pulled it. This step is critical with every body part because many children don't believe their body is still good when someone has hurt or abused them. Therapists should encourage the children to continue to participate in the discussion by praising their responses.

Each body part is addressed in the same way, continuing with eyes, ears, mouth, head/brain, neck, arms, hands, trunk, private parts, legs, and feet. Ideas for questions and activities associated with separate body parts include the following:

1. When discussing positive aspects of eyes, therapists can direct the children to talk about things they can see in the room.
2. When ears are drawn, the group leader can ask the children to stop talking, close their eyes, and listen to sounds they hear both inside and outside the room.
3. When discussing appropriate contact with the mouth, a therapist may ask the children, "What would you do if someone gave you a big slobbery kiss?"
4. When heads are drawn, the children can imagine a big butterfly landing in the room to help them understand that their brains have the power to imagine.
5. When discussing legs and feet, some children can demonstrate their ability to jump or walk around the room.
6. For private parts, the therapist conducts the discussion in the same sequence, "What are private parts good for? Are boys' and girls' private parts different? Is it okay for kids to touch others' private parts? What would you say if someone tried to touch your private parts? Would your private parts still be good?"

Precautions

As with other exercises that focus on victim issues, it is important to make sure that sexually abusive children do not misunderstand this exercise or use the concepts taught to rationalize their own abusive behaviors. Therapists should affirm that sexually abusive behavior is always hurtful. The fact that private body parts are still good despite abuse does not take away the negative effects of abuse.

Adaptations

With older children, this activity can be used to initiate more in-depth conversation about the body. It is also a useful tool in individual therapy with children who claim that their body is "bad" because of their prior trauma.

ACTIVITY: THE GREAT BIG STOP SIGN*

Target Group

Young children.

Objective

To assist young children in formulating a strategy to manage sexual feelings.

Materials

Drawing paper, red construction paper, scissors, paste, crayons or markers.

Description

This activity applies the cognitive-behavioral "thought stopping" approach (Wolpe, 1969) to therapy with young children. It provides children a concrete way to manage sexual feelings and interrupt inappropriate thoughts that can lead to sexual acting-out behavior. The "stop sign" can be an integral part of a young child's relapse prevention plan.

Children are asked to brainstorm what they can do when they find themselves "thinking about touching." Their responses typically include various distractions (e.g., playing Nintendo, riding bikes, watching TV), and talking to people they trust (e.g., parents, therapists). The group leaders then ask the children to close their eyes and imagine "a GREAT, BIG stop sign, the biggest stop sign in the whole world, the biggest stop sign in the universe." The children are told to think of this stop sign whenever they want to touch someone in their private parts or hurt someone and to say to themselves "STOP!!!!" They are asked to either draw their stop sign or to make a stop sign using red construction paper.

The children then focus on identifying the events that occurred prior to their offenses, using the stop sign to mark points where they

*The authors acknowledge the collaboration of Machelle D.M. Thompson, LCSW, and Ronda Nelson, RN, MS, in the development of this exercise.

could have chosen to stop. Therapists ask the children to draw a picture of the place where they engaged in inappropriate touching (e.g., a bedroom, a backyard). The children are given red construction paper and are asked to cut out several small stop signs. The group leaders tell the children to paste the stop signs on their pictures where they think they could have made better choices and stopped themselves from touching.

The stop sign also can be used to help children avoid high-risk situations. Therapists direct the children to draw a floor plan of their house and a map of their yard. They ask the children to identify danger points in the house or yard where another sexual offense could potentially occur and to mark these danger points by pasting on the small stop signs. The children then brainstorm what they could do at each danger point to avoid inappropriate touching. Therapists emphasize the option of talking to a parent or another trusted adult about inappropriate sexual thoughts.

The children are required to develop relapse prevention plans before they can graduate from group. Ben, age eight, presented a number of specific strategies of "what to do if I think about touching." Ben's plan is presented in Table 9.1. He also drew a picture of himself "thinking of the great big stop sign."

Process

The stop sign activity gives children a concrete procedure to help them identify the poor choices they made when they acted out

TABLE 9.1. Ben's Prevention Plan: "What to Do if I Think About Touching"

1. Think of the great big stop sign.
2. Talk to my mom.
3. Talk to my dad.
4. Talk to my therapist.
5. Go watch TV.
6. Play Nintendo.
7. Go run around the block.
8. Ride my bike.
9. Play with my Legos.
10. Stay away from little kids.

sexually and to plan alternatives to prevent reoffending. Trevor, age seven, put a stop sign on the door of his three-year-old sister's bedroom explaining, "If I hadn't gone in her room, I wouldn't have touched her privates." Similarly, Danny, age eight, put a stop sign on his little brother's bed and drew an arrow to the TV, showing that he could have stopped himself from touching by watching TV instead of playing with his brother on the bed.

When asked to identify the danger points in his house where another offense might occur, Alex, age eight, put a stop sign on the stairs to his basement. He explained that his two younger sisters slept downstairs. By not going downstairs to their bedroom, he could avoid placing himself in a situation in which he might be more likely to think about touching. Similarly, seven-year-old Diana placed stop signs on the shed in her backyard. In this shed, Diana had molested several little girls in her neighborhood. She understood that preventing herself from reoffending included avoiding the location where the sex offenses took place.

Precautions

If children become aroused when drawing a location of an offense, therapists can remind them to imagine the big stop sign and tell themselves to "Stop!!!!" The therapists can then change the focus by moving to another work activity, such as drawing or role-playing.

Adaptations

The image of the stop sign can be combined with more complex imageries. For example, children can be asked to imagine themselves encountering one of their victims and having thoughts about touching. This image is then paired with that of the "great, big stop sign," which reminds them to stop thinking about touching. They can then imagine leaving the situation and going to "a safe place" where they will not be hurt and where they will not hurt anyone else.

After the imagery exercise, the children can draw pictures of their "safe place." Children's ideas of what makes a safe place vary. Some children include other people with them in their safe place, while others depict themselves alone. Dylan, an eight-year old boy with a history of physical abuse, drew a picture of a monster in his safe place. He explained to the other group members that the monster was a friend who would protect him from getting hurt and keep him safe.

If parents are educated about the stop sign and safe place imageries in parent group, they can encourage their children to use them to manage sexual thoughts and feelings. In individual and family therapy, therapists can remind the children to think of the stop sign when they are aware of having sexual thoughts and feelings.

ACTIVITY: A TOUCH IS A TOUCH

Target Group

Latency-age children.

Objectives

To help children:

1. understand feelings of sexual arousal they may have experienced when sexually abused, and
2. discuss worries or perceptions about becoming gay or lesbian due to being touched by someone of the same sex.

Description

This exercise is divided into two parts. The first part involves a demonstration in which two therapists, a male and a female, touch the open palm of a volunteer. The child describes the similarities between the two touches. The therapists explain that the palm feels the same, whether the touch comes from the male or the female therapist. They stress that gender does not affect the body's response to the physical sensation. Children are helped to understand that physical sensations, like sexual feelings, are natural responses. They cannot control physical sensations; they can only control what they do with their sexual feelings. In the second part of this exercise, therapists challenge group members to consider whether molestation by a same-sex perpetrator affects the personality and sexual identification of the victim.

Process

A therapist begins by saying, "We are going to talk about the physical feelings and sensations people have when they are touched." The therapists explain that they would like to make a point by touching someone and assure the children it won't hurt. A volunteer is asked to hold up his/her palm with closed eyes, while fanning out his/her fingers. A therapist then says, "You will feel a sensation in just a moment, and we want you to describe it to the group."

One therapist lightly presses the volunteer's palm with his/her own. The therapist asks the volunteer to describe the feeling as thoroughly as possible. Next, the other therapist does the same, and the child again describes how the touch felt. The therapists ask the child to compare the two touches. As the child responds, the therapists highlight the similarities in the two sensations. A therapist may then summarize, "It doesn't matter who touches you, male or female, or how old they are; it feels much the same."

The therapists then ask the children to think about how they felt (physically) when they were molested. Even if they felt the sexual activity was wrong, it is normal to have sexual feelings when one is touched in a sexual way. The physical sensation occurs regardless. A therapist may say, "When someone gets touched in a sexual way, his/her body usually responds with a feeling. Can anybody think of a name for that feeling?" After the children respond, the therapist can summarize, "So touches can cause arousal." Next, a therapist asks the group members to describe what they learned from the palm touch example. "All touches create a physical sensation whether the 'toucher' is male or female. In the same way, sexual touches can cause arousal whether the 'toucher' is male or female."

In the final part of the activity, therapists lead the children in a discussion about the effects of same-sex molestation on victims. The following suggested questions may be asked concerning either sex:

1. If a boy was abused by a male perpetrator does that make the boy victim gay? Does that make the male perpetrator gay?
2. If the male perpetrator is married and has children can he be gay?
3. If the male perpetrator was sexually molested by another male perpetrator when he was a little boy does that make him gay?
4. If a female perpetrator molests little girls does that make her a lesbian?

5. If a twelve-year-old boy found himself being aroused when seeing other boys or young men in the school locker room undressed is he gay?
6. If a girl was molested by a woman and later becomes aroused when she thinks about older girls does that make her lesbian?
7. If several boys (or girls) engage in mutual masturbation are they gay (or lesbian)?

Therapists can conclude the discussion by affirming, "Sexual abuse cannot cause a heterosexual person to be gay or lesbian. Some people are gay or lesbian; some are heterosexual. If someone is gay or lesbian, it isn't because they were sexually abused. If a child molests another child of the same sex, that does not necessarily mean they are gay or lesbian." Therapists can further clarify that as children grow older they know if they are heterosexual, gay, lesbian, or bisexual.

Precautions

Therapists should be aware of the abuse histories of children in the group and anticipate the concerns that may need to be addressed. Individual therapists should be told this activity is being conducted in group so that follow-up can be provided if needed. Parents also need to be informed and be prepared for questions their children may later ask them. Individual and family therapists can help integrate a child's concerns with his/her family's values about sexual orientation.

Adaptations

This exercise can be used with parents as well as children. It is helpful for parents to understand their children's confusion concerning these sexual issues. They can learn to help their children resolve such personal dilemmas.

ACTIVITY: RELAPSE PREVENTION "FIRE SAFETY PLAN"*

Target Group

Latency-age children.

Objectives

To help sexually abusive children:
1. create a workable and effective relapse prevention plan; the plan includes "internal" self-management strategies to enhance a child's self-control and an "external," supervisory prevention team to monitor the child's behaviors and model appropriate behaviors (Gray and Pithers, 1993); and
2. practice self-management skills to avoid high-risk situations and interrupt their abuse cycles.

Materials

"Fire Inspection Safety Plan" worksheet and "Safety Plan Definitions" (see Table 9.2), fire helmets, badges, etc.

Description

This activity uses the metaphor of a fire to help sexually abusive children learn and use relapse prevention strategies. A therapist tells the children that a sexual abuse cycle can be compared to a fire. Just like a fire, a sexual abuse cycle is a dangerous thing that can hurt people. A sexual abuse cycle starts from an emotional trigger and grows bigger, just like a fire starts from a spark and grows bigger. To prevent a fire from starting, or to stop it before it hurts someone,

---

*The authors gratefully acknowledge the assistance of Denzil Grimshaw, LCSW, in the development of this exercise. The authors also acknowledge Alison Gray and Bill Pithers for their application of the relapse prevention model to sexually aggressive children (Gray, A.S. and Pithers, W.D. [1993]. Relapse prevention with sexually aggressive adolescents and children: Expanding treatment and supervision. In H. Barbaree, W. Marshall, and S. Hudson [Eds.], *The Juvenile Sexual Offender* [pp. 289-319]. New York: The Guilford Press).

people need to make a fire safety plan. Sexually abusive children also need to make a safety plan to prevent their sexual abuse cycle from starting and to help them escape from or stop their cycle if it gets started.

To create their safety plan, children take the role of a "fire inspector" and conduct a "fire inspection" to understand how their sexual abuse cycle started and grew. The children use the worksheet, "Fire Inspection Safety Plan," and the "Safety Plan Definitions" (see Table 9.2) to identify their own "flammable areas," "sparks," "safety patrol," "fire alarms and smoke detectors," "fire extinguishers," and "fire exits."

Recognizing Risky Situations and Triggers

Children learn to identify and avoid flammable areas, or risky situations, where sexually abusive behavior is most likely to happen. Examples of flammable areas may include baby-sitting, sleep-overs, looking at pornographic magazines or watching X-rated videos, playing with younger children, or playing in isolated or secretive locations. The children identify sparks or events that may trigger their sexual abuse cycle. Sparks could include feeling rejected by peers, being embarrassed or humiliated by an adult, or experiencing events that provoke feelings of powerlessness. When children repress their feelings about these kinds of events, the sparks may trigger compensatory responses that start their sexual abuse cycle. Children may then begin to use thinking errors or develop get-back fantasies that lead to offending.

Establishing a Prevention Team

Assembling a "safety patrol" is a critical component of the safety plan. The safety patrol, or prevention team, consists of trusted adults who help the children avoid flammable areas, identify and correct thinking errors, and prevent their sexual abuse cycle from starting. The safety patrol can include parents, therapists, caseworkers, school personnel, extended family members, and trusted friends.

In the next step of the "Fire Inspection," children identify "fire alarms" and "smoke detectors" that can warn them if their sexual

TABLE 9.2. Safety Plan Definitions

FIRE—A sexual abuse cycle that leads to sexually abusive behavior. *(Just like a fire, a sexual abuse cycle is a dangerous thing that starts from a spark and grows bigger and bigger. Fires can be prevented from starting, or stopped before they hurt someone. So can your sexual abuse cycle.)*

FIRE INVESTIGATION—A search to understand how your sexually abusive behavior started and got worse. You are a "fire inspector" when you investigate your sexually abusive behavior. *(People investigate fires to find out how they started and grew bigger.)*

SAFETY PLAN—A plan you make that will help you prevent your sexual abuse cycle from starting and help you escape from or stop your sexual abuse cycle if it gets started. *(Fire safety plans help people prevent fires from starting and tell them how to escape from or put out fires once they start.)*

FLAMMABLE AREAS—Risky situations in which sexually abusive behavior is most likely to happen. *(e.g., A lighted cigarette near a gas pump is a risky situation, just like a child with a touching problem baby-sitting is a risky situation.)*

SPARKS—Events that trigger your sexual abuse cycle. *(Just like sparks start fires.)*

SAFETY PATROL—Parents and other adults who help you identify and avoid risky situations to prevent your sexual abuse cycle from ever starting. *(Fire safety patrols keep sparks away from flammable areas to prevent fires from starting.)*

FIRE ALARMS/SMOKE DETECTORS—Signals that warn you when your sexual abuse cycle has started. *(Just like a fire alarm or smoke detector warn people when a fire has started.)*

FIRE EXITS—Ways you can escape from your sexual abuse cycle after it has started. *(Just like people use fire exits to escape from a fire.)*

FIRE EXTINGUISHERS—Ways you can stop your sexual abuse cycle after it has started. *(Just like people use fire extinguishers to stop a fire.)*

FIRE DRILLS—Practicing your safety plan so you'll know what to do if your sexual abuse starts. *(Fire drills show people what to do in case of a fire.)*

Fire Inspection Safety Plan

1. Identify your **flammable areas** *(risky situations):*

_____
_____
_____
_____
_____

List of possible **"flammable areas"**:

    Being alone in a bedroom with another child
    Baby-sitting
    Sleepovers
    Swimming
    Playing alone in secluded areas
    Being alone in abandoned buildings
    Camping
    Taking baths or showers with another child
    Being alone in a bathroom with another child
    Letting a child sit on your lap
    Playing video games alone with another child
    Playing "truth or dare" games
    Playing "house"
    Playing sexually oriented games such as strip poker

2. Identify your **sparks** *(events that trigger your sexual abuse cycle)*:

_____

_____

_____

_____

_____

List of possible **"sparks"**:

    Feeling lonely
    Feeling left out
    Feeling put down
    Feeling angry
    Feeling powerless
    Having flashbacks
    Hearing or seeing sexual things
    Feeling revengeful

3. Identify your **fire alarms and smoke detectors** *(signals that warn you that your sexual abuse cycle has started)*:

_____

_____

_____

_____

_____

TABLE 9.2 *(continued)*

List of possible **"fire alarms"** and **"smoke detectors"**:

Get-back fantasies
Showing off to others
Using thinking errors
Covering up your behavior
Thinking about getting a child alone
Thinking about touching someone's private parts
Thinking about setups
Giving excuses to your parents
Being secretive about your behavior
Lying
Feeling sorry for yourself
Trying to get other people to feel sorry for you
Rationalizing your behavior
Minimizing—saying your bad behaviors aren't serious
Avoiding dealing with your feelings
Being phony—not saying how you really feel
Trying to make other people do what you want

4. List some **fire exits** *(ways you can escape from your sexual abuse cycle after it has started):*

_____
_____
_____
_____
_____

List of possible **"fire exits"**:

Don't be alone with a younger child. Find an adult.
Go home from the sleepover.
Change activities to get your mind on something else.
Just get out of the risky situation! Leave!!!

5. List **fire extinguishers** *(ways you can stop your sexual abuse cycle after it has started):*

_____
_____
_____
_____
_____

List of possible **"fire extinguishers"**:

> Correct your thinking errors.
> Think about the consequences of reoffending.
> Think about the embarrassment of being caught.
> Think of what your friends would think if they knew what you did.
> Stop the sexual thought.
> Call your therapist.
> Talk to a parent.
> Talk to a trusted friend.
> Talk to yourself about why you don't want to reoffend.
> Think about how your victim might feel.
> Think about how your past victims looked or felt.
> Think about how you felt when you were molested (or when you were hurt really badly by someone else).
> Talk about it!

Copyright © 1995, Lucinda A. Rasmussen, PhD, Denzil Grimshaw, LCSW, and Steven C. Huke, MS.

abuse cycle starts. A fire alarm or smoke detector could be a journal in which a child keeps track of his/her body sensations, feelings, thoughts, thinking errors, get-back fantasies, sexual fantasies, actions, and feedback from others. Sharing journal entries with parents, therapists, or other members of the safety patrol can prevent the secrecy that often enables sexually abusive behavior.

Stopping the Sexual Abuse Cycle

Children must develop self-management skills to interrupt their sexual abuse cycle. They can escape their cycle through "fire exits" or stop the cycle with "fire extinguishers." Fire exits are strategies that interrupt offending (e.g., thinking of consequences, distracting oneself with other activities, walking away from an opportunity to offend). Although fire exits interrupt the sexual abuse cycle, they do not address the underlying motivation for offending. "Fire extinguishers," on the other hand, are positive strategies for resolving feelings that motivate offending. Fire extinguishers include (1) identifying feelings (including bodily sensations of sexual arousal), (2) identifying and correcting thinking errors, (3) interrupting get-back fantasies and setups, (4) talking about feelings to trusted individuals, and (5) developing empathy for the feelings of others (especially victims).

Practicing the Relapse Prevention Plan

As sexually abusive children build self-management skills and establish a prevention team, they need opportunities to practice what they have learned. When children have completed their "Fire Inspection" worksheets, they can do "fire drills" in group to practice their safety plan. Therapists explain that fire drills are often held to help people practice what to do in case of a fire. In a fire drill, people act as if a fire were really happening. They identify exits to escape the fire, make a plan, and carry out the plan. In the fire drill, a child identifies a risky situation (i.e., situation in which he/she is vulnerable to acting out sexually); identifies possible fire exits to avoid and escape the risky situation; and discusses the fire extinguishers he/she plans to use to stop the sexual abuse cycle.

Writing the Relapse Prevention Plan

Relapse prevention plans outline what the children will do to interrupt their sexual abuse cycles and prevent reoffending. Children use their completed "Fire Inspection Safety Plan" worksheet and insight gained from participation in fire drills to write their relapse prevention plans. Their plans must include exits and fire extinguishers that the children plan to use at each step of their cycles to interrupt their inappropriate thought processes and stop themselves from reoffending. Children must be able to identify members of their safety patrol whom they can trust enough to talk to about their thoughts and feelings. Children must demonstrate that their relapse prevention plans are workable and effective before they can be discharged from therapy.

Process

It may take several sessions to complete this activity. Children should complete the "Fire Inspection Safety Plan" worksheet before volunteering for fire drills. As with the "hot seat," (see Chapter 5), a child can volunteer to do several fire drills at different times during treatment.

Precautions

It is important for therapists to ensure that sexually abusive children are as specific as possible when identifying high-risk situations. Individual therapists should also work with the children to identify situations in which the child is particularly vulnerable to acting out sexually. Relapse prevention plans must be realistic and include strategies the child would actually do when confronted with a high-risk situation.

Adaptations

This activity is designed for older children. It should be used concurrently with work in family therapy on relapse prevention. An effective prevention team is critical for a successful relapse prevention plan. Therapists should work with parents in family therapy to help them develop skills to support their children's relapse prevention plans. Communication about the specific details of the relapse prevention plan is essential.

ACTIVITY: COMMUNICATING SEXUAL VALUES

Target Group

Parents.

Objectives

To help parents:

1. identify their own values and feelings about sexual behaviors, and
2. give parents practice talking about sex, to decrease their discomfort when discussing sex with their children.

Materials

The worksheets "Sexual Values Quiz" and "Communicating Healthy Values About Sexuality" (at the end of this chapter), poster paper, markers, tape or thumb tacks, pens, and pencils.

Description

This activity involves three separate exercises completed in succession and may require several group sessions. It is possible to use any of these exercises separately. However, we have found that parents gain more from all three exercises when they are presented in consecutive weeks.

Sexual Development

Discussions about sexual development most often begin when parents ask what is "normal" sexual behavior in children. Many parents feel discomfort regarding their children's sexuality. They wish their children would not have sexual feelings until they are at least twenty-five years old. It is often helpful to invite a pediatrician or pediatric nurse to the group to discuss sexual development of children with them. Many parents are surprised to learn that even infants have sexual responses. The use of a medical professional to facilitate the discussion helps parents feel comfortable asking questions they may not have been able to ask therapists (e.g., how much masturbation is normal?) It also keeps initial sexual discussion on a clinical level, which helps parents begin to talk more openly about sexual issues. Information about normal sexual development is contained in Table 9.3.

Clarifying Sexual Values

Talking about their sexual feelings to a trusted adult is a critical component of relapse prevention for sexually abusive children. Children with sexually abusive behavior problems frequently grow up in homes in which values regarding sexuality are confusing, distorted, and in some cases, deviant and abusive. They often lack correct knowledge about sex.

In order to build an environment in which sexually abusive children may feel free to talk about their sexual feelings, parents themselves need to become aware of their sexual values. They should feel at ease using correct terminology to describe private body parts. Parents have a responsibility to provide their children with age-appropriate information and to communicate sexual values that are clear and self-caring and which affirm the rights of others.

In the second part of this activity, the therapists ask participants to identify "healthy" and "unhealthy" values regarding sexuality. The responses are written on poster paper. The healthy values list should include items that affirm sex as a positive expression of affection and caring between consenting adults. It is emphasized that sexual expression should be sensitive to the needs and rights of others. When communicating sex education to children, adults need to consider the developmental level of the child and provide clear, correct, and age-appropriate information.

Unhealthy values about sexuality include items that degrade sex or emphasize deviant, abusive, or violent sexual expressions. Sexual repression also can be an unhealthy value. Parents who are sexually repressed may conceal information about sex, define sexual expression as "dirty" or "nasty," and react punitively to their children's natural curiosity about sex.

TABLE 9.3. Normal Sexual Development in Children from Infancy Through Late Childhood

I. Infancy, 0-1 year

A. In the uterus, the fetus may suck his/her thumbs, fingers, and toes.
B. Periodic erections and vaginal lubrication (reflexive rather than sexual).
C. Genital stimulation for pleasure.
D. Physical closeness with primary caregivers, consisting of holding, clinging, cuddling, nursing, dressing, playing.

II. Early Childhood, 2-5 years

A. Interest in one's body and its functioning.
B. Curiosity about gender differences.
C. Body exhibitionism (running nude through the sprinklers or after a bath).
D. Beginnings of peer sexuality explorations, including genital examination.
E. Seeking names for body parts, sensual feelings, and body functions.
F. Fascination with "obscene" words, jokes about sex, genitals and body functions.
G. Modeling of parental interactions of expressing affection; continued responding to another with hugs, kisses, and cuddling.
H. Possible jealousy of intimacy shared by parents.

III. Middle Childhood, 5-9 years

A. Continued self-stimulation, in private.
B. Continued sexual play and exploration between same- and opposite-sex peers (secretive and hidden from adults).
C. Peer discussions regarding sexual behavior.
D. Keen interest in children of opposite sex.
E. Increased need for personal privacy.
F. Nocturnal emissions in males (wet dreams) may begin by age 9.

IV. Late Childhood, 9-12 years

A. The development of secondary sexual characteristics are well established.
B. Menarche occurs (average age of 11.5 years).
C. Peer sexuality explorations, including genital examination.
D. The sexual activity of both boys and girls tends to be within their general age range and may be either same or opposite sex.
E. Masturbation continues and may be mutual with both boys and girls, although self-stimulation is most common. Mutual masturbation may involve boy-girl mutual fondling and stimulation to orgasm.

Source: Tharinger, D. (1988). "Behavioral characteristics of normal childhood development." Presented at conference, Albuquerque, NM.

Next, parents complete the worksheet "Sexual Values Quiz." They are asked to share their responses with one another. The therapists may want to note that everyone has values about sexuality that were formed in childhood. These values include ideas regarding sexual play between children, masturbation, sexual orientation, sexual abuse, and consensual sex between adults.

Communicating Sexual Values

In the third exercise, parents discuss each step in the "Communicating Healthy Values about Sexuality" worksheet. They work together as a group to identify their sexual values, evaluate whether each value is healthy or unhealthy, and determine how best to communicate these values to their children. It is important for parents to be cognizant of their own sexual values and to evaluate whether these ideas are healthy and functional in adulthood.

Process

It will be difficult for parents to honestly examine and verbalize their sexual values unless they have trust in the other group members and therapists. They are not likely to actively participate unless the sexual values exercises are presented in a supportive environment.

Precautions

It is important that the group leaders keep the objectives in mind as they facilitate these activities. Discussions about sexuality can be awkward. Therapists must be comfortable using all the terminology and discussing sexual issues frankly. They also must be willing to share their own feelings in order to model openness in the discussion. It has been helpful to use these activities with therapists to help them clarify their own sexual values and train them to talk to clients about sex.

It is helpful to warn parents in advance that these activities will be presented. If this is done with some humor—"Wait until you go through the next activity! You'll really get used to talking about sex"—parents seem to anticipate the upcoming exercise in a positive way.

SEXUAL VALUES QUIZ*

Answer the following questions for each of these issues:

- Sexual behavior between children
- Masturbation
- Sexual orientation
- Sexual expression between consenting adults
- Sexual abuse

1. What are your three strongest beliefs concerning this issue?
   a.

   b.

   c.

2. How do you think you acquired these beliefs?

3. Have your beliefs concerning this issue undergone any change in the past ten years? If so, why?

4. Are you comfortable with your current beliefs concerning this issue, or would you like to change the beliefs?

COMMUNICATING SEXUAL VALUES WORKSHEET*

1. Be aware of your own sexual values. Identify your values about the following:
   - Sexual behavior between children
   - Masturbation
   - Sexual orientation
   - Sexual expression between consenting adults
   - Sexual abuse

2. Examine each of your values:

   Is it healthy?
   - Does it affirm sex as a positive expression of caring and affection between consenting adults?
   - Does the value help you nurture yourself?
   - Does it affirm the rights of others?

   Or is the value unhealthy?
   - Does it degrade sex?
   - Does it promote deviant, abusive, or violent sexual expressions?
   - Does it conceal information and enable secrecy?

3. Think about each of your healthy sexual values. Identify ways you can communicate these values to your children.

4. Now, carefully examine each of your unhealthy sexual values:
   - Why do you think you have the value?
   - Can you change it?
   - What do you need to do?
   - Should you seek professional help?

5. Identify those unhealthy values that you feel you cannot change, at least not at the present time.
   - How does the value affect your relationship with your children?
   - What do you need to do to avoid imposing your unhealthy value(s) on your children?

---

*Copyright © 1995, Lucinda A. Rasmussen, PhD. In Rasmussen, L. A. (1995). *Caring for children with sexually abusive behavior problems: A training course for foster and shelter care parents.* Salt Lake City, UT: Utah State Division of Family Services, Department of Human Services.

Chapter 10

The Power of the Treatment Team

ACTIVITY: COLLABORATION

Target Group

Therapists.

Objectives

To help therapists:

1. develop activities to help clients address therapeutic issues,
2. keep their work exciting and rewarding, and
3. maintain a supportive and creative work environment.

Materials

Yellow legal pads, pens or pencils.

Description

Therapists collaborate to create effective interventions to address the issues of sexually abusive children and their families. They evaluate their interventions, identify gaps in services, and engage in discussions of cases and theoretical issues. Collaboration provides therapists with opportunities to obtain support from one another.

Process

It is challenging to present materials in ways that are understandable and engaging to both children and their parents. Therapist collaboration is essential to create, implement, and evaluate therapeutic activities. The joy of the creative process helps compensate for the adverse experience therapists sometimes have listening to accounts of abuse. These experiences are offset when a new intervention facilitates positive changes in a family.

Precautions

Therapeutic work with sexually abusive children and their parents is personally demanding and presents diverse challenges to therapists. They must monitor themselves and one another to ensure that their personal issues or biases do not interfere with the quality of the services they provide. The team approach to treatment helps clarify issues of countertransference that arise when treating sexually abused children and their families (Conte, 1995). Periodic reviews of cases by a team help keep treatment objectives clear. A team is less likely to miss problematic salient issues than an individual therapist working alone.

Therapists working with child sexual abuse victims and children with sexually abusive behavior problems must have a clear sense of professional boundaries. Family members in crisis may depend on their therapist to make decisions. Therapists must avoid becoming a rescuer, allowing their clients' crises to become their own. Awareness of their own feelings can help therapists remain objective and keep their clients' problems in perspective. Therapists need to nurture their clients' sense of autonomy, encourage independent thinking, and help them be responsible for their decisions and actions.

Therapists must also have the capacity to deal with clients who are hostile and resistant to intervention. Family members who are court ordered into therapy are often angry when they begin treatment. It is important to confront the resistance of these clients without developing a punitive style. Communicating empathy for the feelings of powerlessness these family members often have, can help diffuse their anger and establish a positive working relationship.

Therapists must confront their own power and control issues, as they are often in a position of authority when working in the area of abuse. It is critical that therapists confront their own thinking errors and avoid becoming defensive when their thinking is challenged by clients. For example, one therapist initially assumed a child was minimizing the extent of his offense. After more information was obtained, it was important for that therapist to acknowledge that this assumption was false. As therapists model the ability to acknowledge inaccurate perceptions or admit mistakes, they may help their clients learn to become more accountable.

Therapists often experience empathy for sexual abuse victims. When working with children with sexually abusive behavior problems, it is important to balance empathy with objectivity and supportive confrontation. A therapist must not be so empathic to a sexually abusive child's victim issues that he/she does not hold the child accountable for sexually abusive behavior. In contrast, therapists must also be careful to contain any anger they may feel about a sexually abusive child's offenses. Dislike of perpetrators can interfere with the development of therapeutic relationships with sexually abusive children. To be helpful, therapists need to accept the child, despite his/her abusive behavior, and build upon the child's strengths.

Therapists need to be comfortable discussing sexuality. They must actively initiate discussions of sexual topics to address the children's presenting problems. Sexually abusive children know they are in therapy because of their inappropriate sexual behavior. When a therapist does not deal directly with sexuality, it may reinforce a child's perception that sex is too embarrassing and scary to talk about. Training, modeling, and practice can help therapists become more comfortable discussing sexual topics. Therapists can complete the "Sexual Values Quiz" and the "Communicating Sexual Values Worksheet" in Chapter 9 to become aware of their own sexual values and overcome any discomfort they have discussing sexuality.

Therapists who have their own history of sexual victimization may find it particularly difficult to initiate discussions of sexual issues. Moreover, therapists struggling with prior victimization issues must remain aware of how their own self-victimization and abuse cycles can be triggered by interactions with sexually abusive children and/or their families. Those who do not have personal histories of victimization may experience trauma vicariously (Neumann and Gamble, 1995) as they listen to accounts of abuse. Even experienced therapists who have "heard everything" can become emotionally unraveled by especially disturbing information. At these times, it is helpful to talk with a cotherapist or colleague. It may occasionally be necessary for therapists to seek professional help to ensure that personal issues do not interfere with the quality of their work. Whether they have been abused themselves or vicariously traumatized, it is helpful for therapists to routinely assess themselves and determine where they are in their own Trauma Outcome Process. Sharing feelings related to past or present trauma can help therapists stay in recovery and remain effective in helping their clients.

It is easy for therapists to become discouraged when they fail to successfully impact family systems. One therapist became disillusioned when a sexually abusive boy reoffended. This child's reoffense was particularly distressing because all therapists involved had believed he was ready to graduate from the program. He had made considerable progress on all treatment goals and appeared accountable and empathic. His therapist began to question her own skills as well as the effectiveness of the program. Her colleagues reminded her that the boy had made a poor choice, and other children had benefited from the program.

Finally, therapists working in the area of sexual abuse must take active measures to avoid burnout. Self-awareness is critical for self-care. Some individuals cope with stress by expressing their feelings to someone they trust; others engage in social or leisure activities. In either case, a personal support system of family and close friends both distracts one from the pain of abuse and provides a contrasting perspective of pleasure in life.

Adaptations

The adaptations are as diverse as the individuals who choose to do this work.

EPILOGUE

Keep in mind that Robert Fulghum's kindergarten rules also apply to you: "Warm cookies and cold milk are good for you. Live a balanced life—learn some and think some and draw and paint and sing and dance and play and work every day some. Take a nap every afternoon" (or at least whenever possible). And when you go out into the world of clients, watch out for crises, hold hands, and stick together.

References

Abel, G.G., Mittelman, M., and Becker, J.V. (1985). Sex offenders: Results of assessment and recommendations for treatment. In H.H. Ben-Aron, S.I. Hucker, and C.D. Webster (Eds.), *Clinical criminology: Current concepts* (pp. 191-205). Toronto: M & M Graphics.

American Psychiatric Association. (1994). *Diagnostic and statistical manual of mental disorders* (fourth edition). Washington, DC: American Psychiatric Association.

Araji, S.K. (1997). *Sexually aggressive children: Coming to understand them.* Thousand Oaks, CA: Sage.

Araji, S.K. and Finkelhor, D. (1986). Abusers: A review of research. In D. Finkelhor (Ed.), *Sourcebook on child sexual abuse* (pp. 89-119). Newbury Park, CA: Sage.

Bagley, C. and Ramsey, R. (1986). Sexual abuse in childhood psychological outcomes and implications for social work practice. In J. Gripton and M. Valentich (Eds.), *Social work practice in sexual problems* (pp. 33-47). Binghamton, NY: The Haworth Press.

Beitchman, J., Zucker, K., Hood, J., DaCosta, G., Akman, D., and Cassavia, E. (1992). A review of the long-term effects of child sexual abuse. *Child Abuse and Neglect, 16,* 101-118.

Belsky, J. and Vondra, J. (1989). Lessons from child abuse: The determinants of parenting. In D. Cicchetti and V. Carlson (Eds.), *Child maltreatment: Theory and research on the causes and consequences of child abuse and neglect* (pp. 164-169). Cambridge, MA: Cambridge University Press.

Bengtsson, H. and Johnson, L. (1992). Perspective taking, empathy, and prosocial behavior in late childhood. *Child Study Journal,* 22(1), 11-22.

Berenson, D. (1987). Choice, thinking and responsibility: Implications for the treatment of the sex offender. *Interchange,* January, 1-9.

Berliner, L., Gray, A., Friedrich, W. N., and Pithers, W. (1996, November). *Trends in classification and differentiating treatments of children with sexual behavior problems: Current descriptive research.* Paper presented at the Fifteenth Annual Research and Training Conference of the Association for the Treatment of Sexual Abusers, Chicago, Illinois.

Berliner, L. and Rawlings, L. (1991). *A treatment manual: Children with sexual behavior problems.* Seattle, WA: Harborview Sexual Assault Center.

Berstein, J.E. (1983). *Books to help children cope with separation and loss,* Second Edition. New York: R. R. Bowker.

Bonner, B.L., Kaufman, K.L., Harbeck, C., and Brassard, M.R. (1992). Child maltreatment. In C.E. Walker and M.C. Roberts (Eds.), *Handbook of clinical child psychology* (Second edition, pp. 967-1008). New York: John Wiley.

Bowen, M. (1978). *Family therapy in clinical practice.* New York: Aronson.

Breer, W. (1987). *The adolescent molester.* Springfield, IL: Charles C Thomas.

Briere, J.N. (1988). The long-term correlates of childhood sexual victimization. In R.A. Prentky and V. Quinsey (Eds.), *Human sexual aggression: Current perspective (V. 528)* (pp. 327-334). New York: Annals of New York Academy of Science.

Briere, J.N. (1992). *Child abuse trauma: Theory and treatment of the lasting effects.* Newbury Park, CA: Sage.

Briere, J.N. (1997, April). *Assessment and treatment of trauma.* Conference presentation, Utah State University, Logan, Utah.

Briere, J. and Runtz, M. (1988). Post sexual abuse trauma. In G.E. Wyatt and G.J. Powell (Eds.), *Lasting effects of child sexual abuse* (pp. 85-99). Newbury Park, CA: Sage.

Brown, A.H. and Rasmussen, L.A. (1994, November). *Environmental contributors to sexually offending behavior: A family systems application to the trauma outcome process.* Paper presented at the Thirteenth Annual Research and Treatment Conference of the Association for the Treatment of Sexual Abusers (ATSA), San Francisco, California.

Browne, A. and Finkelhor, D. (1986). Impact of child sexual abuse: A review of the research. *Psychological Bulletin, 99,* 66-77.

Burkett, L.P. (1991). Parenting behaviors of women who were sexually abused as children in their families of origin. *Family Process, 30,* 421-434.

Burnette, E. and Murray, B. (1996, October). Conduct disorders need early treatment. *American Psychological Association Monitor, 27*(10), 40.

Cantwell, H.B. (1988). Child sexual abuse: Very young perpetrators. *Child Abuse and Neglect, 12,* 579-582.

Carnes, P. (1983). *Out of the shadows. Understanding sexual addiction.* Minneapolis, MN: Compcare.

Conte, J. (1995, January). *Unrecognized conflicts of interest in the therapy of abused children: Issues in countertransference.* Paper presented at the San Diego Conference on Responding to Child Maltreatment, San Diego, California.

Conte, J. and Schuerman, J. (1987). Factors associated with an increased impact of child sexual abuse. *Child Abuse and Neglect: The International Journal, 11,* 201-211.

Cosentino, C.E., Meyer-Bahlburg, H.F.L., Albert, J.L., Weinberg, S.L., and Gaines, R. (1995). Sexual behavior problems and psychopathology symptoms in sexually abused girls. *Journal of the American Academy of Child and Adolescent Psychiatry, 34*(3), 1033-1042.

Courtois, C. (1988). *Healing the incest wound: Adult survivors in therapy.* New York: W. W. Norton.

Cunningham, C. and MacFarlane, K. (1991). *When children molest children: Group treatment strategies for young sexual abusers.* Orwell, VT: Safer Society Press.

Cunningham, C. and MacFarlane, K. (1996). *When children abuse: Group treatment strategies for children with impulse control problems.* Brandon, VT: Safer Society Press.

Damon, W. (1988). *The moral child: Nurturing children's natural moral growth.* New York: Free Press.

Deblinger, E., McLeer, S.V., Atkins, M.S., Ralphe, D., and Foa, E. (1989). Post-traumatic stress in sexually abused, physically abused, and nonabused children. *Child Abuse and Neglect, 13,* 403-408.

Doleski, T. (1983). *The hurt.* Mahwah, NJ: Paulist Press.

Donaldson, M.A. and Gardner, R., Jr. (1985). Diagnosis and treatment of traumatic stress among women after childhood incest. In C.R. Figley (Ed.), *Trauma and its wake: The study and treatment of post-traumatic stress disorder* (pp. 356-377). New York: Brunner/Mazel.

Einbender, A.J. and Friedrich, W.N. (1989). Psychological functioning and behavior of sexually abused girls. *Journal of Consulting and Clinical Psychology, 57*(1), 155-157.

Elliott, D.M. and Briere, J. (1992). Sexual abuse trauma among professional women: Validating the Trauma Symptom Checklist-40 (TSC 40). *Child Abuse and Neglect, 16,* 391-398.

Erickson, E.H. (1963). *Childhood and society* (Second edition). New York: W.W. Norton.

Eth, S. and Pynoos, R.S. (1985). *Post-traumatic stress disorder in children.* Los Angeles, CA: American Psychiatric Association.

Everitt, B. (1992). *Mean soup.* San Diego, CA: Harcourt Brace Jovanovich.

Everson, M.D., Hunter, W.M., Runyan, D.K., Edelsohn, G.A., and Coulter, M.L. (1989). Maternal support following disclosure of incest. *American Journal of Orthopsychiatry, 59,* 197-207.

Everstine, D S. and Everstine, L. (1989). *Sexual trauma in children and adolescents: Dynamics and treatment.* New York: Brunner/Mazel.

Fatout, M.F. (1990). Aggression: A characteristic of physically abused latency-age children. *Child Adolescent Social Work, 7*(5), 365-376.

Feshbach, N.D., and Feshbach, S. (1969). The relationship between empathy and aggression in two age groups. *Developmental Psychology.* Cited in *Second step: A violence prevention curriculum.* Grades 1-3. Seattle, WA: Committee for Children.

Feshbach, N.D., Feshbach, S., Fauvre, M., and Ballard-Campbell, M. (1983). *Learning to care.* Glenview, IL: Scott, Foresman.

Finkelhor, D. (1988). The trauma of child sexual abuse: Two models. In G.E. Wyatt and G.J. Powell (Eds.), *Lasting effects of child sexual abuse* (pp. 61-82). Newbury Park, CA: Sage.

Finkelhor, D. and Browne, A. (1985). The traumatic impact of child sexual abuse: A conceptualization. *American Journal of Orthopsychiatry, 55*(4), 530-541.

Finkelhor, D. and Browne, A. (1988). Assessing the long-term impact of child sexual abuse. In L.E.A. Walker (Ed.), *Handbook on sexual abuse of children* (pp. 55-72). New York: Springer.

Fraser, M.W. (1996). Aggressive behavior in childhood and early adolescence: An ecological-developmental perspective on youth violence. *Social Work: Journal of the National Association of Social Workers, 41*(4), 347-361.

Friedrich, W.N. (1990). *Psychotherapy of sexually abused children and their families.* New York: W. W. Norton.

Friedrich, W.N. (1995). *Psychotherapy with sexually abused boys: An integrated approach.* Thousand Oaks, CA: Sage.

Friedrich. W.N., Grambsch. P., Broughton, D., Kuiper, J., and Beilke, R.L. (1991). Normative sexual behavior in children. *Pediatrics, 88,* 456-464.

Friedrich, W.N., Grambsch, P., Damon, L., Hewitt, S., Koverola, C., Lang, R., Wolte, V., and Broughton, D. (1992). Child sexual behavior inventory: Normative and clinical comparisons. *Psychological Assessment, 4*(3), 303-311.

Friedrich, W.N., and Luecke, W.J. (1988). Young school-age sexually aggressive children. *Professional Psychology Research and Practice, 19*(2), 155-169.

Friedrich, W.N., Luecke, W.J., Beilke, R.L., and Place, V. (1992). Psychotherapy outcome of sexually abused boys: An agency study. *Journal of Interpersonal Violence, 7*(3), 396-409.

Fromuth, M.E. (1986). The relationship of childhood sexual abuse with later psychological and sexual adjustment in a sample of college women. *Child Abuse and Neglect, 10,* 5-15.

Fulghum, R. (1986). *All I really needed to know I learned in kindergarten.* New York: Ballantine.

Gale, J., Thompson, R.J., Moran, T., and Sack, W.H. (1988). Sexual abuse in young children: Its clinical presentation and characteristic patterns. *Child Abuse and Neglect, 12,* 163-170.

Garbarino, J., Dubrow, N., Kostelny, K., and Pardo, C. (1992). *Children in danger: Coping with the consequence of community violence.* San Francisco, CA: Jossey-Bass.

Garbarino, J., Guttmann, E., and Seeley, J.W. (1986). *The psychologically battered child: Strategies for identification, assessment, and intervention.* San Francisco, CA: Jossey-Bass.

Gale, J., Thompson, R.J., Moran, T., and Sack, W.H. (1988). Sexual abuse in young children: Its clinical presentation and characteristic patterns. *Child Abuse and Neglect, 12,* 163-170.

Gil, E. (1987). *A guide for parents of young sex offenders.* Walnut Creek, CA: Launch Press.

Gil, E. (1991). *The healing power of play: Working with abused children.* New York: The Guilford Press.

Gil, E. (1993a). Age-appropriate sex play versus problematic sexual behaviors. In E. Gil and T.C. Johnson (Eds.), *Sexualized children: Assessment and treatment of sexualized children who molest* (pp. 21-40). Rockville, MD: Launch Press.

Gil, E. (1993b). Etiologic theories. In E. Gil and T.C. Johnson (Eds.), *Sexualized children: Assessment and treatment of sexualized children who molest* (pp. 53-66). Rockville, MD: Launch Press.

Gil, E. (1993c). Family dynamics. In E. Gil and T.C. Johnson (Eds.), *Sexualized children: Assessment and treatment of sexualized children who molest* (pp. 101-120). Rockville, MD: Launch Press.

Gil, E. and Johnson, T.C. (1993). *Sexualized children: Assessment and treatment of sexualized children who molest*. Rockville, MD: Launch Press.

Glasgow, D., Horne, L., Calam, R., and Cox, A. (1994). Evidence, incidence, gender, and age in sexual abuse of children perpetrated by children: Toward a developmental analysis of child sexual abuse. *Child Abuse Review, 3*, 196-210.

Goldston, D.B., Turnquist, D.C., and Knutson, J.F. (1989). Presenting problems of sexually abused girls receiving psychiatric services. *Journal of Abnormal Psychology, 98*(3), 314-317.

Goodwin, J. (1985). Post-traumatic stress disorder in incest victims. In S. Eth and R.S. Pynoos (Eds.), *Post-traumatic stress disorder in children* (pp. 157-168). Los Angeles, CA: American Psychiatric Association.

Gray, A.S. (1989, October). *New concepts in sexual abuse recovery: Healing the effects of trauma*. Paper presented at the Fourth Annual Training Conference on the Treatment of Juvenile Sex Offenders, Salt Lake City, Utah.

Gray, A.S. (1991, October). *Modifying relapse prevention with sexually aggressive and sexually reactive children: Building the prevention team*. Paper presented at the First National Conference on Sexually Aggressive and Sexually Reactive Children, Burlington, Vermont.

Gray, A.S., Bonner, B., Berliner, L., and Friedrich, W. (1993, October). *Children with sexual behavior problems*. Paper presented at the Twelfth Annual Research and Treatment Conference of the Association for the Treatment of Sexual Abusers, Boston, Massachusetts.

Gray, A.S., Bonner, B.L., Friedrich, W., Berliner, L., and Walker, C.E. (1994, November). *Children with sexual behavior problems: A research update on two NCCAN studies*. Paper presented at the Twelfth Annual Research and Treatment Conference of the Association for the Treatment of Sexual Abusers, San Francisco, California.

Gray, A.S. and Friedrich, W. (1996, November). *Precursors to sexual aggression: Research implications for changing treatment of sexual misbehavior in young children*. Paper presented at the Fifteenth Annual Research and Treatment Conference of the Association for the Treatment of Sexual Abusers, Chicago, Illinois.

Gray, A. S. and Pithers, W. D. (1993). Relapse prevention with sexually aggressive adolescents and children: Expanding treatment and supervision. In H. Barbaree, W. Marshall, and S. Hudson (Eds.), *The juvenile sexual offender* (pp. 289-319). New York: The Guilford Press.

Green, A. (1985). Children traumatized by physical abuse. In S. Eth and R.S. Pynoos (Eds.), *Post-traumatic stress disorder in children* (pp. 133-154). Washington, DC: American Psychiatric Press.

Groth, A.N., Longo, R.E., and McFadin, J.B. (1982). Undetected recidivism among rapists and child molesters. *Crime and Delinquency, 128,* 450-458.

Hamilton, J., Decker, N., and Rumbart, R. (1986). The manipulative patient. *American Journal of Psychotherapy, 40*(2), 189-200.

Hammond, D.C., Hepworth, D.H., and Smith, V.G. (1977). *Improving therapeutic communication.* San Francisco, CA: Jossey-Bass.

Harter, S., Alexander, P.C., and Neimenyer, R.A. (1988). Long-term effects in incestuous child abuse in college women: Social adjustment, social cognition, and family characteristics. *Journal of Consulting and Clinical Psychology, 56,* 5-8.

Hartman, A. and Laird, J. (1983). *Family-centered social work practice.* New York: The Free Press.

Hazen, B. (1987). *The knight who was afraid of the dark.* New York: Dial Press.

Herman, J.L. (1992). *Trauma and recovery.* New York: Basic Books.

Hindman, J. (1989). *Just before dawn.* Ontario, OR: Alexandria Associates.

Hindman, J. (1991). *The mourning breaks.* Ontario, OR: Alexandria Associates.

Howes, C. and Eldredge, R. (1985). Responses of abused, neglected, and non-maltreated children to the behaviors of their peers. *Journal of Applied Developmental Psychology, 6*(2-3), 261-270.

Isaac, C. and Lane, S. (1990). *The sexual abuse cycle in the treatment of adolescent sexual abusers.* Shoreham, VT: Safer Society Press.

James, B. (1989). *Treating traumatized children: New insights and creative interventions.* Lexington, MA: Lexington Books.

Johnson, T.C. (1988). Child perpetrators: Children who molest other children: Preliminary findings. *Child Abuse and Neglect, 12,* 219-229.

Johnson, T.C. (1989). Female child perpetrators: Children who molest other children. *Child Abuse and Neglect, 13,* 571-585.

Johnson, T.C. (1993a). Childhood sexuality. In E. Gil and T.C. Johnson (Eds.), *Sexualized children: Assessment and treatment of sexualized children who molest* (pp. 1-20). Rockville, MD: Launch Press.

Johnson, T.C. (1993b). Sexual behaviors: A continuum. In E. Gil and T.C. Johnson (Eds.), *Sexualized children: Assessment and treatment of sexualized children who molest* (pp. 41-52). Rockville, MD.

Johnson, T.C. (1993c). Clinical evaluation. In E. Gil and T.C. Johnson (Eds.), *Sexualized children: Assessment and treatment of sexualized children who molest* (pp. 137-178). Rockville, MD: Launch Press.

Johnson, T.C. (1995a). *Treatment exercises for child abuse victims and children with sexual behavior problems.* Pasadena, CA: Author.

Johnson, T.C. (1995b). *Child sexuality curriculum for abused children and their parents.* Pasadena, CA: Author.

Johnson, T.C. and Aoki, W. T. (1993). Sexual behaviors of latency age children in residential treatment. *Residential Treatment for Children and Youth, 11*(1), 1-22.

Johnson, T.C. and Berry, C. (1989). Children who molest: A treatment program. *Journal of Interpersonal Violence, 4*(2), 182-203.

Kahn, T.J. (1990). *Pathways: A guided workbook for youth beginning treatment.* Orwell, VT: Safer Society Press.

Karpman, S.B. (1968). Fairy tales and script drama analysis. *Transactional Analysis Bulletin, 7*(26), 39-40.

Katherine, A. (1991). *Boundaries: Where you end and I begin.* Park Ridge, IL: Parkside.

Katz, S. and Mazur, M.A. (1979). *Understanding the rape victim.* New York: John Wiley.

Kaufman, K.L., Hilliker, D.R., and Daleiden, E.L. (1996). Subgroup differences in the modus operandi of adolescent sexual offenders. *Child Maltreatment, 1*(1), 17-24.

Kendall-Tackett, K.A., Williams, L.M., and Finkelhor, D. (1993). Impact of sexual abuse on children: A review and synthesis of recent empirical studies. *Psychological Bulletin, 113*(1), 164-180.

Klimes-Dougan, B. and Kistner, J. (1990). Physically abused preschoolers responses to peers' distress. *Developmental Psychology, 26*(4), 599-602.

Knopp, F.H. and Freeman-Longo, R. (1997). Program development. In G. Ryan and S. Lane (Eds.), *Juvenile sexual offending: Causes, consequences, and correction* (Revised edition, pp. 183-200). San Francisco, CA: Jossey-Bass.

Kolko, D.J., Moser, J.T., and Weldy, S.R. (1988). Behavioral/emotional indicators of sexual abuse in child psychiatric inpatients: A controlled comparison with physical abuse. *Child Abuse and Neglect, 12*, 529-541.

Landry, S., and Peters, R. (1992). Toward an understanding of a developmental paradigm for aggressive conduct problems. In R. Peters, R. McMahon, and V. Quinsey (Eds.), *Aggression and violence through the life span.* Thousand Oaks, CA: Sage.

Lane, S. (1991a). Special offender populations. In G.D. Ryan and S.L. Lane (Eds.), *Juvenile sexual offending: Causes, consequences, and correction* (pp. 299-332). Lexington, MA: Lexington Books.

Lane, S. (1991b). The sexual abuse cycle. In G.D. Ryan and S. Lane (Eds.), *Juvenile sexual offending: Causes, consequences, and correction* (pp. 103-141). Lexington, MA: Lexington Books.

Lane, S. (1997a). Special populations: Children, females, the developmentally disabled, and violent youth. In G. Ryan and S. Lane (Eds.), *Juvenile sexual offending: Causes, consequences, and correction* (Revised edition, pp. 322-359). San Francisco, CA: Jossey-Bass.

Lane, S. (1997b). The sexual abuse cycle. In G. Ryan and S. Lane (Eds.), *Juvenile sexual offending: Causes, consequences, and correction* (Revised edition, pp. 77-121). San Francisco, CA: Jossey-Bass.

Lane, S. and Zamora, P. (1984). A method for treating the adolescent sex offender. In R. Mathias (Ed.) *Violent juvenile offenders: An anthology* (pp. 347-363). Washington, DC: National Council on Crime and Delinquency.

Larson, N.R. and Maddock, J.W. (1986). Structural and functional variables in incest family systems: Implications for assessment and treatment. *Journal of Psychotherapy and the Family, 2*(2), 27-44.

Levitan, S. (1991). *The man who kept his heart in a bucket.* New York: Dial Books for Young Readers.

MacFarlane, K. and Cunningham, C. (1988). *Steps to healthy touching.* Mount Dora, FL: Kidsrights.

Maddock, J.W. and Larson, N.R. (1995). *Incestuous families: An ecological approach to understanding and treatment.* New York: W.W. Norton.

Madonna, P.G., Van Scoyk, S., and Jones, D.P.H. (1991). Family interactions within incest and nonincest families. *American Journal of Psychiatry, 148*(1), 46-49.

Main, M. and George, C. (1985). Responses of abused and disadvantaged toddlers to distress in agemates: A study in the day care setting. *Developmental Psychology, 21*(3), 407-413.

Mandell, J. and Damon, L. (1989). *Group treatment for sexually abused children.* New York: The Guilford Press.

Martinson, F. (1976). Eroticism in infancy and childhood. *Journal of Sex Research, 12,* 251-262.

Martinson, F.M. (1991). Normal sexual development in infancy and childhood. In G.D. Ryan and S.L. Lane (Eds.), *Juvenile sexual offending: Causes, consequences, and correction* (pp. 57-82). Lexington, MA: Lexington Books.

Martinson, F.M. (1997). Sexual development in infancy and childhood. In G. Ryan and S. Lane (Eds.), *Juvenile sexual offending: Causes, consequences, and correction* (Revised edition, pp. 36-58). San Francisco, CA: Jossey-Bass.

Mayer, M. (1968). *There's a nightmare in my closet.* New York: Dial Books for Young Readers.

McCann, I.L. and Pearlman, L.A. (1990). *Psychological trauma and the adult survivor: Theory, therapy, and transformation.* New York: Brunner/Mazel.

McGovern, K.B. (1985). *Alice doesn't baby-sit anymore.* Portland, OR: McGovern and Mulbacker Books.

McNamera, J. (1990). Structure for safety: Parenting adoptive children who were sexually abused. In J. McNamera and B.H. McNamera (Eds.), *Adoption and the sexually abused child* (pp. 47-59). Portland, ME: University of Southern Maine.

Mellody, P. (1989). *Facing codependence: What it is, where it comes from, how it sabotages our lives.* San Francisco, CA: Harper & Row.

Mennen, F.E. and Meadow, D. (1994). A preliminary study of the factors related to trauma in childhood sexual abuse. *Journal of Family Violence, 9*(2), 125-142.

Miller, P.A. and Eisenberg, N. (1988). The relation of empathy to aggressive and externalizing/antisocial behaviors. *Psychological Bulletin, 103*(3), 324-344.

Miller, S., Nunnally, E.W., and Wackman, D.B. (1975). *Alive and aware: Improving communication in relationships.* Minneapolis, MN: Interpersonal Communication Programs, Inc.

Minde, K. (1992). Aggression in preschoolers: Its relation to socialization. *Journal of the American Academy of Child and Adolescent Psychiatry, 31*(5), 853-862.

Minuchin, S. (1974). *Families and family therapy.* Boston, MA: Harvard University Press.

Narimanian, R. (1990). *Secret feelings and thoughts.* Philadelphia, PA: Philly Kids Play It Safe.

National Task Force on Juvenile Sexual Offending. (1993). The revised report from the National Task Force on Juvenile Sexual Offending, 1993 of the National Adolescent Perpetrator Network. *Juvenile and Family Court Journal, 44*(4), 1-120.

Neumann, D.A. and Gamble, S.J. (1995). Issues in the professional development of psychotherapists: Countertransference and vicarious traumatization in the new trauma therapist. *Psychotherapy, 32*(2), 314-323.

Neumann, D.A., Houskamp, B.M., Pollock, V.E., and Briere, J. (1996). *Child maltreatment, 1*(1), 6-16.

Osofsky, J.D. (1995). The effects of exposure to violence on young children. *American Psychologist, 50*(9), 782-788.

Patterson, G.R. (1976). The aggressive child: Victim and architect of a coercive system. In E.J. Mash, L. A. Hamerlynch, and L.C. Handy (Eds.), *Behavior modification and families* (pp. 267-316). New York: Brunner/Mazel.

Patterson, G.R. (1982). *Coercive family process.* Eugene, OR: Castalia.

Perls, F.S. (1969). *Gestalt therapy verbatim.* Lafayette, CA: Real People Press.

Peters, S. (1988). Child sexual abuse and later psychological problems. In G.E. Wyatt and G.J. Powell (Eds.), *Lasting effects of child sexual abuse* (pp. 101-117). Newbury Park, CA: Sage.

Pianta, R., Egeland, B., and Erickson, M.F. (1989). Results of the mother-child interaction research project. In D. Cicchetti and V. Carlson (Eds.), *Child maltreatment: Theory and research on the causes and consequences of child abuse and neglect* (pp. 203-253). New York: Cambridge University Press.

Pithers, W.D. (1990). Relapse prevention: A method for enhancing maintenance of therapeutic change in sexual aggressors. In W. Marshall, D.R. Laws, and H. Barbaree (Eds.), *The handbook of sexual assault: Issues, theories, and treatment of the offender* (pp. 343-361). New York: Plenum.

Pithers, W.D., Gray, A.S., Cunningham, C., and Lane, S. (1993). *From trauma to understanding: A guide for parents of children with sexual behavior problems.* Brandon, VT: Safer Society Press.

Pithers, W.D., Kashima, K.M., Cumming, G.F., and Beal, L.S., (1988). Relapse prevention: A method of enhancing maintenance of change in sex offenders. In A.C. Salter (Ed.), *Treating child sex offenders and victims: A practical guide* (pp. 131-170). Newbury Park, CA: Sage.

Pithers, W.D., Kashima, K.M., Cumming, G.F., Beal, L.S., and Buell, M.M. (1988). Relapse prevention of sexual aggression. In R.A. Prentky and V.L. Quinsey (Eds.), *Human sexual aggression: Current perspectives. Annals of the New York Academy of Sciences* (Volume 528, pp. 244-260). New York: New York Academy of Sciences.

Pithers, W.D., Marques, J.K., Gibat, C.C., and Marlatt, G.A. (1983). Relapse prevention: A self-control model of treatment and maintenance of change for sexual aggressives. In J. Greer and J.R. Stewart (Eds.), *The sexual aggressor: Current perspectives on treatment* (pp. 214-239). New York: Van Nostrand Reinhold.

Pynoos, R.S. (1993). Traumatic stress and developmental psychopathology in children and adolescents. In J.M. Oldham, M.B. Riba, and A. Tasman (Eds.), *American Psychiatric Press Review of Psychiatry* (Volume 12). Washington, DC: American Psychiatric Press.

Rasmussen, L.A. (1995). *Caring for children with sexually abusive behavior problems: A training course for foster and shelter care parents.* Salt Lake City, UT: Utah State Division of Family Services, Department of Human Services.

Rasmussen, L.A., Burton, J., and Christopherson, B.J. (1992). Precursors to offending and the trauma outcome process in sexually reactive children. *Journal of Child Sexual Abuse, 1*(1), 33-48.

Rasmussen, L.A. and Cunningham, C. (1995). Focused play therapy and non-directive play therapy: Can they be integrated? *Journal of Child Sexual Abuse, 4*(1), 1-20.

Ray, J. and English, D.J. (1995). Comparison of female and male children with sexual behavior problems. *Journal of Youth and Adolescence, 24*(4), 439-451.

Regina, W.F. and LeBoy, S. (1991). Incest families: Integrating theory and practice. *Family Dynamics Addiction Quarterly, 1*(3), 21-30.

Roesler, T.A. and McKenzie, N. (1994). Effects of childhood trauma on psychological functioning in adults sexually abused as children. *Journal of Nervous and Mental Disease, 182*(3), 145-150.

Rohnke, K. (1984). *Silver bullets.* Hamilton, MA: Project Adventure.

Rutter, M. (1989). Intergenerational continuities and discontinuities. In D. Cicchetti and V. Carlson (Eds.), *Child maltreatment: Theory and research on the causes and consequences of child abuse and neglect* (pp. 317-348). New York: Cambridge University Press.

Ryan, G. (1989). Victim to victimizer: Rethinking victim treatment. *Journal of Interpersonal Violence, 4*(3), 325-341.

Ryan, G. (1991a). Perpetration prevention. In G.D. Ryan and S.L. Lane (Eds.), *Juvenile sexual offending: Causes, consequences, and correction* (pp. 393-408). Lexington, MA: Lexington Books.

Ryan, G. (1991b). Theories of etiology. In G.D. Ryan and S.L. Lane (Eds.), *Juvenile sexual offending: Causes, consequences, and correction* (pp. 41-55). Lexington, MA: Lexington Books.

Ryan, G. (1991c). The juvenile sexual offender's family. In G.D. Ryan and S.L. Lane (Eds.), *Juvenile sexual offending: Causes, consequences, and correction* (pp. 143-160). Lexington, MA: Lexington Books.

Ryan, G. (1997a). Perpetration prevention. In G. Ryan and S. Lane (Eds.), *Juvenile sexual offending: Causes, consequences, and correction* (Revised edition, pp. 433-454). San Francisco, CA: Jossey-Bass.

Ryan, G. (1997b). Theories of etiology. In G. Ryan and S. Lane (Eds.), *Juvenile sexual offending: Causes, consequences, and correction* (Revised edition, pp. 19-35). San Francisco, CA: Jossey-Bass.

Ryan, G. (1997c). Phenomenology: A developmental-contextual view. In G. Ryan and S. Lane (Eds.), *Juvenile sexual offending: Causes, consequences, and correction* (Revised edition, pp. 122-135). San Francisco, CA: Jossey-Bass.

Ryan, G. (1997d). The families of sexually abusive youth. In G. Ryan and S. Lane (Eds.), *Juvenile sexual offending: Causes, consequences, and correction* (Revised edition, pp. 136-154). San Francisco, CA: Jossey-Bass.

Ryan, G. and Blum, J. (1994). *Childhood sexuality: A guide for parents.* Denver, CO: Kempe Center, University of Colorado Health Sciences Center.

Ryan, G., Blum, J., Sandau-Christopher, D., Law, S., Weber, F., Sundine, C., Astler, L., Teske, J., and Dale, J. (1988). *Understanding and responding to the sexual behavior of children: Trainer's manual.* Denver, CO: Kempe Center, University of Colorado Health Sciences Center.

Ryan, G., Lane, S., Davis, J., and Isaac, C. (1987). Juvenile sexual offenders: Development and correction. *Child Abuse and Neglect: The International Journal, 11*(3), 385-395.

Salter, A. (1995). *Transforming trauma: A guide to understanding and treating adult survivors of child sexual abuse.* Thousand Oaks, CA: Sage.

Selman, R.L. (1980). *The growth of interpersonal understanding.* New York: Academic Press.

Sgroi, S.M. (1982). Family treatment. In S.M. Sgroi (Ed.), *Handbook of clinical intervention in child sexual abuse* (pp. 241-267). Lexington, MA: Lexington Books.

Sgroi, S.M., Bunk, B.S., and Wabrek, C.J. (1988). Children's sexual behaviors and their relationship to abuse. In S.M. Sgroi (Ed.), *Vulnerable populations* (Volume I). (1-24). Lexington, MA: Lexington Books.

Shapiro, J.P., Leifer, M., Martone, M.W., and Kassem, L. (1992). Cognitive functioning and social competence as predictors of maladjustment in sexually abused girls. *Journal of Interpersonal Violence, 7*(2), 156-164.

Silverstein, S. (1964). *The giving tree.* New York: Harper & Row.

Slusser, M.M. (1995). Manifestations of sexual abuse in preschool-aged children. *Issues in Mental Health Nursing, 16*, 481-491.

Staub, E. (1996). Cultural-societal roots of violence: The examples of genocidal violence and of contemporary youth violence in the United States. *American Psychologist, 51*(2), 117-132.

Steen, C. (1993). *The relapse prevention workbook for youth in treatment.* Brandon, VT: Safer Society Press.

Stickrod, A. and Mussack, S. (1986, Fall). Thinking errors of juvenile sex offenders. In K. Strong, J. Tate, B. Wehman, and A. Wyss (Eds.), *Project Safe: A sexual assault and perpetration prevention curriculum for junior high and high school students.* Available from Human Growth and Development Program CESA, Cumberland, WI, 54829.

Stickrod Gray, A. and Mussack, S. (1988, March). *Teaching the juvenile sexual offender to clarify the assault cycle.* Workshop handout presented at the Adolescent Sex Offender Symposium, Salt Lake City, Utah.

Stickrod, A. and Ryan, G. (1987). Identifying the young sexual abuse perpetrator. *Interchange,* January, 10-12.

Strayer, J. (1980). A naturalistic study of empathic behaviors and their relation to affective states and perspective-taking skills in preschool children. *Child Development, 51,* 815-822.

Taussig, H.N. and Litrownik, A.J. (1997). Self- and other-directed destructive behavior: Assesment and relationships to type of abuse. *Child Maltreatment, 2*(2), 172-182.

Terr, L. (1983). Play therapy and psychic trauma: A preliminary report. In C.E. Schaeffer and K.J. O'Connor (Eds.), *Handbook of play therapy* (pp. 308-319). New York: Wiley.

Tharinger, D. (1988). *Behavioral characteristics of normal childhood development.* Presented at a conference, Albuquerque, New Mexico.

Thompson, M. and Nelson, R. (1992, September). *Group treatment for preschool victims of sexual abuse.* Workshop presented at Primary Children's Medical Center, Salt Lake City, Utah.

Tong, L., Oates, K., and McDowell, M. (1987). Personality development following sexual abuse. *Child Abuse and Neglect, 11,* 371-383.

Trickett, P.K. and Putnam, F.W. (1993). Impact of child sexual abuse on females: Toward a psychobiological integration. *Psychological Science, 4*(2), 81-87.

Tsai, M., Feldman-Summers, S., and Edgar, M. (1979). Childhood molestation: Variables related to differential impacts on psychosexual functioning in adult women. *Journal of Abnormal Psychology, 88,* 407-417.

Wells, R.D., McCann, J., Adams, J., Voris, J., and Ensign, J. (1995). Emotional, behavioral, and physical symptoms reported by parents of sexually abused, nonabused, and allegedly abused prepubescent females. *Child Abuse and Neglect, 19*(2), 155-163.

White, S., Halpin, B.M., Strom, G.A., and Santilli, G. (1988). Behavioral comparisons of young sexually abused, neglected, and nonreferred children. *Journal of Clinical Child Psychology, 17*(1), 53-61.

Will, D. (1983). Approaching the incestuous and sexually abusive family. *Journal of Adolescence, 6*(3), 229-246.

Wind, T.W. and Silvern, L. (1992). Type and extent of child abuse as predictors of adult functioning. *Journal of Family Violence, 7*(4), 261-281.

Winnicott, D.W. (1965). *Maturational processes and the facilitating environment.* New York: International Universities Press.

Wolpe, J. (1969). *The practice of behavior therapy.* New York: Pergamon Press.

Wyatt, G.E. and Powell, G.J. (1988). Identifying the lasting effects of child sexual abuse: An overview. In G.E. Wyatt and G.J. Powell (Eds.), *Lasting effects of child sexual abuse* (pp. 11-17). Newbury Park, CA: Sage.

Yochelson, S. and Samenow, S.E. (1976). *The criminal personality* (Volumes I and II). New York: Jason Aronson.

Young, R.E., Bergandi, T.A., and Titus, T.G. (1994). Comparison of the effects of sexual abuse on male and female latency aged children. *Journal of Interpersonal Violence, 9*(3), 291-306.

Zahn-Waxler, C., Cole, P. M., Welsh, J. D., and Fox, N.A. (1995). Psychophysio-logical correlates of empathy and prosocial behaviors in preschool children with behavior problems. *Development and Psychopathology, 7,* 27-48.

Zahn-Waxler, C., Radke-Yarrow, M., and King, R.A. (1979). Child rearing and children's prosocial initiations toward victims of distress. *Child Development, 50*(2), Wind, T.W. and Silvern, L. (1992). Type and extent of child abuse as predictors of adult functioning. *Journal of Family Violence, 7*(4), 261-281. 319-320.

Ziegler, E., Taussig, C., and Black, K. (1992). Early childhood intervention: A promising preventive for juvenile delinquency. *American Psychologist, 47,* 997-1006.

Index

Parents *(continued)*
  stressed, 42
  and Trauma Outcome Process,
    31,52-55
  of victim, 144
  victimization history, 41,75
Patterson, G. R., 13,53
Pearlman, L. A., 13,16
Peers
  affection seeking, 35
  approval seeking, 47-48
  monitoring relationships, 78
  rejection by, 19,238
  sexual explorations, 247
Penetration, 8
Perls, F. S., 139
Perpetration issues, 89
Perpetrators, 89,157
Personal space, 106,217-218,
    219-220. *See also* Privacy
Peters, R., 20,37
Peters, S., 15
Phony, being, 135
Physical abuse, 11-12,21
Pianta, R., 30
Pithers, W. D., 5,41,45,98,237
Place, V., 17
Play, age-appropriate, 7,8
Policemen, 204-205
Pollock, B. E., 12
Post-traumatic stress disorder
    (PTSD), 14,45
Powell, G. J., 13
Power, 18,25,96,136,174-176
Powerlessness
  family members', 252
  and offense setup, 48
  time line activity, 173
  triggering abuse cycle, 34,125,238
Prevention team, 238-242
Privacy, 24,37-38,68,76,215-216,247
Problem solving, 19
Progress Rating Form, 83,84-87
Prosocial behaviors, 13
Psychiatric problems, 87

PTSD. *See* Post-traumatic stress
  disorder
Puppets, 117,175,179
Putnam, F. W., 19
Pynoos, R. S., 14

Radke-Yarrow, M., 21,37
Ralphe, D., 10,14
Ramsey, R., 17
Rasmussen, L. A.
  on children's literature, 150
  Empathy Rating Form, 67
  The Fire, 179-185
  Flight Manual, 208-213
  Progress Rating Form, 84-87
  relapse prevention plan, 239-242
  sexual values, 249,250
  Steps and Slides, 120-122
  Thinking Errors, 133
  Trauma Outcome Process, 9,31,33
Ray, J., 11,19
Recovery, 48-49
Regina, W. F., 23
Rejection, 19,129,238
Relapse prevention plan
  activities, 126-130,231-232,
    237-244
  in group therapy, 97-99
  in individual therapy, 76-77
  parents' role, 44
Relationship skills, 100-101
Removal, from home, 80,87-88
Resource books, 45,111,150
Respect, 216,217,221
  for body, 225-229
Responsibility. *See also*
    Accountability
  activities, 116-118,126-130,
    142-147,174-176
  assessing responsible party,
    174-176
  avoidance of, 17-19,51
  for household tasks, 220-221
  parents' abdication of, 24

Trauma Outcome Process
  activity, 179-185
  and children, 50-52
  description, 31-32
  and parents, 31,52-55
Traumagenic dynamics, 13-14
Traumatization, 10-17
  assessing responsibility, 174-176
  disclosure, 157-159,168-173,178,
    179-185
  effects, 14-16,52,99,168-173,178
    179-185
  and empathy, 51-52
  environmental support, 33
  individual responses, 31,45-49
  and other life experiences,
    168-173
  therapists', 253-254
Treatment. *See* Therapy
Trickett, P. K., 19
Triggers, 45,61,123,165-167,238
Trust, 192-200,202,207-208
Tsai, M., 15

Values, sexual, 236,246-250,253
Van Scoyk, S., 23
Victim playing, 135,136
Victimization
  and arousal, 33
  protecting self from, 225-229
  reporting to parents, 157-159
  therapist's attitude, 253
  witnessing, 12
Victims
  conjoint therapy, 77,80,89,229
  conversation with, 139-141
  letters to, 142-148
  parents of, 144

Victims *(continued)*
  and perpetrator's parents, 66
  response to disclosure, 17
  role-playing, 139-141,150
Vondra, J., 52
Voris, J., 10

Wabrek, C. J., 8
Wackman, D. B., 46
Weber, F., 8
Weinberg, S. L., 10
Wells, R. D., 10
Will, D., 23
Williams, L. M., 13,14,16
Wind, T. W., 12
Winnicott, D. W., 24,35
Witnessing
  sexual abuse, 13-14
  victimization, 12,21-22
Wolpe, J., 230
Wolte, V., 63
Wyatt, G. E., 13

Yochelson, S., 17,40
Young, R. E., 10,11,19
Young children
  activities, 113-115,116-118,
    145,149-156,174-176,188,
    191,196,201-205,225-229
  apology letters to, 144
  dressing and bathing, 223
  and empathy, 37
  older children friendships, 98,238
  and oral sex, 61
  and premeditation, 50
  and sexuality, 225-229,247
  therapy, 33-34,81-82

Zahn-Waxler, C., 21,37
Zamora, P., 25,47
Ziegler, E., 21
Zucker, K., 13,16,19

Order Your Own Copy of
This Important Book for Your Personal Library!

TREATING CHILDREN WITH SEXUALLY ABUSIVE BEHAVIOR PROBLEMS
Guidelines for Child and Parent Intervention

_____ in hardbound at $49.95 (ISBN: 0-7890-0472-0)

_____ in softbound at $29.95 (ISBN: 0-7890-0473-9)

COST OF BOOKS_____

OUTSIDE USA/CANADA/
MEXICO: ADD 20%_____

POSTAGE & HANDLING_____
*(US: $3.00 for first book & $1.25
for each additional book)
Outside US: $4.75 for first book
& $1.75 for each additional book)*

SUBTOTAL_____

IN CANADA: ADD 7% GST_____

STATE TAX_____
*(NY, OH & MN residents, please
add appropriate local sales tax)*

FINAL TOTAL_____
*(If paying in Canadian funds,
convert using the current
exchange rate. UNESCO
coupons welcome.)*

Prices in US dollars and subject to change without notice.

☐ **BILL ME LATER:** ($5 service charge will be added)
(Bill-me option is good on US/Canada/Mexico orders only;
not good to jobbers, wholesalers, or subscription agencies.)

☐ Check here if billing address is different from
shipping address and attach purchase order and
billing address information.

Signature_____

☐ **PAYMENT ENCLOSED: $**_____

☐ **PLEASE CHARGE TO MY CREDIT CARD.**

☐ Visa   ☐ MasterCard   ☐ AmEx   ☐ Discover
☐ Diner's Club
Account # _____

Exp. Date _____

Signature _____

NAME _____

INSTITUTION _____

ADDRESS _____

CITY _____

STATE/ZIP _____

COUNTRY _____ COUNTY (NY residents only) _____

TEL _____ FAX _____

E-MAIL_____
May we use your e-mail address for confirmations and other types of information? ☐ Yes   ☐ No

Order From Your Local Bookstore or Directly From
The Haworth Press, Inc.
10 Alice Street, Binghamton, New York 13904-1580 • USA
TELEPHONE: 1-800-HAWORTH (1-800-429-6784) / Outside US/Canada: (607) 722-5857
FAX: 1-800-895-0582 / Outside US/Canada: (607) 772-6362
E-mail: getinfo@haworthpressinc.com
PLEASE PHOTOCOPY THIS FORM FOR YOUR PERSONAL USE.

BOF96